3-38

England
in the age of
Thomas More

DEREK WILSON

England
in the age of
Thomas More

Edward Stafford
Duke of Buckingham

Henry by the Grace of God King of E

HART-DAVIS, MACGIBBON
GRANADA PUBLISHING
London Toronto Sydney New York

Published by Granada Publishing in
Hart-Davis, MacGibbon Ltd 1978

Granada Publishing Limited
Frogmore, St Albans, Herts AL2 2NF
and
3 Upper James Street, London WIR 4BP
1221 Avenue of the Americas, New York, NY 10020, USA
117 York Street, Sydney, NSW 2000, Australia
100 Skyway Avenue, Toronto, Ontario, Canada M9W 3A6
Trio City, Coventry Street, Johannesburg 2001, South Africa
CML Centre, Queen & Wyndham, Auckland 1, New Zealand

ISBN 0 246 10943 2

Printed in Great Britain by
Richard Clay (The Chaucer Press) Ltd
Bungay, Suffolk

PREFACE

T HE SCOPE of this book is very considerable. It spans, in theory at least, the whole of early Tudor life and society. It therefore cannot claim to be a work of completely original research. It rests firmly upon the labours of a multitude of specialist scholars each of whom has published in book, article, paper or thesis his findings on his own small area of study. My indebtedness is, thus, far greater than I can possibly acknowledge. My fascination with the England of Henry VII and Henry VIII was first aroused by those who taught me at Cambridge twenty years ago in the era when G. R. (now Professor) Elton was upsetting previous ideas about the period with his reappraisal of Thomas Cromwell's role in the constitutional 'revolution' of the 1530s. So great has been the interest in the Reformation epoch since then that it has been no easy task to keep pace with the spate of publications.

Surprisingly, throughout those years no one has attempted a social and economic survey of this vibrant period for popular consumption. It is this gap that I have attempted to fill, drawing as fully as possible on recent and current scholarship, as well as going back to the original sources for the bulk of the information. On many issues which are still the subject of academic debate I have had to over-simplify or baldly state my own considered opinion; the present book would not have been the place for detailed consideration of the major, prevailing points of view. In the Select Bibliography and the Notes readers will find references to most of the works I have consulted and to which they may refer for fuller treatment of specific issues.

While it is impossible to mention all those scholars and friends whose work and encouragement over the years have made this book possible, there are a few special 'thank yous' that must be said. The library and archive staffs of the British Library, Public Record Office and Cambridge University Library have been courtesy itself. Mrs Joan Stephens and her assistants of the West Somerset Library Service have been tireless in locating volumes and delivering them to my very door. Professor A. G. Dickens very kindly read the draft typescript and made numerous comments which enabled me to eradicate errors, re-examine opinions and remove some ambiguities.

It would be too much to hope that I have obliterated all suggestion of inaccuracy and silenced every diligent critic. It would *not* be too much to hope that this book may contribute towards a wider interest in and deeper understanding of a turbulent and creative period of our history. Such, indeed, is my hope.

Derek Wilson

Contents

PROLOGUE

The Man and the Age

I T WAS one of the most vital periods in the history of England and he was one of the most remarkable men of that or any other period. The sceptical reader may well expect a historian to make exaggerated claims for his own particular field of study and, therefore, my first task should, perhaps, be to defend that opening statement. In so doing I shall inevitably have to define the subject-matter of this book and to make some general statements about it. This may be no bad thing, for the scope of the chapters which follow is vast and it may help the reader if he gains a bird's-eye view of the terrain we are to travel together before we begin to tread the streets and lanes of early Tudor England and to rub shoulders with all sorts and conditions of men.

Thomas More lived from 1478 to 1535. In trying to paint a picture of the world he knew we cannot, of course, be restricted by those two dates. What we are really concerned with here is England during the years when a mature More influenced and was influenced by the contemporary scene. His was the age of the first two Tudors (1485–1547); the age when the Renaissance and the Reformation came to England; the age when Englishmen began to venture into the world of which Europe and the Mediterranean were only a small part; the age which pointed England clearly along the road towards parliamentary democracy and limited monarchy. It was, if the word has any meaning at all, a 'revolutionary' age.

The build up to this revolution was gradual until the mid-1520s. Religious, political and cultural ideas infiltrated slowly from the continent, affecting, first of all the centres of learning and the major towns and ports where the sophisticated, cosmopolitan minority congregated. The invention and rapid exploitation of the printing press ensured that these influences would not be ephemeral. Johanne Gutenberg had perfected the techniques of printing from movable type in the 1430s and the new invention had spread with astonishing rapidity. By 1500 there were 1700 presses scattered throughout the major towns of Europe and something of the order of 40,000 individual titles had been published. It was, indeed, the appearance of a new book in 1526 – William Tyndale's English *New Testament* – which caused the explosion which gave the forces of change a new impetus. From then on more and more people were committed to radical views, and a government, which had its own motives for transforming society, could depend on the support of a growing volume of public opinion.

Thomas More belonged to that group which we call the humanists, disciples of a 'new learning' which they believed could direct European society towards a golden age of harmony and progress. The impetus for English humanism came originally from Italy where philosophers like Marsilio Ficino and Pico della Mirandola challenged the basic assumptions upon which medieval scholasticism rested; where Niccolo Machiavelli propounded a new concept of statecraft; where Copernicus mastered those principles which were to change completely the sciences of astronomy and cosmography; where Michelangelo and Leonardo were only the brightest stars in a galaxy of artists who were rediscovering the human form and liberating the human spirit. Yet the leading figure of the northern Renaissance was not an Italian; he was the illegitimate son of a Dutch priest and no other intellectual radical of the age was more desirous of change or more cynically critical of the establishment than Desiderius Erasmus: '. . . the whole proceedings of the world are nothing but one continued scene of Folly, all the actors being equally fools and madmen . . .'[1] So wrote Erasmus in his *In Praise of Folly* (1509), and one by one all the sacred and secular institutions of Europe were placed under the microscope of his wit. In more serious vein Thomas More exposed the social evils of sixteenth-century England in *Utopia*, some seven years later. The pioneers were followed by Thomas Starkey, Robert Crowley and a host of reformist authors and pamphleteers, whose objective was the establishment of a Christian commonwealth where justice, good order and true faith should thrive.

Some humanists belonged to the Protestant camp and as such were members of a group possessing an even stronger determination to revolutionise the lives of individuals and of society. They aimed at a religious revival which involved the overthrow of papal antichrist and the triumph of evangelical truth.

What inspired many of the radicals with hope was the fact that

England had a new, strong dynasty capable of carrying out a wide programme of reform. Under the first 'Tudors royal government became more efficient and more powerful. Inevitably, Henry VII and his son used their power in ways which did not always meet with the approval of the humanists. They were extremely efficient in reordering society by removing wealth and privilege from those groups which had abused their position of semi-independence. They were less able in redistributing the confiscated resources for the greater well-being of the realm. Largely by financial pressures the first Tudor broke the local territorial authority of the large magnates. Henry VIII stripped the Church of lands, buildings, stock and standing crops, farm equipment and the plate and jewels with which centuries of devotion had decked the shrines and altars of the great religious houses.

All this activity brought about major changes throughout the country, changes which could only be bewildering and alarming for the mass of simple people who had come to regard agricultural practices and hereditary landholding as fixed by immutable laws of custom and economics. Other traditions were also swept away, and the power of the monarchy is, perhaps, seen most convincingly in this ability to put an end to age-hallowed customs. In the 1530s Thomas Cromwell, as Vicar-General, removed objects of superstition from parish churches, put an end to pilgrimages, struck many saints days and holy days from the calendar and caused every churchwarden to procure 'one book of the whole Bible of the largest volume in English'. No parishioner had to walk far to observe the most permanent memorials of all to religious change; gaunt and roofless, the 'bare ruined choirs' stood deserted among the fields or busy with the clamour of masons and carpenters who were turning them into fine houses for the new squires. No English king since the Conqueror would have dared to undertake such sweeping and insensitive changes.

The Reformation, however, was not something forced on unwilling people for political motives. It certainly was, looked at from one point of view, a political movement whereby Henry VIII, proclaiming that 'this realm of England is an empire', put an end to papal authority and thus exploded the medieval myth of 'Christendom'. It was also and more fundamentally a religious revival more far reaching than the Wesleyan revival of the mid-eighteenth century. It was based upon a rediscovery of the written word of God, translated (for the first time officially) into a language 'understanded of the people'. For the first time every man (at least, every literate man) was his own theologian, able to challenge his parish priest from the pages of holy writ, able to find his own way to heaven without the ministrations of monk or clerk. The new Protestantism was an exciting, liberating force which impelled the allegiance of thousands of English men and women; so much so that, within a decade of 1547, over three hundred of them went through the flames of martyrdom for their faith.[2]

Religious revival is something with which we are unfamiliar in the last quarter of the twentieth century; the same cannot be said of another factor of early Tudor life – inflation. During the reign of Henry VIII the cost of living increased three hundred per cent and it was still rising in 1547.[3] The reasons for this price rise were many and complex, and they are as imperfectly understood by economic historians now as they were then. Growing population, use of land for wool rather than crop production, an over-buoyant property market, increased use of credit, the influx of bullion from the mines of Germany, Bohemia and the New World – these were all factors tending towards the devaluing of money. When a bankrupt Treasury (for, incredibly, Henry VIII squandered first the funds garnered by his father, then the spoils of the church) turned to such measures as the savage debasement of the coinage (the coins of 1545 contained only one-third silver), the situation was made worse. Landlords who had granted long-term and copyhold tenancies found themselves squeezed between the upper and nether millstones of fixed rents and rising prices. Wiser landlords refused to give long leases, thus passing on the insecurity of the times to their tenants. As for the poor peasant and the town labourer, they could only watch with dismay as the prices of food and clothing increased, wages fell and jobs became scarce. One contemporary observed simply and gloomily, 'The state of England was never so miserable as it is at present.'[4]

We need not take the pessimistic words of Becon as being solely representative of the spirit of the age. There were, doubtless, thousands of English men and women who managed, either by geographical isolation or an effort of will, to be untroubled by change. The manorial framework of society survived for a century or more in many places. Government still lacked the power to make its will felt everywhere. The priest and the lord remained as the leaders of the community. Local issues engaged men's minds more than national issues. Yet no one could fail to notice that new ideas were in the air, that old institutions were collapsing and that authority was being transferred from spiritual to secular agents – in short, that revolutionary changes were sweeping through society.

We are fortunate to have in Thomas More an ideal 'window' on this changing and turbulent world. More was a man of conscience, personally involved in the social, political and religious life of the realm. He was also a man of acute consciousness who perceived more clearly than most contemporaries just what was happening to the European Christendom which he loved. In *Utopia* he diagnosed more accurately than any other humanist the diseases from which society was suffering. Yet it is not merely as a man of independent and penetrating intelligence that More made such an impression on his own and on succeeding ages.

He was, first and foremost, a man of faith. This was a characteristic he shared not only with the men and women of the religious life whom he admired so much, but also with many of the Protestant reformers he so completely despised. On 3 September 1529 he wrote to his wife from the royal court at Woodstock. Dame Alice was greatly distressed because the family's barns at Chelsea, containing corn stored for the winter by the Mores and their neighbours, had been burned down. The Lord Chancellor's reply to his distraught wife is one of the most moving of all More's collected letters:

> . . . it were great pity of so much good corn lost, yet since it hath liked him [God] to send us such a chance, we must and are bounden not only to be content but to be glad of his visitation. He sent us all that we have lost and since he hath by such a chance taken it away again his pleasure be fulfilled; let us never grudge thereat but take it in good part and heartily thank him as well for adversity as for prosperity and [it may be that] we have more cause to thank him for our loss than for our winning, for his wisdom better seeth what is good for us than we do ourselves. Therefore I pray you be of good cheer and take all the household with you to church and there thank God both for that he hath given us and for that he hath taken from us and for that he hath left us, which if it please him he can increase when he will and if it please him to leave us yet less, at his pleasure be it.[5]

No Calvinist ever expressed more clearly or practically the doctrine of the sovereignty of God.

The depth and sincerity of religious conviction which marked More as representative of his age inevitably led him into bitter controversy. Though highly critical of the corruption of the church, he was an obedient son of that church and a devoted supporter of papal authority. Those who sought to challenge that age-old authority and replace it by the authority of Scripture were fools and knaves. Moreover they were dangerous men who sought to undermine the whole edifice of Christendom. Thomas More devoted the last years of his life to a violent literary conflict with the heretics. He believed it vital to persecute them out of existence. In his exhaustive and bitter works of Catholic apologetic there is little trace of the elegant, witty author of *Utopia*:

> There be fled out of this realm for heresy a few ungracious folk . . . priests, monks and friars that neither say mass nor matins, nor never come at church, talking still of faith [yet] full of false heresies [who] would seem Christ's apostles but play the devil's disciples, speaking much of the spirit with no more devotion than dogs, divers of them not hesitating to wed harlots and then call them wives.[6]

Thomas More found it impossible to forgive monks and priests who had forsaken their vows. The vituperation he directed at such failed ascetics betrays more than outraged principle; More was bitter because he was himself a failed ascetic. As a young man he seriously contemplated taking up the religious life, only to reject the idea finally because he could not pledge himself to a life of chastity.

It is as well for us that this was so. Had it been otherwise we should never have seen another, delightful side of More's life: More the family man. In *Utopia* the family was the basic unit of society; the centre in which education was imparted and the young brought up in the *mores* of the state; the place where skills were learned; the cultural nucleus where civilised conversation, art and music were indulged in by all the adult members. Though family life in *Utopia* was idealised and highly organised to a preconceived pattern, it was, in essence, the same as family life in the well-to-do homes of Tudor England. The merchant's house or the nobleman's mansion provided shelter for a large extended family – children, parents, grandparents, uncles, aunts, cousins, servants, apprentices and boys and girls sent from other families to learn the ways of polite society. Every English household was a patriarchy and in *Utopia* also, 'the wyfes bee ministers to theire husbandes, the children to theire parentes, and . . . the yonger to theire elders'. It would never have occurred to More to question the authority of fathers or the duty of children. He, himself, obeyed his own father in the matter of a career; he would far rather have lived the life of a scholar but John More had decided that his son should be a lawyer and Thomas bowed to parental wishes. (It is interesting to note that in *Utopia* sons were expected to follow their fathers' careers but were not forced to do so if they felt some other vocation. Clearly, Thomas More

12   VTOPIAE INSVLAE TABVLA.

The Island of Utopia from the *Utopia* of Sir Thomas More, 1595

believed that in an ideal world children should not have to share his
own fate.)

Thomas More married twice. At the age of about twenty-seven he
took to wife Jane Colt, a girl some ten years his junior. She bore him
four surviving children in as many years and died in 1511. Within
weeks More wed again. This time he chose a forty-year-old widow,
Alice Middleton. There were no children by this second marriage and
it would seem that what attracted More to Alice was her abilities as a
housewife rather than feminine charm, of which she was, apparently,
almost devoid. Indeed, More's intimate friends wondered what had
possessed him to saddle himself with a woman they regarded as a
shrew (or, as one of them unkindly dubbed her, 'a hook-nosed harpy').
For More, as for most contemporaries, marriages were business arrangements. He selected Jane Colt because she was the eldest of three
sisters even though he was more attracted to one of the younger girls.
When he had daughters of his own to marry he exercised the same cool
judgement in selecting husbands. Two of the girls were betrothed in
early adolescence to More's own wards, wealthy young men whose
wardship he had purchased from the crown.

They are all there in the sketch of More's family made by Holbein in
1527 – the grandfather, the children, the second wife, the fool, even the
pet monkey. They are stiffly, formally posed yet it is impossible to miss
the relaxed good humour as though they were all waiting for the
painter to finish with them so that they could get on with some game or
some mock-serious debate. It is not fanciful to see the Holbein picture
as a symbol of life at Bucklersbury and Chelsea – warm and exuberant
within the confines of a strict and demanding daily routine. The household rose early for prayer and study. At mealtimes there were readings
from devotional books. Family prayers were held every evening. Dic-
ing, cards and loose talk were forbidden; gardening, disputation in
Latin and Greek and music were encouraged. Yet despite, or perhaps
because of, this disciplined regimen the household was one of the
happiest in the land. More's wit and geniality presided over a home
where friends were always welcome, where learning was reverenced
and where ingenuity was always devising new entertainments and
diversions.

Even in his own lifetime More's household was held up as a model
of Christian family life and as a pattern for the education and upbringing of children. The head of the house employed the best tutors and
was always entertaining leading scholars. Erasmus, Vives, Ammonius
and others – all were intimates of More and his family and all spoke

FAMILIA THOMÆ MORI ANGL: CANCELL:

Sir Thomas More: family group by Holbein

glowingly of the standards achieved by those who were educated at Bucklersbury or Chelsea. Especially was More praised for his attitude to the education of girls. More was not a supporter of women's lib any more than he was a communist. He believed that women had a divinely ordained role of subservience to men. It was their task to bear and rear children and to tend the home, making it as pleasant a place as possible for their husbands and their husbands' friends. He accepted that, by and large, women lived shorter lives than men and often died as a direct or indirect result of having many babies. There was no alternative; in an age of high infant mortality it was important for a wife to bear as many children as possible. Yet More also believed that girls should have as full a grounding as boys in the classics, the sciences and in works of piety. He tried, with little result, to train his wives in philosophy and astronomy. With his daughters he was more successful. Like the boys of the household they were instructed by tutors and took part in learned debates. They were expected to write Latin letters to their father and to make their own translations of classical authors. All More's children were accomplished scholars but none more so than the eldest, his beloved Meg. She disputed in philosophy before the king, she debated as an equal with her father's guests, she made a translation of Erasmus's treatise on the Lord's Prayer. She was first among a band of learned and pious women whose upbringing was affected by humanist ideas, a band which includes such names as Catherine Parr, Lady Jane Grey and Queen Elizabeth I. It was the upbringing of Margaret More and her sisters that John Vives must have had largely in mind when he wrote his revolutionary treatise *De institutione foeminae Christianae* (a book which, incidentally, was translated into English by Richard Hyrde, a tutor in More's household, under the title *The Instruction of a Christian Woman*).

It is as England's foremost humanist scholar that More stands out most clearly as a representative of his age. His formative years were spent in that humanist golden dawn of intellectual liberation dominated by John Colet, Erasmus, William Lilly, Thomas Linacre and William Grocyn – all of whom became his close friends. He thrilled to the rediscovery of scripture through the study of Greek. He applauded Colet's pulpit denunciations of clerical abuses and the devastating comparison of early church simplicity with the luxury, pomp and liturgical complexity of contemporary practice. It was in More's house at Bucklersbury that Erasmus wrote *In Praise of Folly*, destined to be received by the humanist brotherhood as their manifesto against the contemporary evils of church and state. (The work was dedicated to More and its very title is a pun on his friend's name, for the Greek for 'fool' is μωρια, latinised in the title of the book as *Moriae Encomium*.) Thomas More even wrote a few Latin epigrams in the same satirical vein, in which the inconsistencies between the practices of the church and the precepts of its Founder were pointed out. The young More emulated his Dutch friend as a cruelly witty satirist who wanted to shock and shame the establishment into re-examining its conduct and customs.

Yet Erasmus and More were not entirely twin souls. The Englishman could never maintain the aloof, scholarly detachment of his friend. Their circumstances and some of their basic attitudes were different. Erasmus had been forced to become a monk and spent the rest of his life trying to escape the restraints of the religious life. More was increasingly drawn into secular politics but would far rather have lived in a monastery. Erasmus spent much of his life travelling. He had no family and few professional commitments. Therefore, he could claim to speak from 'pure', impartial motives. More, on the other hand, was a servant of his king, something for which he often felt it necessary to apologise in his letters to his colleague. 'My thoughts and heart had long been set upon a life of retirement, when suddenly, without any warning, I was tossed into a mass of vital business affairs . . . The more I realize that this post involves the interests of Christendom, my dearest Erasmus, the more I hope it all turns out successfully . . . Farewell dearest Erasmus, more than half my soul.'[7] So, More excused his acceptance of the office of Lord Chancellor when he wrote to Erasmus on 28 October 1529.

Erasmus remained something of an optimistic idealist, little affected by the realities of human nature and day-to-day politics. When he produced his fresh Latin version of the New Testament, the *Novum Instrumentum*, he saw it as heralding a new age of simple, pure faith.

> Wisdom . . . may be drawn from these few books, as from a crystalline source, with far less trouble than is the wisdom of Aristotle from so many thorny books and with much more fruit . . . The equipment [for the Christian's pilgrimage] is simple and at everyone's immediate disposal. This philosophy is accessible to everybody. Christ desires that his mysteries shall be spread as widely as possible. I should wish that all good wives read the Gospel and Paul's Epistles; that they were translated into all languages; that out of these the husbandman sang while ploughing, the weaver at his loom; that with such stories the traveller should beguile his wayfaring.[8]

Thomas More could not follow his friend along this path. He was not so sanguine about human nature. Neither England nor any other state in the real world could be transformed into a Utopia, as he fully realised, because men lacked charity and the true love of equity and justice. More welcomed the publication of the *Novum Instrumentum* and thought it excellent that scholars should have access to a translation purer than the Vulgate, but as to vernacular Scriptures, that was a different matter. Indeed, once the Reformation debate had got under way he went further:

> in these dayes . . . in whyche men by theyr owne defaute mysseconstre and take harme of the very scrypture of god, vntyll menne better amende, yf any man wolde now translate Moria [*Moriae Encomium*] in to Englyshe, or some workes eyther that I have my selfe wryten ere this, all be yt there be none harme therein folke yet beynge (as they be) geuen to take harme of that that is good I wolde not onely my derlynges [my darling's, i.e. Erasmus's] bokes but myne owne also, helpe to burne them both wyth myne owne handes, rather then folke sholde (though thorow theyr own faute) take any harme of them, seynge that I se them lykely in these dayes so to do.[9]

More came to believe that heresy should be fought with every
available weapon, a conviction which led him to debase his literary gifts
in a battle of words with Tyndale. This exercise struck Erasmus as
totally futile. As he stressed in a letter to Bishop Tunstall, you cannot
fight fire with fire.[10]

These fundamental differences between two humanists who, according to a mutual friend had a likeness of 'minds, tastes, feeling and
interest such that twin brothers could not more closely resemble one
another'[11] highlight a very important aspect of Christian humanism –
its diversity. Cuthbert Tunstall, diplomat, bishop, councillor, the
friend who urged More to become a religious controversialist was a
humanist. So was William Tyndale, the arch heretic against whom
More's wrath was principally turned. Men of the New Learning
formed the backbone of Tudor administration throughout four reigns.
In the front rank were politicians of the stamp of Stephen Gardiner,
William Paget, William Cecil and Nicholas Bacon. The diplomatic
corps and the lower echelons of central and local government were
thronged with 'new men'. For years great teachers and tutors such as
Roger Ascham, John Cheke, Nicholas Udall and Anthony Cooke
ensured a succession of royal servants whose minds were trained to
question and probe for the truth and who could express themselves in
elegant Latin or English. Yet they were by no means united on the
great issues of the day. Indeed, many of them found themselves in rival
political factions, working to overthrow each other. Most of More's
friends, for example, could not follow him in the stand he made over
the Succession oath. It was not that they lacked his courage; they
genuinely could not understand his point of view.

'What did nature ever create milder, sweeter or happier than the
genius of Thomas More?'[12] So wrote Erasmus and the opinion was
supported by most men who knew More well. 'More is a man of an
angel's wit and singular learning. I know not his fellow. For where is
the man of that gentleness lowliness and affability? And, as time
requireth, a man of marvellous mirth and pastimes, and sometime of as
sad gravity.'[13] Gay, sensitive, kind, generous, pious, quick to praise
and slow to take offence, we do not need to read the eulogies of
biographers anxious to turn More into a Catholic saint to realise what a
delightful companion and friend he must have been.

There was, of course, another side to his personality. He could be
stubborn. He was vicious in his attacks on those he considered to be
enemies of the truth. He was sometimes less than honest with his
friends (and, perhaps, with himself). For example, although he

Tho: Moor L. Chancelour

Sir Thomas More: whether making finished paintings in oil or sketching with pen and chalk, Hans Holbein portrayed flawlessly the characters of his sitters

protested his reluctance to enter royal service, he deliberately sought the patronage of Wolsey and the king. He did not notably distinguish himself in public office. To be sure, he gained a reputation for incorruptibility and impartiality on the bench but he could no more keep his hands clean than could any other Tudor statesman. His bitter attack on Wolsey in parliament turned the knife in the disgraced Cardinal's wound. He was involved in the government decision to murder the Duke of Buckingham. He helped to extort money from parliament (for which a grateful king gave him £200). He accepted the fees and pensions attendant upon his office. His period as Chancellor left no

positive contribution. Indeed, the only cause he pursued with
enthusiasm during his years in office was the persecution of heretics.

But all this is of little consequence for the purposes of the present
book. We are here concerned with More as a representative and a
recorder of his age. Lawyer, scholar, writer, politician, diplomat,
polemicist, landowner, householder, courtier, family man, champion of
a great cause (albeit a lost one) – Thomas More was a man involved
with life at all levels. At the same time he was a man apart. He was the
satirical, and sometimes impassioned, observer who wrote *Utopia*. In
that book More held a mirror up to his age. The image is not an
attractive one: kings more interested in fleecing their subjects to finance
futile foreign wars than attending to the common weal; landowners
dispossessing tenants and peasants in order to turn their land over to
sheep farming; courts which discriminate against the poor; savage sen-
tences out of all proportion to the crimes committed; education of
children entrusted to ill-equipped tutors; artisans and craftsmen slav-
ing for inadequate reward; growing vagabondage; and a crime rate
increasing alarmingly as a result of poverty and idleness. It is More's
deep understanding of the human condition, his appreciation of the
timeless subtleties of the human heart, which in the last analysis are the
only explanation of current events, that make him not only a representative of his own age, but a man for all ages.

He understood more clearly than most contemporaries what was
happening in early-sixteenth-century England. Most of what he
understood he did not like. He had no answer. *Utopia* was certainly not
set forth as an ideal pattern for England's lawgivers and administrators.
His own talents did not lie in the direction of framing policy and drafting
statutes. He was even cynical about the ability of kings and councillors to
accept wise advice.

> These thinges (say they) pleased our forefathers and auncestours:
> wolde God we coulde be so wise as thee were: and as though thei
> had wittely concluded the matter, and with this answere stopped
> every mans mouth, thei sitte downe againe. As who should sai, it
> were a very daugerous matter, if a man in any pointe should be
> founde wiser then his forefathers were.[14]

And yet perhaps he did have an answer, the answer of example
rather than precept – to exercise compassion widely, to live simply, to
go among unscrupulous and ambitious men honestly, to hold his truth
tenaciously, to serve his God faithfully, to die bravely and to become a
legend.

In the following chapters I have used Thomas More's life as a base from which to explore early Tudor England. For example, I have started with London, the first world which he knew as a young boy. Then I have discussed school and university education, and so on. But it has only been possible to adhere very loosely to this convention. For the reader who might like a more secure point of reference I set out here a brief outline of More's career.

1478	Born in London
c. 1487–90	At St Anthony's School
c. 1490–2	In Archbishop Warham's household
c. 1492–4	At Oxford
c. 1494–1503	At the inns of court. Under the influence of John Colet
1499	First meeting with Eramus
1504	Member of the House of Commons
c. 1505	Married Jane Colt
c. 1511	Married Alice Middleton
1516	Published *Utopia*
1517	Entered the royal service. Master of the Court of Requests
1521	Became Under-Treasurer
1523	Became Speaker of the Commons
1528	Wrote the *Dialogue Concerning Heresies*
1529	Became Lord Chancellor
1532	Resigned the Chancellorship
1532–3	Wrote *Confutation of Tyndale's Answer*
1534	Refused the oath of Succession. Imprisoned
1535	Tried and executed

1

'Your world and impery of England'

I Town Life

EEP IN AN April night when most honest citizens were abed
some excited Londoners were very much awake.

> ... the self night in which King Edward died, one Mystlebrooke,
> long ere morning, came in great haste to the house of one Pottyer,
> dwelling in Red Cross Street without Cripplegate. And when he was
> with hasty rapping quickly letten in, he showed unto Pottyer that
> King Edward was departed. 'By my troth, man,' quoth Pottyer,
> 'then will my master the Duke of Gloucester be king!'[1]

A few months later, in the summer of 1483, the City was buzzing with
rumours that the late king's two young sons had been smothered and
secretly buried somewhere within the confines of the Tower.

London, the base of England's itinerant Yorkist and Lancastrian
kings, was used to such alarms. It was much more than the largest city
and principal commercial centre in the kingdom. Within its boundaries
and in the adjacent countryside were to be found the mansions of the
temporal and spiritual nobility. In nearby Westminster its burgesses
from time to time assembled with their provincial peers in the lower
house of parliament. Many of its merchants enjoyed the patronage of
king and court. All its citizens were familiar with occasional displays of
royal pageantry. All witnessed, if they were so inclined, the comings
and goings of foreign embassies, the mustering of royal armies and the
death of traitors on Tower Hill. All were proud of their City and its
ancient liberties which had been won from a succession of sovereigns as
dependent on London as Londoners were dependent on the crown.

This was the little world which Thomas More knew first and which
for all his subsequent travels, he knew best. He was just five years old

on that spring night in 1483 when Mystlebrooke rushed through the unlit streets with the news of Edward IV's death. He was seven and a half on an August evening in 1485 when dusty messengers clattered through Bishopsgate shouting out that Richard III, last of the Plantagenets, lay slain on Bosworth field. The Mores were an old-established London family. At the time of Thomas's birth his father, John More, was a young, and no doubt struggling, lawyer living in the parish of Cripplegate with his wife Agnes (daughter of a prominent City merchant) and his three-year-old daughter Joan. (Five children appear to have survived the high rate of infant mortality: Joan, Thomas, Agatha, John and Elizabeth. They were probably not all borne by Agnes, for John More married four times.) John was a conscientious and much loved man who rose ultimately to be a justice of King's Bench. Thomas's first companions were the sons of other lawyers and merchants and his haunts the narrow streets and small, enclosed gardens of the City.

London, busy, rich, sophisticated London, was an international city, steadily taking over from Antwerp and Venice the role of the world's business centre. Within the realm it dominated almost completely commercial and cultural life. Symbolically watched over by St Paul's at its western end and the Tower in the east, the capital was a compact, untidy sprawl of teeming life. Its citizenry, already some 60,000 strong, overflowed into crowded tenements beyond the walls, filled the towns of Southwark, across the bridge, and of Westminster, a mile or so upriver beyond the stately Thameside houses of the nobility. Downstream from the bridge sprawled a mile of wharves where merchants from Hamburg, Antwerp, Bordeaux, Venice and the Levant unloaded their wines, spices, glassware, pottery, carpets, silk, pitch, timber, and filled their holds with woollen cloth. (England did have other exports – wool, corn, tin, coal, timber, salt, etc, but at this period cloth was by far the dominant commodity.) Most foreigners were impressed by London's wealth and when the Scottish friar, William Dunbar, visited it in 1501 he extolled it as 'the flour [sic] of cities all' in a famous seven-stanza panegyric.

> Gem of all joy, jasper of jocunditie,
> Most mighty carbuncle of virtue and valour;
> Strong Troy in vigour and in strenuitie;
> Of royal cities rose and geraflour;
> Empress of townes, exalt in honour;
> In beautie bearing the crown imperial;

> Sweet paradise precelling in pleasure:
> London, thou art the flour of cities all.

What we know of Tudor London from other sources tempts us to
believe that Dunbar's muse was taking him for a ride, or perhaps he
was just trying to commend himself to the city fathers. For many
citizens London was far from being a paradise.

Behind the waterfront lay the slums, the hastily-built dwellings
inhabited by hopefuls come up to seek their fortunes, by foreigners,
sailors and travellers in transit. Steadily, uncontrollably the wretched
dwellings sprawled eastwards, 'a continual street, or filthy straight
passage, with alleys of small tenements or cottages builded . . . along by
the river of Thames, almost to Radcliffe'.[2]

When Thomas More wrote his greatest work, *Utopia*, he created a
kind of distorting mirror in reverse. In its shining surface we see
Tudor England with its vices, its squalor, its injustice and its inconsistencies smoothed out. Utopia was not an ideal state but through the
medium of this imagined land the author expressed many of his own
profoundest wishes and aspirations. For example, in his description of
Amaurote, the main city of that fabulous land, we see clearly the sort of
town that More's beloved London was not – ideally situated, provided
by conduits with fresh spring water, clean and laid out to a preconceived plan.

> The stretes be appointed and set furth very commodious and hand-
> some, both for carriage, and also againste the windes. The houses be
> of faire and gorgious building, and on the strete side they stande
> joyned together in a long rowe through the whole streate without
> any partition or separation. The stretes be twentie foote brode. On
> the backe side of the houses throughe the whole length of the streete,
> lye large gardens inclosed round aboute wyth the backe part of the
> streetes . . . They set great store by their gardeins. In them they have
> vineyards, all maner of fruite, herbes, and flowres, so pleasaunt, so
> well furnished, and so fynely kepte, that I never sawe thynge more
> frutefull, nor better trimmed in anye place . . . the houses in the
> beginning were [originally] very low, and like homely cotages or
> poore sheppard houses, made at all adventures of everye rude pece
> of tymber, that came firste to hande, with mudde walles, and ridged
> rooffes, thatched over with strawe. But nowe the houses be curi-
> ouslye buylded after a gorgious and gallante sorte, with three
> storyes one over another . . . They kepe the winde oute of their
> windowes with glasse, for it is ther much used, and som here also

with fine linnen cloth dipped in oyle or ambre ... For by thys meanes more lighte commeth in, and the winde is better kepte oute.[3]

Medieval London was not a planned city with fine public buildings and open squares like Amaurote or even the great commercial centres of North Italy. It had grown much more pragmatically according to the demands of trade. Because trade was booming the demand for business and living space within the square mile was intense. Houses pressed shoulder to shoulder as plots were divided and subdivided. The main thoroughfares were paved and provided with conduits or open sewers but this counted for little as one foreigner observed:

> All the streets are so badly paved that they get wet at the slightest quantity of water, and this happens very frequently owing to the large numbers of cattle carrying water, as well as on account of the rain, of which there is a great deal in this island. Then a vast amount of evil-smelling mud is formed, which does not disappear quickly but lasts a long time, in fact nearly the whole year round.[4]

Fine houses there were but they stood cheek by jowl with thatched hovels having 'mudde walles' and unglazed windows. The city skyline was changing all the time as wealthy citizens and speculators, untrammelled by planning restrictions, tore down, remodelled or built anew. While Thomas Wood was erecting Goldsmith's Row, a dazzling development of shops and dwellings between Bread Street and Cheap, Bucklersbury Manor, a fine old medieval mansion, was being divided into overcrowded tenements. When a great man like Thomas Cromwell wanted to build a new town house, streets of rickety dwellings might be torn down and neighbouring gardens mercilessly encroached upon.[5]

Gardens there were but only attached to the houses of the wealthy. They were tucked into corners and enclosed by high walls and certainly did not give London the green and open appearance of beauteous Amaurote. Noblemen and merchants who, like More, loved grass, flowers and trees had mostly moved out to Westminster or to such riverside villages as Chelsea and Lambeth. London was probably the only town in the land whose inhabitants had become totally urbanised. For More and for most Englishmen town life was a thing unnatural. It was not only the languorous courtier who affected to despise city life, though he expressed better than most of his contemporaries the pleasure and relief of retiring to the country.

This maketh me at home to hunt and to hawk,
And in foul weather at my book to sit,
In frost and snow then with my bow to stalk:

No man doth mark whereso I ride or go,
In lusty lease [pasture] at liberty I walk,
And of these news I feel nor weal nor woe,
Save that a clog doth hang yet at my heel –
No force for that [never mind about that], for it is ordered so
That I may leap both hedge and dike full well . . .
But here I am in Kent and Christendom
Among the muses where I read and rhyme,
Where if thou list, my Poyntz, for to come,
Thou shalt be judge how I do spend my time.[6]

However unnatural city life was, England's capital was *par excellence* the place for fortune seekers. For centuries the ancient livery companies had been growing in both size and number, until by 1500 there were well over a hundred, though it was the twelve great companies (Mercers, Grocers, Drapers, Fishmongers, Goldsmiths, Skinners, Merchant Taylors, Haberdashers, Salters, Ironmongers, Vintners and Clothworkers) which dominated the political and social life of the city. Aldermen and lord mayors were very rarely chosen from a wider circle than that which encompassed the great twelve. Each craft had its own quarter. The skinners' workshops, stalls and guild hall were in the Wallbrook Ward and were flanked by the premises of the vintners and cord-wainers. 'In one single street, named the Strand, leading to St Paul's, there were fifty-two goldsmiths' shops, so rich and full of silver vessels, great and small, that in all the shops in Milan, Rome, Venice and Florence put together, I do not think there would be found so many of the magnificence that are to be seen in London.'[7] The Venetian visitor who wrote those words was deliberately using hyperbole to impress the armchair travellers of his own land but he was far from being the only foreigner to be struck by the enormous wealth of the city.

The leading members of the guilds did not derive their riches merely from the practice of their trade. They were import and export agents, members of the Merchant Adventurers, dealers in all manner of merchandise which passed across the Narrow Seas. They and their factors were constantly travelling to and from the continental markets of Calais and Antwerp to haggle with their foreign counterparts over the price of wine, wool and cloth. It was a hazardous business and many a well-found ship went down off the coast of Zeeland or France, but substantial fortunes were consistently made.

Most of them were made from cloth. The changeover from wool to

cloth as England's principal export took place during the late fourteenth and fifteenth centuries for reasons which need not concern us
here. By 1495 the cloth trade was booming; demand far exceeded
supply and, as in every buoyant market situation, it was the middlemen
who controlled the flow of merchandise and took the biggest slice of
the cake. The Merchant Adventurers of London were the middlemen
because they held the monopoly of cloth exports. Clothiers from all the
major clothmaking areas – Somerset, the Cotswolds, East Anglia and
Yorkshire – travelled up to the capital with their laden packhorse trains
and unloaded them, at last, in Blackwell Hall, Basinghill Street. There
the bales were weighed and sealed by market officials and the provincial clothiers began haggling with their prospective buyers. The
London dealers were all freemen of the city for only such were allowed
to buy at Blackwell Hall and by agreeing among themselves beforehand
they could fix the prices to be paid for the various grades of cloth –
'double worsted', 'motley', 'camlet', 'bombazine', 'red stamel' and
'marbre'. The vendors had little alternative but to accept the price;
they could not take their goods all the way home again, or offer them
for sale elsewhere. Not content with this degree of control, many of the
wealthier London merchants bought themselves country estates and
sheep runs which enabled them to control the whole chain of production as far as their own fleeces were concerned.

Not all the wealth earned from trade went into country estates.
Noblemen, bishops and leading merchants kept large establishments in
the city. Most of them were timbered but a few were of stone. The
fifteenth-century Guildhall and the headquarters of the livery companies were among the secular splendours of the city. Londoners spent
generously on the embellishment of their many churches and especially
on the massive cruciform St Paul's. Until the 1530s all the religious
orders had establishments in London. The ecclesiastical presence was a
continuing source of resentment for not only were the friaries, monasteries, nunneries, churches, chantries, hospitals, episcopal and abbatical
residencies exempt from municipal control, but the church owned
tenements, houses and plots of land all over the city which were also
outside the jurisdiction of the lord mayor and aldermen. When competition for space was acute and business opportunities were being lost
for want of premises, it angered master drapers, vintners and skinners
to see so much city property being wasted. When, in the 1530s, the
monasteries and friaries were dissolved there was a rush to acquire
these London premises, clear the sites, and build shops and houses.

The physical difference between London and other cities was one of

degree rather than of kind but its proximity to the centre of government assured for it a very special character and importance. It was
there that the king staged spectacles and pageants to impress his subjects with what he was doing for them.

> ... the xiij day of June after was Wytsonday, and ther was a gener-
> alle processione from Powlles un to sent Peters in Cornehylle with
> alle the chelderne of Powlles scole, and a crosse of every parishe
> church, with a banner and one to ber it in a tenache, alle the clarkes,
> alle the presstes, with parsons and vekeres of every church in
> coppys, and the quere of Powlles in the same manner, and the
> byshoppe bereynge the sacrament under a canapy with the mayr in a
> gowne of cremsone velvet, the aldermen in scarlet, with alle the
> crafttes in their best aparelle; and when the mayer came betwene the
> crosse and the standert there was made a proclamacyon with dyvers
> harhoddes [heralds] of armes and pursevanttes in their cote armeres,
> with the trompettes, and ther was proclamyd a unyversalle pes for
> ever betwene the emperar, the kynge of Ynglonde, the French
> kynge, and all crystyne kynges for ever.[8]

Thus was the Universal Peace of 1518 proclaimed in London.

The river was a splendid stage for such spectacles. When Anne
Boleyn was brought up from Greenwich to the Tower in May 1533 in
preparation for her coronation she was met by a concourse of boats and
barges. From one a dragon breathed sheets of fire over the water. On
another stood 'terrible monsters and wylde men castyng fyer, and
makyng hideous noyses'.[9] The gaily-decked official barges of the lord
mayor and all the leading citizens were on the river, each with its
complement of minstrels and musicians. The height of the spectacle
was a waterborne pageant depicting a mountain strewn with singing
virgins and bedecked with red and white roses and Anne's emblem, the
white falcon. The royal marriage was unpopular but the city fathers
knew that a colourful display of enthusiasm was expected of them.

Sometimes the entertainments laid on by the court partook more of
the nature of horseplay but there was always a propaganda objective
behind the merriment. In June 1539 two barges were prepared,

> ... with ordinance of warre, as gonnes and dartes of reede, one for
> the Bishop of Rome and his cardinalles, and the other for the Kinges
> Grace, and so rowed up and downe the Thames from Westminster
> Bridge to the Kinges Bridge; and the Pope [and his cardinals] made
> their defyance against England and shot their ordinaunce one at

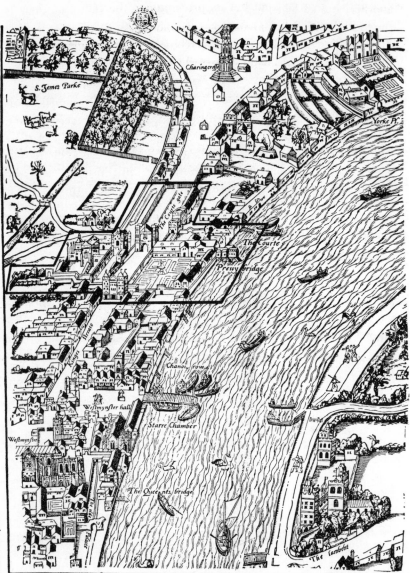

In the 1530s Henry VIII built the palace of Whitehall (outlined
on the map) not far from the old residence/administrative office
complex of Westminster, largely destroyed by fire in 1512.
Increasingly this area, a brief journey from London via the river
or the Strand, became the centre of government, although the
sovereign only resided there in the winter months

another, and so had three courses up and downe the water; and at
the fourth course they joynid togither and fought sore; but at last the
Pope and his cardinalles were overcome, and all his men cast over
the borde into the Thames; howbeyt there was none drowned, for
they were persons chosen which could swimme, and the Kinges
barge lay by hoveringe to take them upp as they were cast over the
borde, which was a goodly pastime.[10]

The special relationship between the crown and the merchant aristo-
cracy of London was founded squarely upon mutual self-interest. The
loyalty of London was essential to the survival of the dynasty and the
royal treasury relied heavily on loans from city financiers. The disposal
of wool from the royal estates and the bulk purchase of wines and
continental furnishings for the royal household all relied on the cooper-
ation of the London merchant body. The merchants for their part
looked to the crown for sympathetic treatment regarding customs
duties and for support in their relations with foreign corporations and
governments. Trade was just as important an element in international
politics in the sixteenth century as it is now. When, in 1493, Henry VII
became exasperated with the Emperor Maximilian for supporting
Perkin Warbeck one strand in his retaliatory policy was the imposition
of economic sanctions. English merchants were forbidden to trade with
Antwerp. Despite the protests of the Merchant Adventurers the ban
remained in force for two and a half years until, by the *Intercursus
Magnus* of 1496, full commercial relations were restored and the opportunity was taken to obtain the redress of certain grievances suffered in
the past by English traders in the Low Countries.

For recreation Londoners resorted to the many open spaces around
the city, such as Spitalfields, Moorfields (grassed over since the great
drought of 1498 had destroyed the allotments there) and Smithfield,
scene of horsefairs and the occasional burning of heretics. There the
wilder elements could indulge in football, handball, or hockey, sports
much rougher than their modern counterparts. There the butts were
set up for men to sharpen their skill with the long-bow. Thither came
the annual fairs, the mummers, the minstrels and the puppeteers. All
entertainments were not out of doors. It was to the taverns that the
professional gamblers, minstrels and players resorted. Despite the official disapproval of these pastimes all sections of London society from
the beribboned courtier to the dock labourer indulged in them. They sang
the latest bawdy songs, they applauded the mummers, they lost their
money at cards, shuffleboard, dice or tables (backgammon) to men who

played with crooked 'Fulham' dice (so called because Fulham village was a notorious resort of cheats and rogues). Those whose mind turned to other pleasures did their drinking at the houses kept by ladies of the town. It was after an evening of roistering at such an establishment run by Mistress Arundel that the young Earl of Surrey and his cronies went on a rampage through the streets of London one March night in 1543, shying stones through the windows of respectable citizens. They paid for their pleasure with a few months in the Fleet prison.

Mistress Arundel's was not the most notorious London bordel. That distinction was reserved for the 'stews' across the bridge in Southwark. The city fathers seem habitually to have banished to Southwark the activities of which they did not officially approve. There were situated the arenas for bull and bear baiting. There the grandchildren of Henry VIII's generation would build the first English theatres. The stews were, in theory, innocent enough; they were public bathhouses, licensed originally by the bishop of Winchester. But they had, early on, become houses of ill repute against which preachers tiraded. It took the arrival of the 'pox' or the 'French disease' or (as the French called it) the 'English disease' – in other words, syphilis – to stir the government to action. This infection, probably brought from the New World by Columbus's crew, made its first appearance in England at the turn of the century. In 1506 Henry VII had closed the stews. But not for long – they were to flourish and to play their part in spreading the wretched contagion for another forty years before Henry VIII by proclamation ordered the shutting down of 'any house wherein is kept and holden any hot-house or sweating-house, for ease and health of men, to which be resorting or conversant any strumpets or women of evil name or fame'.

The growth of monopolistic London and the economic changes of which that growth was a symptom had had a detrimental effect on some other towns. Boston, on the Lincolnshire coast, had grown fat on the wool trade controlled by the merchants of the Hanseatic League. Alas, it was another story that was reported to John Leland when he visited the town sometime in the 1530s.[11]

Mr Paynel a gentilman of Boston tolde me that syns that Boston of old tyme at the great famose fair there kept was brent that scant syns it ever came to the old glory and riches that it had: yet sins hath it beene manyfold richer then it is now. The staple and the stiliard [i.e. 'Steelyard', the headquarters of the Hanse merchants] houses yet there remayne: but the stiliard is litle or nothing at alle occupied.[12]

Thomas Paycock's prestigious house at Coggeshall, Essex, is typical of the town dwellings wealthy provincial merchants built for themselves in the fifteenth and sixteenth centuries

It was the same story at York, Exeter, Grimsby, Chester and other towns which were slow to adapt to changing economic conditions.

But the swings and roundabouts of economic fortune brought great prosperity to other towns. Three areas profited enormously from the cloth industry. One was the southern half of East Anglia; another was the West Riding of Yorkshire and the third was the Gloucestershire–Somerset hinterland of Bristol. The Suffolk–Essex border had become, by 1500, the industrial heart of England – a boom region. It had been prosperous in the days when England's main export was wool, and through its ports of Ipswich and Dunwich it had close contact with the Low Countries. When the Flemish textile industry fell on evil days many of the more enterprising weavers travelled across the North Sea and it was to East Anglia that they came. Equipped with wool, labour, professional expertise and a well-established trading network, the region was well placed to take advantage of the new situation. Insignificant villages were put on the map – Long Melford, Cavendish, Clare and Lavenham, Lindsey and Kersey (which live on as names of cloth to this day). Old market centres blossomed into populous, bustling towns – Hadleigh, Colchester, Thaxted, Sudbury. And the towns filled

with the outward and visible signs of prosperity – timbered wool halls
and guildhalls, the impressive houses of the clothiers, and the soaring,
Perpendicular splendours of new and enlarged parish churches, in
which the wealthy merchants were ultimately laid to rest beneath monuments in brass and alabaster. In the region as a whole, lay wealth had
increased more than fourfold in the period from 1334 to 1524 and in a
town like Lavenham the leading citizens were eighteen times better off
by the end of this period.[13]

The cloth industry introduced the first real capitalist entrepreneurs
to England. Clothmaking was a series of complex processes each of
which was carried out by a specialist working in his own home. The
man who was responsible for keeping the chain of production going
was the clothier. It was his agents who brought the cartloads of shorn
fleece from the farms into his barn for sorting into various qualities
and lengths. Other employees washed and scoured the wool, oiled it,
and laid it out layer upon layer to become supple enough for working.
Only the master's expert fingers could determine when the wool was
ready to be sent out for processing.

Ipswich Borough Council

This magnificent
memorial brass to
Ipswich wool merchant
Thomas Pownder, his
wife and children, was
made by a Flemish
craftsman. As well as
the couple's armorial
bearings it depicts
Thomas's wool mark

When the clothier gave the order, the hanks were baled up again and taken by packhorse to the carders. Using their spiked boards the carders pummelled the fibres into a tight, thick mass – hot and dusty work which sent them to bed weary and sweating after twelve hours or more of back-breaking toil. Every batch had to be ready when the clothier's men came to take it to the spinners. This process was done almost entirely by the village women who would sit outside their cottages on fine days, gossiping with their neighbours as they twiddled their distaffs and spun the wool into threads. Time and again the weavers complained of the uneven yarn produced by this old-fashioned process and urged their masters to buy spinning wheels such as were used in the West Country but either the clothiers were too mean or the spinsters too conservative, for it was many decades before this new-fangled invention reached East Anglia.

The weavers were the lynch-pins of the whole operation. Proud master craftsmen, they were organised in their own guilds and for many years preserved their independence and their right to negotiate prices. However, by 1495, this happy era had passed for many of them. The clothiers had obtained such a stranglehold on all other aspects of the industry that they were able to force the weavers into the status of mere wage-earners. The pattern of exploitation which we tend to associate with the worse aspects of the Industrial Revolution was obviously well established two and a half centuries earlier: '. . . the rich men, the clothiers, be concluded and agreed among themselves to hold and pay one price for weaving, which price is too little to sustain households upon, working night and day, holiday and weekday, and many weavers are therefore reduced to the position of servants.'[14] The clothiers did not have things all their own way. The weavers' guilds in the larger towns such as Ipswich and Hadleigh were able to resist pressure from the capitalists. Yet even they were driven to complain in 1539 that the entrepreneurs were trying to push them out of business by bringing cheap labour into the area from Flanders.

After weaving, the cloth had to go to the fulling mill. These mills were usually jointly owned by groups of clothiers or by town corporations. After soaking in clear water, the cloth was beaten with wooden paddles driven by water power, then scrubbed with fuller's earth (aluminium oxide). Now the pieces were brought back to the warehouse for the clothier to supervise the important final operations. First they were stretched on tenterhooks so that they dried out in the required shape and were fully bleached. Then they were sheered to ensure an even finish. The clothier either now sold the cloth 'white' or called upon the services of local dyers. They could offer him a range of colours – saffron yellow from plants grown in the fields around Saffron Walden, other shades of yellow and green from onions, cow parsley, nettles, oakbark or privet leaves, blues and purples from the fruit of sorrel or yellow ladies-bedstraw, shades of grey and black from alder bark and the yellow iris.

Thus, only after several months of careful and patient work, could the clothier see his material made into tight bales, weighed, stitched into protective bags, sealed with his own mark, loaded and off on its way by the packhorse routes to London. During those months he had had to pay his workers, feed his animals, buy wool, hire the fulling mill, pay for professional services, and he knew that his margin for haggling with the London staplers was very narrow. Clothmaking was a hazardous business but for those hard enough and sharp enough the profits were considerable. When Thomas Paycock of Coggeshall, Essex, died in 1518 in the main bed-chamber of his beautiful house of brick and carved timber with the quiet garden behind, he could afford to leave hundreds of pounds to be expended on his obsequies, money for the building of an elaborate chantry in the parish church, bequests to local churches and charities, legacies to many of his workmen and friends, without greatly affecting the bulk of his patrimony, which passed to his widow and children. It comes as no surprise to learn that the wealthiest merchant in England, outside London, was a clothier. When Thomas Spryng of Lavenham died in 1523 his goods were assessed at over £6,000, he owned twenty-seven manors and lands in 130 parishes.

Life for a growing minority of Englishmen was becoming town centred but it remained country based. Even large towns were fringed by cultivated fields in which the citizens had an interest. Norwich was the second city of the realm. It was one of those centres which by turning to cloth had maintained the momentum of an earlier prosperity based on wool. With a population of around 20,000 it was far smaller than London but considerably larger than any other town. Next in size were provincial centres like Exeter, York, Bristol and Shrewsbury, the number of whose inhabitants did not exceed 10,000. County towns with between 800 and 2000 inhabitants were small enough for most of the inhabitants to know each other, at least by sight. To all of them there was a compactness, a sense of identity which was reflected in their physical appearance. They sprawled outwards from clearly-defined bustling centres, usually bounded by the old town walls. All regular business and occasional markets took place in the town centre,

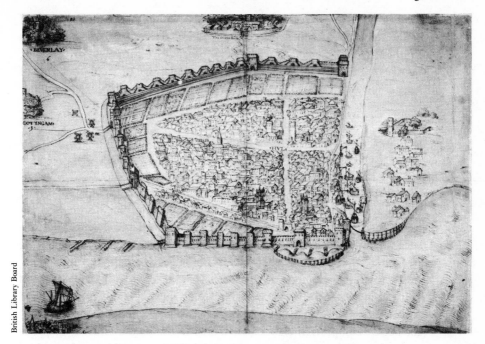

At the beginning of Henry VIII's reign Kingston-upon-Hull, like
many English towns, was still a walled, self-contained unit

where shops, stalls and workrooms were clustered together in guild
groups. Prominent citizens built their houses in the centre and, to some
degree, social status could be measured by the distance a man lived
from the urban nucleus. Another reason why folk were reluctant to
build in the suburbs was that this usually meant further encroachment
on the arable fields or common pasture. England's small towns were
still rural communities dependent on the surrounding country for their
food. There was a distinct unwillingness to see good land lost for ever.

The demand for houses in town centres led, paradoxically, to
depopulation and dilapidation. Owners of urban properties let them at
exorbitant rents and when the poor householders failed to keep the
property in good repair they were evicted. Rather than reduce the rents
the landlords allowed houses to stand empty. Whole urban areas fell
into decay. Bristol corporation petitioned the king for help in repairing
nine hundred houses which were in a semi-derelict state. This was the
first in a spate of such requests. In the 1530s and 1540s Norwich,
Nottingham, Shrewsbury, Gloucester and sixty-three other towns
obtained, by Act of Parliament, powers to rebuild ruined quarters.[15]

We have here the beginnings of town and country planning: local municipalities were receiving government support and even direction in the task of rebuilding. This is not to say that town authorities had not long since displayed considerable municipal pride and made decisions affecting the health, safety and comfort of citizens. Certain trades, for example, were traditionally excluded from town centres. The tile-makers of York had their workshops in Bishop Fields. Tanners, fishmongers and butchers in most towns were allocated quarters where the smell connected with their trades would cause least offence. But in what was basically a free economy situation the average citizen had little redress against powerful or influential pressure groups. Stow recalls, for instance, that at Houndsditch in London three gunfounders were allowed to set up their dangerous workshops. The vainly-protesting neighbours had had to flee for their sanity. Their dwellings were pulled down and replaced by hovels which 'do rather want room than rent' and were peopled by such commercial riff-raff as dealers in second-hand clothes.[16] The state of the streets had traditionally been left to householders and shopkeepers who were responsible for the surfacing and cleanliness of the public way before their premises. The system had, of course, never worked properly and now town authorities were beginning to assume responsibility for the uniform condition of public thoroughfares. In 1482 Southampton appointed a municipal paviour and paid for his services by levying a rate on householders. In 1501 Nottingham had its first man appointed to 'make and mend all the defaults in all places of the said town in the pavements'. He was paid 33s 4d a year plus a gown.[17]

The maintenance of roads and bridges within the borough boundaries was the responsibility of the local authorities though often, in practice, left to private charity or neglected altogether. At Culham, Leland found a substantial stone bridge and noted 'Geffray Barbar of Abbandune gave monie chefly towards makynge the bridge and procurynge lands for the maynteynaunce of it. Ther wrowght that somer 300 men on the bridge.' But at Keynsham the stone bridge of six arches was 'now al yn ruine'. Of roads Leland had little to say because there was little to be said. Most of them were mere tracks whose width and definition were directly proportionate to the amount of traffic they carried. In bad weather Leland must, like most horsemen, have eschewed the highways wherever possible, preferring to ride cross country with a local guide. For, as an Act of 1523 affirmed, 'Many common ... ways in Kent be so deep and noyous, by wearing and course of water, and other occasions, that people cannot have their carriages, or passages by horses upon, or by the same, but to their great pains, peril and jeopardy.[18] For some distance out of important towns roads might be marked and surfaced with gravel or stone. In places where the terrain was particularly bad a special effort might be made to keep the roads in reasonable condition. 'From Oxford to Hinkesey fery a quartar of a myle or more. Ther is a cawsey of stone fro Oseney to the ferie, and in this cawsey be dyvers bridges of plankes. For there the streme of Isis breketh into many armelets.'[19] For the rest the roads were rutted, uneven and pitted at the best of times and totally useless at the worst of times.

Most carts and waggons had spiked wheels, and blacksmiths whose forges stood beside busy highways did a lucrative business in keeping horses well shod and repairing broken wheels. Large tracts of fenland, moor and hill country were cut off in wet or snowy weather. There were no signposts, habitations were few and far between, and it was the easiest thing in the world to get lost. Into such areas as the Isle of Ely and Exmoor strangers ventured without guides at their peril. It was not unusual for men and horses to disappear without trace into dyke, fen or bog.

Leland certainly did not travel unarmed or without trusted servants, for human hazards were as real as natural ones along the common ways of England. Two hundred years before the first Tudor came to the throne the Statute of Winchester had ordained that the land beside highways should be cleared two hundred feet on either side to remove all cover for brigands and highwaymen. Like most inconvenient medieval legislation it was imperfectly obeyed. By 1500 an Italian visitor could confidently assert 'There is no country in the world, where there are so many thieves and robbers as in England; insomuch that few venture to go alone, excepting in the middle of the day, and fewer still in the towns at night, and least of all in London.'[20] As we shall see in a later chapter (pp. 155–61) poverty and unemployment were driving increasing numbers of Englishmen into a life of crime. Such wandered the main roads singly and in bands so that every journey carried a high element of risk. People travelled in groups whenever possible but there was not always safety in numbers. 'It hath often ben seen in England, that three or four thefes, for Povertie hath sett upon seven or eight true Men, and robbed them al. There be more Men hangyd in England in a Yere, for Robberye and Manslaughter, than ther be hangyd in France for such Cause of Crime in seven years.'[21] Wooded areas such as Epping and Sherwood were notorious haunts of these highway robbers and though the legend of Robin Hood, who only robbed the rich and gave alms to the poor, was immensely popular in Tudor England, there was a world of difference between the desperate, murderous rogues who infested the main roads and the merry men of the greenwood.

The state of bridges and highways was a subject of widespread concern. Many wealthy men and women left money in their wills for the 'repair of bridges and highways, and other pious and charitable uses'. Margaret Paston allocated five shillings for 'the reparation of the highway in Woollerton'. The commercial and official classes knew better than most the extent of this national problem. Not surprisingly we find many London merchants making bequests for road works; men like John Plot who left £5 'to be yspendyth betwene London and Ware of fowle ways . . . there most nede ys'.[22] But private charity and even action on the part of local authorities were inadequate to deal with these problems.

The Tudor period saw the beginning of legislation to tackle them at a national level. The Statute of Bridges (1531) empowered JPs to levy a rate upon towns and parishes responsible for the upkeep of bridges. Where responsibility for a particular edifice could not be assigned to a community the charge was to be borne by the shire. Similar legislation was introduced covering roads in 1555, and this authorised magistrates to impress men into work on the highways, together with their waggons and draught animals, their picks and shovels. It was a beginning but it would be centuries before England had an efficient system of roads. For the time being John Marshall's report to Cromwell would be an all too common complaint, 'The highways be cried out upon; every flood makes them impassable.'[23]

Few generalisations hold good for England's towns and cities. The sharp-eyed Leland found squalor and gracefulness, prosperity and decay. In Southampton the broad thoroughfare running from the Barrgate to the Watergate was 'one of the fairest streates that ys yn any town of al England, and it is welle buildid for timbre building',[24] and the town boasted a new covered market at Holy Rood. Bristol of the nine hundred decayed houses had fair streets fifty feet in width and an abundance of fresh water brought to the town in four conduits. Winchester, Hull, Leicester, Southampton and Exeter, as well as the capital, boasted public latrines. At Wells Leland found another excellent piece of urban development.

There be xij exceding fair houses al uniforme of stone high and fair windoid in the north side of the market place, joining hard to the north west part of the bishop's palace. This cumly peace of work was made by

Bisshop Bekington, that myndid, yf he had lyvid lengger, to have buildid other xij on the south side of the market steede, the which work if he had complished it had bene a spectable to al maket places in the west cuntery.[25]

Sutton Coldfield, a decayed town, had been refounded in recent years by the industry of the Bishop of Exeter who had built 'dyvars praty howsys' there, deforested the chase, turning it into arable land, and founded a grammar school.[26] No such benefactor had rescued the 'auncient towne' of Ribchester which Leland found 'now a poore thing'.[27] Appleby, the shire town of Westmorland 'is but a poore village, having a ruinus castel wherin the prisoners be kept'.[28] Carlisle was only a shadow of its former self, 'For wher as the stretes were and great edifices, now be vacant and garden plottes'.[29] In town after town the traveller noted crumbling walls, derelict castles and abbeys and evidence of departed prosperity.

Wealth was, thus, a highly variable commodity and the fluctuations from region to region were great. One factor in determining prosperity was industry. Here we have to unthink all that that word usually means to us – workers concentrated in busy centres of production, highly organised distribution networks, skilful manipulation of labour and raw materials. Apart from the manufacture of woollen cloth no Tudor industry was exploiting more than a fraction of its potential.

One industry which began to organise itself along modern lines was the ancient tin-mining of Cornwall and, to a lesser extent, of Devon. From time immemorial the needs of all Europe had been met almost entirely by small West Country operators washing tin ore out of gravel by the process known as streaming. But by about 1490, largely because of the growing desire for pewter, demand began to outstrip supply. Simple surface mining with pick, shovel and bucket was no longer adequate. Shafts had to be sunk, gangs of labourers employed, mining engineers and expert smelters brought over from Germany. This meant that the industry could not develop without the capitalist. The first heavy investors in tin mining were the large Devon and Cornwall landowners on whose estates tin had always been mined, families like the Courtenays and Godolphins. They were soon joined by substantial merchants from Exeter, Truro and the stannary towns.

Lead came from the hills of Shropshire, Derbyshire, Yorkshire and north Somerset. Demand in the early Tudor period was considerable as pious parishioners and ostentatious gentry built for posterity, for most lead went into roofing the great churches, castles and houses of the land. Production here was more in the hands of peasants and small landowners, but only the landed and mercantile classes could afford to manage the smelting and distribution of the metal. In the sixteenth century there was no means of protecting small industries from economic change. After decades of steady expansion the lead producers were suddenly hit by the dissolution of the monasteries. The old lead which came flooding on to the market from the redundant buildings knocked the bottom out of the business for many years.

Just when lead mining was declining, England's iron industry was experiencing a sudden boom. The only important centre of this essentially small-scale industry was the Sussex Weald and the most ambitious artefacts turned out by the charcoal-fired furnaces were small forged cannon.

2

'Your world and impery of England'

II Rural Life

LONDON WAS not England. Beyond the marshes of Hackney and Harrow's hill lay a variety of other lands, more or less isolated communities with their own customs, allegiances and languages. Though society was much more fluid than it had been in the days of all-pervasive feudalism, the majority of Englishmen still lived and died in their native villages and seldom, if ever, wandered far from them. The rich assortment of regional dialects to which this gave rise was confusing to travellers and posed a considerable problem to a man like William Caxton whose job it was to print books in the vernacular:

> . . . that comyn englysshe that is spoken in one shyre varyeth from another. In so moche that in my dayes happened that certayn merchauntes were in a shippe in Tamyse, for to haue sayled over the see into Selande, and for lacke of wynde thei taryed atte Forlond [on the Kent coast], and wente to lande for to refreshe them; and one of theym named Sheffelde, a mercer, cam in-to an hows and axed for mete; and specyally he axyed after eggys; and the goode wyf answerde, that she coude speke no frenshe. And the merchaunt was angry, for he also coude speke no frenshe, but wolde haue hadde egges and she vnderstode hym not. And theene at laste another sayd that he wolde haue eyren. Then the good wyf sayd that she vnderstod hym wel. Loo, what sholde a man in thyse dayes now wryte, egges or eyren?[1]

It was fashionable among the smart denizens of court and capital to dismiss the provinces as unsophisticated backwaters. Agents sent out from London often complained about the leaders of local society with whom they had to deal. The knights and esquires of Lincolnshire, one of them reported 'are meeter to be bailiffs; men void of good fashion, and, in truth, of wit, except in matters concerning their trade, which is to get goods only'.[2] The inept rural 'gentleman' was a stock figure of fun long before Shakespeare invented Sir Andrew Aguecheek.

There were Londoners, however, for whom the infinite variety of national life was a matter of fascinated interest. One such was Henry VIII, who demonstrated his interest by authorising John Leland's survey of the realm. Most of the cultivated ground Leland covered he called 'champion' or 'champain'. By this he meant land farmed by the old open field system. Each village had three common fields rotated in turn. Every household worked its strips within the fields and held grazing rights on the common. It was a restricted system which allowed all its participants to live more or less at subsistence level. Well might the church pronounce its anathema against 'he that removeth his neighbour's landmark'; the temptation to increase one's productive capacity at the expense of the man who ploughed the adjacent strip was great.

It was because of the economic and social pressures upon it that the old manorial system, described so brilliantly by such historians as Eileen Power (*Medieval People*), had largely broken down. Leland might use 'champain country' as a blanket term but the reality was extremely diverse. In most areas peasants had, by common consent, consolidated some of their holdings in the interests of greater efficiency. Common fields there still were, but these might be anything from five to 150 acres in extent. The growth of the woollen and cloth industries had encouraged many villagers to turn some of their land over to sheep. At Nassington in Northamptonshire, for example, fifty-two cottagers owned a total of 1200 sheep.[3]

Then, there were the more basic differences dictated by variations of soil and climate. Generally speaking, in predominantly arable areas peas, beans and barley were the basic spring-sown crops and were followed by winter wheat and rye. However, the proportions of land allotted to each crop varied considerably. Peas and beans might be the staple on heavier soils, barley on chalk uplands. In the high-yielding fen and marshland of Lincolnshire acreages were small and many villages operated a two-field system since stock, raised on the fallow, was far more profitable. Every village practised a mixed economy. The ingredients of the mixture were much the same from region to region – wheat, barley, peas, oats, rye, hemp (the latter usually grown by cottagers in a garth beside the house), cows, sheep, goats, chickens and geese – but the proportions and methods of mixing were very varied.

The freedom enjoyed by peasant farmers to organise the allocation of arable and pasture is further evidence of the decline of the feudal manor. Originally tenants and tenants-in-chief held land in return for service. At the village level this meant working so many days on the lord's land, making payment in kind at harvest time for common rights and being generally an auxiliary labour force for the landlord. By 1500 most tenants had commuted all these obligations into cash payments. For instance most householders on the roll of Bury St Edmunds Abbey now paid one penny instead of devoting a day to gathering eels for the monks, and a similar sum rid them of their harvest obligations. This had involved a change of attitude on the part of the landlords also. Increasingly land was regarded as an investment, a source of regular income. The spiritual or lay lord with many manors to administer had little interest in how the peasants farmed their fields as long as they paid their fines and rents promptly. Difficulties would only arise (as they soon did; see below, pp. 129–39) when those fines and rents no longer proved adequate to meet the landowner's rising expenses. Then he would be forced to rethink drastically his attitude to his tenants.

Despite the great diversity of agrarian life, there was a discernible pattern which held good for all rural communities. Every village, whether it straggled for a mile along a popular road, like Long Melford, or clustered round its green, like Finchingfield, was an enclosed, inward-looking and, as far as possible, self-contained community. Local issues were far more important than national issues: the miller is increasing his charges; something must be done about the rabbits from the lord's warren which are ruining the crops; young Margaret from the house beside the bridge is pregnant by John the carter's son, and her widowed mother says she can find no dowry; Peter Bull the yeoman who farms on the hill is letting his cattle muddy and foul the common stream; the chancel of the church was badly damaged in a recent storm and someone must take a message to the absentee incumbent.

The villagers grew their crops and hoped for a harvest which would feed themselves and their animals and give them a small surplus to take to market. When the harvests failed it was the villagers who had to go to market as buyers. They used almost everything the animals produced – dung, wool, meat, feathers, hides, hair; even bones were valuable to make needles, bobbins, toys, dice and small tools. The villagers could augment their food supply with fish, wild animals and birds provided they did not take them on enclosed parkland or forest (i.e. land where the game was preserved for royal use and protected by forest laws; such areas were not necessarily wooded) which crime carried heavy fines. In many places this was a considerable boon to the local people for England was rich in edible wildlife. The fenny hinterland of the Wash was particularly well stocked, 'wherein at some times and seasons of the year hath been taken in nets in August at one draught above three thousand mallards and other fowls of the like kind'.[4]

The village contained all the skilled men it needed – smith, carter, miller, carpenter, mason, wheelwright. It had two assembly rooms – the church and the inn. There the folk gossiped and gambled, said their prayers and watched the priest elevate the host. When matters of importance for the whole community arose, such as the reading of a royal proclamation or a message from the lord of the manor, the church bell would summon everyone to the church or the market cross. These places would sometimes be the venue for impromptu meetings when a group of villagers had a grievance to air or a recommendation to make. Such was the social fabric of day-to-day village life.

But the year was punctuated by a large number of 'red letter days'. Sundays and major saints' days were largely free and, according to the season, the people of town and village might resort to a variety of games and pastimes. The men might practise with the longbows which they were obliged by statute to keep and to be proficient with. When they did so the local lads of seven and upwards (seven was the age at which a boy was required to have his own small bow) would flock out with them hoping for a lesson from their neighbourhood champion. Other displays of prowess and strength at which young swains loved to show off were quoits, tossing the horseshoe, tossing the beam, wrestling and combat with staves or cudgels. Many of these sports were very rough but the prize for danger and foolhardiness must go to football, a game castigated by Sir Thomas Elyot as 'nothing but beastly fury and extreme violence; wherefore procedeth hurt and consequently rancour and malice do remain with those that be wounded; whereof it is to be [ought to be] put into perpetual silence.'[5] There were few rules in this game and no restrictions whatsoever on numbers or techniques of play. Boundaries and goals were decided by the terrain over which the game was to be played. Often it was rival villages which participated in these affrays and the object was to strike the inflated bladder on the market cross or some other appointed landmark. The contest might well go on from dawn to dusk – without result, except the traditional score of broken limbs and heads.

In the annual pageant of festivities specific, well-loved pastimes had their place. May Day was the great spring festival. Fairs were held in many towns and thither resorted bands of mummers to act over the familiar old legends. If there were no professionals, local actors made up the deficiency. Every spring the churchwardens of Kingston-on-Thames disbursed monies for the costumes and props of 'Robyn Hode . . . the mores daunsais, the frere [i.e. 'the friar' a stock figure of fun in the Morris dances] and mayde Maryan . . . and little John'.[6] Robin Hood was not then the dispossessed gentleman of nineteenth-century myth; he was set firmly in the yeoman class to which many of his rural admirers either belonged or aspired to belong.

> Roben Hood was the yeman's name,
> That was boyt corteys and ffre;
> Ffor the loffe of owre ladey,
> All wemen werscheped ye [he].[7]

It was in the Tudor period that the originally separate stories of Robin Hood, Friar Tuck and Maid Marion were brought together. Robin was no proto-communist with his own simple theory and practice about the redistribution of wealth; he was a 'goodman', a sixteenth-century John Bull, a down to earth, common-sense fellow, who unseated the proud and the pompous in a series of more-or-less comic adventures. Tudor taste added the buffoonery of Friar Tuck and the romantic (or more often bawdy) Maid Marion to the greenwood epic.

But the Robin Hood plays and dances were only the main attraction in a diverse series of May Day entertainments. On the eve of the festival young men and maidens wandered into the woods to bring back green boughs to decorate their homes and to fell and trim the maypole. This would be triumphantly dragged into the town or village next day, decked with ribbons, and set up in an open space. There then followed hours of dancing and feasting. There would be races and puppet shows for the children, troll madam, and kayles for the women, running at the quintain and straddling the greasy pole (over the village pond) for the bolder young men.

Christmas, though not for the common people the elaborate twelve-day ritual celebrated at court and in great households, was another excuse for boisterous fun and a welcome break from the dull routine of life. There were bonfires and the roasting of sheep and oxen. There was feasting and drinking at the inn, perhaps helped on by a dole of food and ale from the lord of the manor. There was the irreverent sermon preached by the boy bishop. In some places the people were traditionally invited to the manor house or the abbey to share (largely as spectators) in the revels of their betters.

Midsummer, Whitsun, Easter, sheep-shearing, harvest home, Shrove Tuesday, the feast of the local patron saint, Candlemas, Corpus Christi – these and a host of other festivals each with their attendant rituals, composed of sacred and secular elements helped to make life bearable for Tudor men and women. They did not constitute a 'Merrie Englande', nor was the pre-Reformation period an age of innocence and simple faith. Yet the regular pattern of life instilled a sense of security and order. In the 1530s the leaders of the Reformation launched an attack upon this pattern – or rather upon the superstition and idleness engendered by unnecessary saints' days. When Thomas Cromwell, the king's Vicar-General, abolished a number of ancient holy days and decreed that men should work on these days he engendered more genuine distress than was occasioned by any of the religious changes of those tumultuous years.

Not all Tudor Englishmen lived in towns and villages. The houses of the nobility and the richer gentry were in themselves centres of large communities, as were the monasteries before the dissolution. But there were many other people who lived in greater or lesser isolation from their more gregarious fellows. Some of the prosperous yeomen had aggregated holdings and built houses in the centres of their new estates. In highland regions such as the Cotswolds and the Quantocks where the accent was on stock rearing rather than arable farming there were many secluded farmsteads. In the wooded pasture country of Essex and Suffolk there still remain hundreds of moated farmhouses.

The rural peasant occupied with his family and livestock a dwelling which, for centuries, had owed little or nothing to changing fashion. His cottage, built of timber and mud (or stone if that commodity was plentiful locally), had a thatch of reed or straw. The sparsely furnished interior was gloomy with smoke and little light penetrated from the simply-shuttered casements. It was divided into two parts, a hall and a bower. It might have a small upper room. It might also boast one or two lean-to accretions. We would call it a hovel.

> Of one baye's breadth, God wot! a silly cote,
> Whose thatched sparres are furred with sluttish soote
> A whole inch thick, shining like black-moor's brows,
> Through smoke that down the hed-less barrel blows:
> At his bed's-feete feeden his stalled teme;
> His swine beneath, his pullen on the beame:

A starved tenement, such as I gesse
Stands stragling in the wasts of Holdernesse;
Or such as shiver on a Peake-hill side,
When March's lungs beate on their turf-clad hide.

The verse is that of the early-seventeenth-century writer, Joseph Hall, but it describes accurately if picturesquely the kind of dwelling which most Englishmen called 'home' a hundred years earlier. In basic materials and construction techniques there was no difference between the cottage of a farm labourer or poor tenant and the byres erected for the winter protection of livestock. Thus complaints such as the following about the Abbot of Peterborough struck contemporaries as less shocking than, at first sight, they appear to us.

> He hath enlarged his park called Meldesworth, and keepeth wild beasts now in those tenements; and by what he has taken one plough has been put down and 50 persons who were want to dwell in the messuages and cottages aforesaid have gone forth and have been compelled to seek their dwelling elsewhere.

Rural depopulation was a distressing phenomenon and one of considerable concern to Tudor governments (see below, pp. 138–9) but the loss of a cottage was not in itself a great disaster. A poor Englishman's home (and probably 30 per cent of the population lived at or below subsistence level) was not his castle. He had no sentimental attachment to the building in which he lived despite the fact that in all probability his father and grandfather had lived in it before him.

Some peasants prospered as a result of skilful husbandry, canny market dealing or, more likely, by agreeing with their neighbours to consolidate strips and thus farm more profitably. They put their spare profits into more land, acquiring freeholds or good copyholds (see below, pp. 133–4, for systems of land tenure). The independent farmer as he prospered, acquiring yeoman status and, perhaps, aspiring to the ranks of the lesser gentry, was no longer content with the humble cottage of his ancestors. He 'pulled downe the old house quite to the ground' and built 'that strong and large stone house that now stands in its place'[8] – or it might be a large house of timber framing or brick, according to the materials locally available. The dissolution of the monasteries brought on to the market an unprecedented quantity of stone, tile, timber, lead and slate from the buildings and walls no longer required on the ex-monastic estates. This accelerated an already increasing building mania which was raging at all levels of society. As the years passed, more and more substantial farmhouses studded the landscape, houses containing such 'innovations' as glazed windows, separate bed chambers for the children, fireplaces and chimneys and – essential in every 'arriviste' home – a parlour.

As Leland toured the country he was less interested in these humble dwellings than in the more imposing edifices erected by the great. In them he found vivid symbols of a changing world. Abbeys and castles were everywhere in ruins. The long Gothic era of church building had come to an end. The stress now was on domestic architecture and all over the land gentlemen, noblemen and rich merchants were erecting splendid new houses.

At Liskeard 'There was a castel on an hille in the toun side by north from S. Martin. It is now al in ruine. Fragments and peaces of waulles yet stond. The site of it is magnificent and looketh over al the toun. This castelle was the erles of Cornwall; it is now usyd somtym for a pound for catell.'[9] At Doncaster, 'The faire and large paroch chirche of S. George, standing in the very areas, where ons the castelle of the toune stoode, long sins clene decayid. The dikes partely yet be seene and foundation of parte of the waullis.'[10] Near Whitchurch, Shropshire, stood Redcastle 'now al ruinus. It hath bene strong and hath decayid many a day.'[11]

The story told by these and many, many other neglected heaps of moss-covered stone is a story of growing national peace and internal security, of declining baronial power, of the growing use of canon which rendered stout walls no longer impregnable, and of a changing social order. No longer had the peasantry to be kept in check by a baronage lodged safely within mote and bailey. Even on the troublesome western border the coming of a Welsh dynasty had done much to pacify the Celtic subjects of the crown. However, the marcher lordships enjoyed throughout the period a considerable degree of autonomy. Lawlessness was rife in these mountain fastnesses where many of the king's enemies found refuge as an Act of 1534 stated: '. . . the people of Wales and marches of the same, not dreading the good and wholesome laws and statutes of this realm, have of long time continued and persevered in perpetration and commission of divers and manifold thefts, murders, rebellions, wilful burning of houses and other scelerous deeds and abominable malefacts, to the high displeasure of God, inquietation of the King's well-disposed subjects and disturbance of the public weal. . .'[12] This Act, which extended English legal jurisdiction into the principality, was an important step in the full incorporation of Wales into the kingdom. The old Council in the Marches of

Wales was given stronger teeth and in 1536 the marcher lordships were
abolished completely, some land being added to the border counties
and five new Welsh shires being created. The old days of the Welsh
princes and the border lords who could defy the crown from their
impregnable fortresses were gone forever.

Not all the old castles fell into slow decay. The de la Pole's impressive castle at Wingfield in Suffolk still presents its crenellated fourteenth-century face to the passer-by but to the rear its appearance is
altogether different. Its half-timbered gracefulness speaks more of
comfort than defence. Belvoir Castle had suffered greatly during the
Wars of the Roses, as Leland reported:

> 'Then felle alle the Castelle to ruine, and the tymbre of the rofes
> onkeverrid rottid away, and the soile betwene the waulles at the last
> grue ful of elders, and no habitation was there tyl that of late dayes
> the Erle of Rutland hath made it fairer then ever it was . . . In the
> castel be 2 faire gates. And the dungeon is a fair rounde tour now
> turnid to pleasure, as a place to walk yn, and to se al the country
> aboute, and raylid about the round waull, and a garden plot in the
> midle.'[13]

Some castles, then, took on a new lease of life as palaces. The gaunt
towers that could be converted into places 'to walk yn' were so converted. Courtyards were sown with grass. Draughty, severe keeps were
knocked down to be replaced by domestic complexes where ladies and
gentlemen could eat and drink, sleep and dance, read, sew, converse
and make love in comfort and style. This development was to reach its
apogee not many years later at Kenilworth, when the castle fell into the
hands of Elizabeth I's favourite, Robert Dudley.

But the castle as a defensive edifice had not quite come to the end of
its days. Henry VIII was to write the last chapter in the story of the
English castle. In the 1540s a French seaborne invasion was a distinct
possibility (one was actually attempted in the summer of 1545) and the
king ordered the construction of a series of fortresses all along the
south coast. At Deal, Walmer and St Mawes they remain to this day –
squat, solid edifices whose low round towers once bristled with cannon.

If England was studded with crumbling castles it was also dotted
with the empty houses of monks, nuns and friars. Scarcely a page of
Leland's *Itinerary* lacks such references as, 'There was a right goodly
house of White Freres in the mydle of the towne now defacid.' Until
recently these buildings had echoed to the sound of plainsong and
shuffling, sandled feet. Now they were empty and open to the sky or

they had been converted into fine houses for their new owners. Sir William Sharington, master of the Bristol mint acquired Lacock Abbey, Wiltshire. Incorporating the cloisters in his new design, he tore down most of the other buildings and used the stone to erect a fine new mansion in an elaborate, Italianate style. At Wenlock in Shropshire it was just the prior's lodge and the farmery which were converted into a splendid new dwelling and the secular owner was evidently quite unconcerned as he gazed through his windows at the ruins of the massive thirteenth-century church and cloisters.

The dissolution of the monasteries provided the opportunity for private house building but the unprecedented surge of enthusiasm for new building among the wealthier classes did not have to wait for Henry VIII's massive act of spoliation. Indeed (see Chapter 5), it was the ambition and land hunger of these classes which, in part, made the dissolution possible. All over the country landowners were building new houses – houses which, though largely medieval in concept, yet reflected in their design the peace and stability of a new age. Within a few miles Leland observed the following examples of recent building in the East Midlands. At Grooby:

> There remayne few tokens of the olde castelle . . . the late Thomas Marquise filled up the diche of it with earthe, entending to make an herbare there . . . newer workes and buildinges there were erectid by the Lorde Thomas first Marquise of Dorset: emong the which workes he began and erectid the fundation and waulles of a greate gate house of brike, and a tour . . .[14]

> Thefs to Wiscumbe [Withcote] a 4. miles by corne, pasture and wood a 4 miles. Mr. Radeclif buildid here a right goodly house apon Smithe's ground, that now dwelleth yn it, and hath married a sister of the Caves. I take this to be one of the fairest housis in Leircestershire, and to the fairest orchardes and gardines of those quarters: but it stondeth lowe and wete, and hath a pole afore it . . .[15]

All over the land they stood, these new houses of stone or brick. They were semi-fortified mansions, a self-contradictory description which highlights the transitional nature of these buildings. Many were moated and had drawbridges which could be raised and lowered. Most were built on the old square plan around one or more enclosed court-yards, presenting sheer walls to the outside world. They sprouted crenellated towers and gatehouses. But their large windows, extravagant chimneys, external decoration and extensive pleasure gardens belied any serious defensive purpose. The more fashionable owners, indeed, went a step further along the road from security to comfort when they 'opened up' their house plans, designing homes to an H or E plan, but this was a foretaste of Elizabethan architecture.

It may be nothing more than a romantic response to the picturesque, but the house which above all other seems to breathe the atmosphere of early Tudor England is Compton Wynyates, a ramble of rich brick and stone work lying quietly possessive in its peaceful Warwickshire hollow. The rebuilding of the ancestral home was begun by Edmund Compton who inherited it in 1481. His son William, close companion and First Gentleman of the Bedchamber to Henry VIII, continued the work using stone from the demolished castle at Fulbrook. Neither father nor son knew anything of 'style' or felt constrained to obey the dictates of architects. They built as occasion demanded, and so chambers, staircases, turrets and windows proliferated. Within, the principal rooms were a riot of stained glass, gilding, moulded ceilings and bright tapestries, a fitting place, Sir William thought, to entertain Henry VIII and Catherine of Aragon. To the best of our knowledge his royal guests did not disagree.

The new manor house was the centre of amalgamated farmlands extensive enough to support a ménage permanently in residence or, if the owner was a courtier or merchant with pressing business elsewhere, in residence for a substantial part of the year. More and more merchants built their country houses close to the towns where their professional life was centred, and court officials studded the home counties with residences to which they could retire easily.

William Petre, a close colleague of Thomas Cromwell, and destined to become one of the longest serving Tudor administrators (he was councillor under Henry VIII, Edward VI, Mary and Elizabeth I), was well placed to benefit from the dissolution and he was not slow in making the most of his position. 'Would to God, if my lord [Cromwell] go to the King at any time before our return,' he wrote to Cromwell's secretary in 1538, 'it would please his lordship to remember our suit, wherein I 'pray you to remember your goodness. This I write because I think these times most meet for that purpose in which I am occupied in his business . . . I think the more secret the thing is kept the better, for fear of other suitors.'[16] The young official eventually gained, among other properties, the manor of Gynge Abbess (or Ing-at-stone) and here he began, in 1540, to build himself a house suitable to his status.

National Monuments Record

The houses of the great reveal changing patterns of thought.
Compton Wynyates, Warwickshire, was a medieval moated manor
built round an enclosed courtyard but generations of owners
added to it as need or prestige demanded

It may well be that, painstaking civil servant as he was, he read
carefully a treatise published by Robert Wyer in that very year, entitled
*The boke for to Lerne a man to be wyse, in buylding of his howse for the
helth of body to holde quyetnes for the helth of his soule and body*.[17] If he
did so he would have been advised of the need to choose his site with
care, ensuring that it was spacious, well wooded and watered,
preferably on a gravelly or rocky subsoil. Above all he must have his
principal rooms facing east and west, where the dominant winds were
northerlies, for the south wind 'doth corrupt and doth make evil
vapours'. Certainly Petre's design had many features which Wyer
would have approved of. The gatehouse gave on to an outer courtyard
around which were clustered storerooms and quarters for outdoor servants. Beyond that was the middle court flanked on its farthest side
(facing you as you entered the middle court) by the great hall, beyond
which again lay the inner court on to which all the principal rooms
looked. The plan was medieval but the 'feel' of the place was very up to
date. The hall was only one storey high with a massive fireplace in one
wall. Abutting on to it was the family's private dining room, for the
lord of the manor no longer presided over his whole household at
meals. On the first floor Petre had a large 'dining chamber' where he
feasted important guests. On the far side of the inner court was
situated an innovation of which he was very proud; the long gallery

'meet for any man of honour to come into'.[18] From its walls the painted faces of Petre and Henry VIII watched the family play at shove ha'penny, cards or exercise themselves on wet days. 'Let the privy chamber be annexed to the great chamber of estate . . . so that it may have a prospect into the chapel',[19] so Robert Wyer advised and so it was at Ingatestone Hall where a small chamber next to the gallery gave direct access to the chapel beneath. The whole house was built of fashionable brick and equally fashionable were the wide windows arranged symmetrically. Compton Wynyates and Ingatestone Hall display the extremes of architectural taste displayed by well-to-do gentlemen of the early Tudor era.

Wealth was as unevenly spread over the land as were population, rich soil and impressive buildings. The wool-oriented regions of Essex, Suffolk and Norfolk were among the most prosperous but if we take the loan assessment of 1524 as our yardstick we find that, in terms of pounds per acre, Kent was the most rewarding county for the tax commissioners. As well as large flocks, good arable land and the iron-working of the Weald, Kent was fortunate in being close to London and the Channel ports with their insatiable demand for agricultural produce. The Midland areas, where enclosure for sheep farming was well advanced, were among the more wealthy regions. South Devon, with

Ingatestone Hall, Essex, was built in the 1540s to a symmetrical plan in the conceiving of which comfort, convenience and visual appeal were all scientifically considered

Essex County Council

its excellent farmland and its long tradition of supplying the ship chandlers of Plymouth, also prospered.

It is significant that counties which relied largely on industrial output were nearer the bottom of the wealth league table. Magnates such as the Percy earls of Northumberland, the Lords Darcy and the bishops of Durham owned many coal-mines in the northern counties. Cornwall was one of Europe's major sources of tin, important among other uses, for the manufacture of pewter. When Leland visited Birmingham and its surrounding villages he found the air clangorous with noise of nailers, cutlers and lorimers, producing the variety of metal goods for which the region had long been famous. But most English industry was on a small-time, low-capital basis. Mining apart, they were little more than cottage industries, making no great contribution to the local economy. The long progress towards realising England's industrial potential really began in the aftermath of the dissolution of the monasteries. The new landowners, committed to the task of making their new investments pay, started to exploit their mineral resources and the manufactures based on them. It would be two centuries, however, before the ironmaster and the mill owner became more prosperous than the farmer, the tanner and the clothier.

For all England's regional variants, one factor of life was common: all regions shared the benefits of the Tudor peace. All, that is, except one.

> Now Liddesdale has ridden a raid
> But I wat they had better hae stayed at hame,
> For Michael of Winfield he is dead
> And Jock o' the Side is prisoner ta'en.

Leland paid a brief visit to the Scottish border country and found it an uncongenial land of unploughed wastes, castles and heavily fortified market towns. Of Newcastle he reported: 'The strength and magnificens of the waulling of this towne far passith al the waulles of the cities of England and of most of the townes of Europa.'[20] And every fortification was needed. Not here in these desolate northern parts the prospect of decayed castles and crumbling walls; here defence was a daily necessity.

For this was the land of the border reivers, the land of 'Tynedale and Redesdale, a country that William the Conqueror did not subdue, retaining to this day the ancient laws and customs. These Highlanders are famous for thieving; they are all bred up and live by theft. They come down from these dales into the low countries, and carry away horses and cattle so cunningly, that it will be hard for any to get them or their cattle, except they be acquainted with some master thief, who for some money may help them to their stolen goods, or deceive them.'[21]

The territory on each side of the border was divided into three marches – East, West and Middle – and each march had a warden appointed by the crown. But the reiver families were a law unto themselves. Occupying, as they did, a troubled frontier across which national armies sporadically marched in fruitless campaigns of conquest and reprisal, the local clans – the Armstrongs, Carrs, Grahams, Dacres, Fenwicks and their neighbours – had a typical frontier mentality. They recognised no motivation apart from personal advantage, no restraint other than superior force. They were obsessed by their own feuds and conflicts and, though in time of war they followed the banners of St George or St Andrew, in day-to-day life the border was not a rigid barrier between friend and foe. As the Bishop of Ross complained, the borderers,

> assume to themselves the greatest habits of licence ... For as, in time of war, they are readily reduced to extreme poverty by the almost daily inroads of the enemy, so, on the restoration of peace, they entirely neglect to cultivate their lands, though fertile, from the fear of the fruits of their labour being immediately destroyed by a new war. Whence it happens that they seek their subsistence by robberies, or rather by plundering and rapine, for they are particularly averse to the shedding of blood; nor do they much concern themselves whether it be from Scots or English that they rob and plunder.[22]

Scotland had been a thorn in the flesh for centuries. Ever since Edward I's attempt at conquest the people beyond the Cheviots had been hostile and ever ready to ally themselves with England's principal enemy, France. Henry VII's patience with the Scots was sorely tried when James IV supported and gave shelter to the pretender, Perkin Warbeck. Parsimonious Henry got as far as levying a tax to pay for a campaign against the Scots. In the event his love of peace and hatred of expense overcame him. Instead of war a new treaty was drawn up and cemented by the marriage of Princess Margaret to James IV in 1502. The uneasy peace lasted little more than a decade. In 1513 England and France were at war and Louis XII appealed for help to his old ally. James brought 20,000 men across the border to tragic annihilation at Flodden. At the end of the battle Margaret Stuart was a widow as were 10,000 other Scottish women.

It was a terrible warning, and the Scottish leaders had no stomach for further conflict until time had softened the memory. The infant James V became the pawn of rival aristocratic factions backed by English and French money. Henry VIII considered that his relationship to James gave him proprietory rights over the young man but the Scottish king showed increasing independence of spirit, proof of which was his marriage to a French princess, Mary of Guise. A series of rebuffs whittled away Henry's slender reserves of patience and in 1541 he ordered his marcher wardens to harry the Scottish lowlands. The upshot of this renewal of hostilities was another humiliating defeat for the Scots at Solway Moss a year later. James received the news at Edinburgh – and died.

Henry now sought a permanent peace cemented by the betrothal of his own four-year-old heir, Edward, to the newly-born Queen of Scots. The negotiations were bungled on both sides, and upset by Scottish factionalism and French interference. Enraged, Henry ordered another army northward to exact a ruthless vengeance. Edinburgh and the country around were to be put to fire and sword, 'a perpetual memory of the vengeance of God . . . upon them for their falsehood and disloyalty'. His orders were carried out although, as the king's calmer advisers had foreseen, such rough-wooing was counter-productive.

These, in brief, were the major political events. Their intermittent nature conceals an almost perpetual goading of the marcher wardens by the central government to take resolute action and make the Scots aware of English power. Such action was usually ruled out by the border leaders' limited resources and conflicting interests. Neither force nor friendship could impress upon the Scots the will of a distant English king who lacked the money and men to carry through a consistent, determined, long-term policy. Much the same was true of the land on this side of the border. In the fourteenth and fifteenth centuries royal authority had been restricted in those parts by the overweening power of the Percys and Nevilles. That power was now greatly weakened but that did not make it any easier for the Tudor kings to rule their subjects in the far north. For the government still needed the leaders of border society – the Dacres, Darcys, Cliffords and the various branches of the Percy family – needed them and mistrusted them. Preoccupied with their own territorial concerns and resentful of the attitude taken by distant bureaucrats who knew nothing of life on the border, these northern magnates were not the men most likely to make the best of a basically impossible situation.

Just how difficult life was for the marcher lords is demonstrated by the history of the Dacres of Gilsland. They owned many castles and estates throughout Northumberland and Cumberland and their chief seat was at Morpeth on the banks of the Wansbeck near Newcastle where they had a 'fayre castle stondinge apon a hill . . . The towne is longe and metely well buyldyd with low howsys, the stretes pavyd. It is far fayrar towne then Alenwike [i.e. Alnwick, the seat of the Percys]'.[23] In 1509 the forty-two-year-old Lord Thomas Dacre was made warden of the west march, a position held by many of his ancestors before him. The post involved espionage and diplomacy as well as military prowess, for he had to organise government missions to the Scottish court (on one occasion his duties included the pleasant task of entertaining James IV and the pleasanter task of taking £2 6s 8d off him at cards) and to keep Westminster informed of what his northern neighbours were up to. Lord Thomas served with notable courage and promptness at Flodden when, the official report tells us, '. . . Edmonde Howard was thries feled, and to his relief the Lord Dacres cam with 1500 men, and put to flight all the said Scottes, and had aboute 8 score of his men slayne'.[24] After the battle, he and his brother, Sir Christopher, led the savage reprisals against the Scots. They razed towns and villages and destroyed the standing crops. Nor did they stop until Liddesdale, Ewesdale and Teviotdale 'lies all, and every of them, waist now; noo corne sawne upon none of the said grounds'.[25]

His correspondence with Wolsey and other councillors in the ensuing years shows us a man both industrious and competent in keeping his march under control. But it was as a brave, if reckless soldier, that he was most accomplished. According to the Earl of Surrey, one of Henry VIII's principal generals, there was 'noo herdyer, nor battir knyght, but often time he doth not use the most sure order'.[26] No man better understood or exploited the border situation; the loyalty of Thomas Dacre was worth a great deal to the English crown. He bribed English and Scottish reivers to play havoc with the lands of the pro-French Scottish nobility, and his paid informants were well installed in the royal court at Edinburgh. In 1523, though fifty-six years of age and sorely afflicted with gout, he took to the field at the head of his lightly-armoured borderers in a further round of savage official raiding in the Lowlands. In 1525 he was appointed warden-general of the Scottish marches but a few months later he died – characteristically, it was as the result of a fall from his horse.

For all Lord Thomas's talents he bequeathed his family, and the English government, a problem. As a young man he had fallen in love with and abducted Elizabeth Greystoke, the seventeen-year-old ward of Lord Clifford. This began a bitter feud which erupted into serious trouble soon after Dacre's death. He was succeeded as warden by Henry Clifford, recently created Earl of Cumberland. William, the new Lord Dacre, challenged Clifford over the ownership of Carlisle Castle, the warden's headquarters. The feud seriously disturbed the border for over two years until a temporary truce was patched up by the Duke of Northumberland in 1528, when Dacre was appointed warden. He now became a scourge of the reivers, determined to put down lawlessness and particularly to bring the notorious Armstrongs to heel.

But the earl had neither forgiven nor forgotten. He took every opportunity to harass Dacre's people and to complain of misconduct on the border. In 1534 he brought a charge of high treason against Lord William. The frivolity of the accusation is attested by the fact that Dacre was acquitted, the only nobleman to escape from a treason charge in the whole of Henry VIII's reign. But the baron's honour had been besmirched and he forfeited the king's trust. The wardenship went once more to Cumberland. When, two years later, the Pilgrimage of Grace broke out (see pp. 89–91) William simply did not know what to do for the best. Many of his tenants joined the rebels and the pilgrims believed that in the aggrieved baron they might well find a champion. However he might protest his loyalty, his enemies could easily find opportunity to carry false information about him to the king. In the end he decided that his only wise course of action was to go to court where his actions might be neutral but at least could not be misconstrued.

In his absence his uncle, Sir Christopher, acquitted himself well, as even the Earl of Cumberland was forced to admit. In February 1537 Sir Thomas Clifford and the Carlisle garrison were besieged by a commons army. Now old feuds were forgotten and urgent messages were sent to Sir Christopher Dacre. At the moment when the rabble made its major assault, Sir Christopher appeared with five hundred mounted spearmen. He rode down the alarmed rebels, killing, by popular estimate, some seven hundred of them, and became the hero of the hour. Yet, even in the midst of the widespread upheaval of the Pilgrimage, reports were coming in to Thomas Cromwell's office of continued feuding between the Cliffords and Dacres. Richard Dacre, the baron's son, came to blows with Lord Clifford's men in Carlisle churchyard, then rampaged through the town with a band of tenants at his back shouting 'A Dacre! A Dacre!' Such were the men who were responsible for law and order on the border.

The time had come for Tudor authority to be extended into the northern shires as it had been into the Welsh marches. Thomas Cromwell took an old institution, the Council of the North, and breathed new life into it. He appointed lawyers and bureaucrats from the central government to sit on the council as well as the great northern magnates. The marcher lords had seen royal councils before; they had always collapsed before the enormous problems of the border and the united hostility of the baronage. They did not take Cromwell's creation very seriously. But they were wrong: there was a new permanence about the administrative machine set up with its headquarters at York which would make it an effective force for change. This was not the end of border reiving but it was the beginning of the end.

Tudor England was, then, a land of close horizons. What lay beyond the hill, or the other side of the forest was the outside world. Pedlars, friars, journeymen who travelled that world were men to be listened to with excitement and wonder for they had strange tales to tell of King Henry, the pope, the grand cham of Tartary and the many other wonders whose realms began at the frontier of the familiar. Some simple countrymen had seen France if they had been unfortunate enough to get involved in one of the king's wars and there were those who made a business out of travelling to and fro across the Narrow Seas. Such men were Merchant Adventurers indeed.

Yet, while local authorities loomed large in men's minds, Englishmen had a very real national consciousness, a consciousness the first Tudors were anxious to encourage and exploit. The idea of the nation state received its clearest expression in the preamble to Henry VIII's Act in Restraint of Appeals (1533)

> ... by divers sundry old authentic histories and chronicles it is manifestly declared and expressed that this realm of England is an empire, and so hath been accepted in the world, governed by one supreme head and king having the dignity and royal estate of the imperial crown of the same, unto whom a body politic, compact of all sorts and degrees of people divided in terms and by names of spiritualty and temporalty, be bounded and owe to bear next to God a natural and humble obedience.[27]

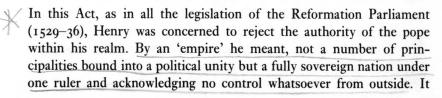

In this Act, as in all the legislation of the Reformation Parliament (1529–36), Henry was concerned to reject the authority of the pope within his realm. By an 'empire' he meant, not a number of principalities bound into a political unity but a fully sovereign nation under one ruler and acknowledging no control whatsoever from outside. It was not an entirely new idea; Englishmen had for centuries felt a sense of national identity which made them different from Scotsmen, Frenchmen, Welshmen, Spaniards and the Infidel Turk. In the past, however, the concept of 'empire' had always had to share a place with the concept of 'Christendom' in the minds of the island race. England, as well as having a temporal identity had a spiritual identity: it was the English church and part of the greater church whose earthly head was the pope. The conflict between these two concepts was one which extended far back beyond the time of Henry II and Becket. One aspect of the Reformation was the culmination of that conflict in the complete triumph of nationalism allied with religious radicalism (see below, pp. 217–30), a triumph which Tudor ministers expertly used parliament and propaganda to bring about.

Henry VII and his son had another reason for asserting the imperial idea, a reason concerned not with powers outside the realm. In 1485 large tracts of country were still dominated by the traditionally powerful noble families – the Percys of the North, the Howards in East Anglia, the Courtenays of Devon and Cornwall. The first two Tudors were to change all this. They would make the monarchy a reality in distant parts of the realm, would banish the national schizophrenia by bringing both church and state under one authority, would give a new meaning to the word 'empire'.

This empire was to play a new role in the affairs of the wider world. Three score years and ten had passed between Agincourt and Bosworth. For Tudor Englishmen the martial glories and continental pretensions of the 'golden age' of Henry V had passed out of living memory and into the realm of legend. The first Tudor concentrated on putting an end to internal strife while maintaining a real but inexpensive influence in continental affairs. His son was determined to cut a more dashing figure as general and statesman. And despite the mistakes and follies of Henry VIII's foreign policy, he and his father won for England a new respect in the councils of Europe.

Men who, like More, were conversant with the international situation found it alarming in the extreme. While Habsburg Spain and Valois France pursued their insane armed rivalry, which occasionally embroiled England; while the Empire disintegrated as German princes and archdukes waged war on each other in the name of religion; and while mercenary armies roamed the continent of Europe, the Ottoman Turks under the invincible Suleiman the Magnificent threw the Christian knights out of Rhodes, destroyed the flower of Hungarian chivalry at the Battle of Mohács, and marched to the gates of Vienna.

In vain the pope called for a crusade. So far from uniting against the
common enemy, Christendom was falling apart. New heresies, bred in
Germany and Switzerland, were exacerbating the growing nationalism
of German states. It seemed that European civilisation no longer
believed in itself, it was decaying from within. That was why More set
himself so staunchly, even vehemently, against the Lutherans, why he
inveighed against war – 'a thing very beastly' – why he urged the king
to avoid involvement in the affairs of Europe, and why he was appalled
when the government cast off England's papal allegiance.

N. World

The early Tudor period saw the beginnings of England's involvement in the world which was opening up beyond Europe and the
Mediterranean. The excitement of new discovery was contagious as
brave captains ventured into the unknown 90 per cent of the earth's
surface. Before Henry VII was fully secure on his throne Christopher
Columbus was exploring the coast of Central and South America.
While the king was keeping the traditional Christmas revels at
Westminster in 1497, Vasco da Gama was visiting a sunny land that
would ever after be called Natal. When Henry of England and Francis
I of France were indulging their sham gilded diplomacy at the Field of
Cloth of Gold, Hernando Cortés was winning Spain a golden empire in
Mexico. Before the end of the second Tudor's reign Spanish and
Portuguese fleets were unloading on to the quays of Lisbon and Cadiz
the treasures of the New World and the spices of the East. And no
Englishman challenged the right of the Iberian lands to all this wealth.
Had not the seal of the church been placed on that right? By the treaty
of Tordesillas (1494) the pope had solemnly drawn a line round the
globe dividing all *Terra Incognita* between Spain and Portugal. It was
only after their rejection of the pope's church that Englishmen seriously began to challenge the primacy the Spaniards and Portuguese
had established in overseas colonisation and trade. In 1545 Robert
Reneger of Southampton set all Europe by the ears when he captured
the Spanish treasure ship *San Salvador* and lifted 124 chests of
sugar, 140 hides and a large, undisclosed, quantity of bar-gold. A new
age, the age of Drake and Hawkins and of overseas expansion had
dawned.

But the old age was not without its excitements. Between 1485 and
1547 England, for all practical purposes, gave up its claims to French
territory. True, Henry VIII made two grandiose military expeditions
across the Channel. True, he added Boulogne to Calais thus giving
England a second toe-hold on the continent. But these were flashes in
the pan, as anachronistic and impractical as Don Quixote. Yet while

England's political claims abroad were evaporating, her commercial claims were taking on substance. London and, to a lesser extent, Southampton were doing a roaring trade with Antwerp and the Baltic; Bristol and Exeter were engaged in lively commerce with Spain; Southampton had a good, though declining, relationship with the Mediterranean ports. In the cosmopolitan atmosphere of England's wharves and waterfront inns native merchants did business with heavily-furred members of the Hanse and ostentatiously wealthy Spaniards. They heard captains tell of the marvels of Mexico and Peru and the fabled riches of Cathay. The more adventurous among them yearned to visit the new found lands for themselves; the more ambitious resented the dominance of foreigners in the carrying trade. They bought more ships and in increasing numbers they petitioned court and parliament for increased privileges. They did not find Henry VII unresponsive.

In a succession of commercial treaties and in no less than fifty Acts of Parliament the government took measures to encourage and assist English merchants. They restricted the privileges of foreign traders and increased the tolls levied on them. They offered bounties to shipowners who laid down new vessels of eighty tons or over. Within the first year of his reign Henry VII had introduced his first Navigation Act (re-enacted with additional clauses in 1489) which restricted to English, Irish and Welsh ships the carrying trade in Gascon wine.

The merchant community responded well. They were men in search of profit but they were also adventurers. From about 1480 pioneer captains, brave and anonymous men, had been sailing westwards from Bristol towards the empty horizon of the grey Atlantic. They had found the 'Isle of Brazil' (Newfoundland?) whose waters teemed with fish. Their exploits were carried along the shipping lanes of the old world and retold wherever sea captains met. At length they reached the ears of the Genoa-born Venetian John Cabot, who had his own ideas about reaching Cathay by a more northerly route than Columbus's. Cabot outlined his plans to the leaders of the Bristol mercantile community and with their backing obtained from the king letters patent authorising him to sail to all parts of the 'eastern, western, and northern sea' and to explore 'whatsoever islands, countries regions or provinces of heathens, and infidels . . . which before this time were unknown to all Christians'. That Henry was genuinely interested in exploration – and particularly its economic possibilities – there is no doubt. He was also flattered at the thought of being the patron of a

By permission of the Master and Fellows, Magdalene College, Cambridge

The *Henry Grâce à Dieu*

second Columbus, especially when Ferdinand and Isabella of Spain tried hard to dissuade him from supporting Cabot's schemes.

Cabot sailed in May 1497. He found the American coast, returned in triumph and became the hero of the hour. 'The King of England is much pleased . . . Cabot . . . is styled the great admiral. Vast honour is paid him; he dresses in silk, and these English run after him like mad people . . .'[28] John Cabot fired the imagination of a whole generation of seafaring Englishmen. Though a foreigner he was taken to their hearts as the first great English adventurer. When he planned another expedition in 1498 an observer stated, 'he can enlist as many as he pleases',[29] and when he failed to return from that expedition there were hundreds of brave spirits anxious to take up the crusade he had left unfinished.

In 1501 Henry VII and leading Bristol merchants backed the Portuguese João Fernandes, who discovered the coast of Labrador. By 1509 it had become obvious that the land mass which lay some six weeks sailing time to the west was not Asia. In that year John Cabot's son Sebastian, backed by a large amount of Bristol money, set off to find a north-west passage around the obstructing land mass. He reached 67 degrees north before being forced back by ice and mutiny. Still the Bristolians clung to their dreams of reaching Cathay and proving that Bristol was the closest European port to the land of the Great Cham. Men, ships and money disappeared into the freezing northern waters but always, it seems, there were more to take their place. They achieved little. It was, in fact, a voyage by John Rut in 1527 which was the most significant of the age: he became the first English captain to sail in the Caribbean – and what a shock he gave the colonial authorities of proud, self-confident Spain.

By the time the second Tudor ascended the throne the possibility was shimmering in a few advanced minds that England might become a major maritime power. Henry VII had rested content to encourage other men to build ships; the royal navy comprised but five vessels when he died in 1509. Within five years it had been increased to thirty-one. Throughout his reign the king paid close attention to enlarging and improving his navy which included such fine capital ships as the *Mary Rose* and the *Henri Grâce à Dieu*. Dockyards were built at Woolwich and Deptford. Portsmouth was enlarged. Trinity House was incorporated in 1514 to advance the study of navigation and pilotage. The office of Lord Admiral gained a new importance and its holder was assisted by a Navy Board with enhanced powers. Henry never tired of showing off his fleet. Even the ladies of the queen's chamber had to be sent to Portsmouth to view the new ships with their massively increased fire power. They confessed themselves dutifully impressed:

> Most gratiouse and benigne sovraigne Lorde, please it your Highnes to understonde that wee have seene and beene in your newe Greate Shippe, and the rest of your shippes at Portismowth, wiche arr things so goodlie to beholde, that, in our liefs wee have not seene (excepting your royall person and my lord the Prince your sonne) a more pleasant sight; for wiche and the most bountiful gifts, the cheere and most gratiouse enterteignment, wich your Grace hath vouchsavid to bestowe upon us your most unworthie and humble servaunts, wee rendre and send unto the same our most humble and entier thanks . . .[30]

The 'world and impery of England' was getting ready to venture into the wider world. Educated Englishmen were developing a taste for travel and a fascination for travellers' tales. Thomas More was certainly such an Englishman, which is why one of his friends introduced More to a Portuguese visitor.

> . . . for there is no man thys day livyng, that can tell you of so manye staunge and unknowen peoples, and Countreyes, as this man can.

And I know wel that you be very desirous to heare of such newes . . .
His patrimonye that he was borne unto, he lefte to his brethern . . .
and for the desire that he had to see, and knowe the farre Countreyes
of the worlde, he joyned himselfe in company with Amerike
Vespuce, and in the iii last voyages of those iiii that be nowe in
printe and abrode in every mannes handes, he continued styll in his
company, savyng that in the last voyage he came not home agayne
with him . . . He was therefore lefte behynde for hys mynde sake, as
one that tooke more thoughte and care for travailyng, then dyenge
. . . after the departynge of Mayster Vespuce . . . he . . . travailed
thorough and aboute many Countreyes . . .[31]

The traveller's name was Raphael Hythloday and among the
'Countreyes' he visited was the incomparable land of Utopia.

3

'*Them that sue for great men's friendship*'

Patronage, Education and Law

JUDGE JOHN MORE gave his boy a good basic education by sending him to St Anthony's, the best school in London. At the age of twelve young Thomas was ready for a change of scene and for the acquisition of a patron. By pulling every string which lay to hand, the judge acquired the support of a very great man indeed. John Morton was Archbishop of Canterbury, Lord Chancellor of England, and Henry VII's closest adviser. His political twists and tergiversations during the York–Lancaster contest as well as his undoubted talents had won for him, at the age of sixty-five, the highest prize. He was the most powerful man in the land below the king. (More's observation of his master was shrewd and incisive: 'a man of gret natural wit, very well lerned, & honorable in behaueor, lacking no wise waies to win fauor . . . [he] hadde gotten by great experience ye verye mother and maistres of wisdom, a depe insighte in politike worldli driftes.')[1]

There was nothing at all remarkable about John More's fervent efforts to win the support and aid of the Archbishop. Patronage was the mortar of Tudor society, binding together the greater and lesser men in an edifice of mutual interest. The social order was clearly defined and understood. It was a pyramid with the king at the summit and descending orders of temporal and spiritual nobility, gentlemen, burgesses, artisans and peasants. Men sensed that this ordering of society was inevitable – hallowed not only by tradition but also by God.

> . . . all Dukes, Erles, Barons, knightes, esquiers, and other gentlemen
> by office or auctorite, [have] nede to lyve in a good conformyte, that
> is to saie, euery man after the honour and degre that god and his

prince hath callid hym vnto, and after that part or porcion to leade
his lyef, and not [to] maligne or envie his superiors nor disdaign or
sett at nought his inferiors. But euery man to know other with his
dewtie and to helpe and guyde as his poower may extend . . .[2]

If stability were to be ensured, injustice and anarchy avoided, men
ought to be content with their lot. But, of course, men and women
were no more contented with their lot then than they are now. The fact
that writers like Edmund Dudley expressed such pious conservative
hopes is in itself sufficient indication that society was not static. Great
magnates were striving, by land deals and marriages, to make themselves greater. Successful merchants were buying estates and marrying
into the gentry. Ambitious tenant farmers worked hard and saved in
the hope of becoming landowners. Men of the humblest status
educated their sons in the hope that, through the church or the law,
they might better themselves.

The system was sufficiently firm to prevent too much change –
particularly among the lower orders – and sufficiently flexible to ensure
that men of exceptional talent or tenacity could reach the top. And the
word 'top' is no exaggeration. The two most powerful men in England
next to the king between 1513 and 1540 were Thomas Wolsey and
Thomas Cromwell. One was the son of a small Ipswich tradesman who
came to the royal service via the church; the other was sired by a
Putney brewer-cum-blacksmith and his path to fame lay through the
common law. Both ministers, and other commoners who rose to high
rank, were despised as upstarts, for there was some contradiction, even
hypocrisy, in society's attitudes. Every man of intelligence and
initiative sought to improve himself and applauded the cleverness or
luck of those who succeeded. At the same time he had an inbuilt regard
for the noble and ancient families who by tradition bore local rule and
were the king's closest advisers. Edmund Dudley – himself of ancient
baronial stock – blamed the nobles themselves for allowing their rightful place to be usurped by lesser men:

> For veryly I feare me, the noble men and gentlemen of England be
> the worst brought vp for the most parte of any realme of christen-
> dom, And therfore the childeren of poore men and meane folke are
> promotyd to the promocion and auctorite that thee childeren of
> noble Blood should haue yf thee were mete therfore.[3]

There was, of course, much more to it than that. Every competent
king since William I had made extensive use of the best talents

available to him, irrespective of rank. People might believe that wisdom, intelligence and the ability to govern only flowed with 'blue' blood but when it came down to the practical task of appointing councillors and household officers medieval monarchs knew that while they could bestow noble titles, the same was not true of such qualities as diplomacy, breadth of vision and a 'good head for figures'.

Nor was this realism evident only in kings. Any man who had great estates to administer or widespread business interests was a fool if he did not employ the most competent people as stewards, captains and factors. This realism had contributed to the breakdown of feudalism, or rather its degeneration into 'bastard feudalism'. By 1495 little trace of original feudalism remained; a system of social bonds based on landholding and service had been replaced by an extensive, amorphous system of feed retainership. First of all there were those maintained in a lord's household. They received a fee or wage and a 'livery', which as well as food and drink might include special clothing and the lord's badge. A man might be retained for life or for an agreed term and he might be employed for almost any function – man at arms, chaplain, steward, farrier or simply a super-numerary attendant paid to increase the lord's retinue and thus enhance his prestige. Display was important; in 1471 the Duke of Suffolk disdained to come to court because 'his servants were from him', many having been given leave of absence for Christmas, and he would not appear in public with a depleted following. Cardinal Wolsey set the ultimate standard in large and ostentatious retinues; 'in his family there were one earl, nine barons and about a thousand knights, gentlemen, and inferior officers'.[4] In one month alone the great minister's kitchen got through 430 oxen and 181 sheep to meet the requirements of those who received Wolsey's livery.[5] Such a large household overshadowed even the royal court (as King Henry eventually realised) and makes the permanent establishments of other Tudor notables appear quite beggarly by comparison. The Duke of Buckingham, for example, could boast only 148 attendants in 1519.[6]

Of much greater concern to king and commoner alike were the large numbers of men retained on an almost casual basis. Small farmers, landless men, even the aimless unemployed might be taken on to a great lord's 'payroll' for unspecified and irregular duties. They might be taken on for shorter or longer periods and their contracts might be terminated without notice. They had loyalty to no one but their paymaster. They enjoyed his protection. In fact, they were effectively beyond the reach of the law. Thomas More described such a one as 'wont with a sworde and buckler by hys syde to jette through the strete with a bragginge loke, and to thynke hym selfe to good to be anye mans mate'.[7] Such retainers might be called upon by their patron to carry out some vendetta, pursue a long-standing feud or simply take part in an ordinary cattle raid. Petitions like the following from a group of Westmorland plaintiffs were all too common in the royal courts:

> ... where your said beseechers were in God's peace and yours, one Robert Warcoppe the elder, of Warcop, Robert Warcoppe the younger, and other riotous and misruled people, to the number of 53 persons and more, the 14th day of the month of October last past, with force and arms, that is to say with bows, arrows, bills, swords and bucklers ... riotously assembled, made assault upon your said beseechers and there beat, wounded and put in jeopardy of their lives without occasion on their part giving, to the great peril of your said beseechers and to the worst example of other like offending unless due punishment be had ...[8]

And we may be sure that for every citizen who plucked up courage to seek justice in the royal courts there were a score who did not.

The abuses of livery and maintenance had been obvious to the crown ever since the reign of Henry IV. Between 1399 and 1485 six Acts of Parliament were enacted to control and limit the practice. They were all ineffective. Henry VII brought in four more. The 1503 statute insisted,

> that no person, of what estate, or degree, or condition he be ... privily or openly give any livery or sign or retain any person, other than such as he giveth household wages unto without fraud or colour, or that he by his manual servant [a servant who works with his hands] or his officer or man learned in the one law or in the other [civil or canon law], by any writing, oath, promise, livery, sign, badge, token or in any other manner wise unlawfully retain; and if any do the contrary, that then he run and fall in the pain and forfeiture for every such livery and sign, badge or token, so accepted, 100s, and the taker and accepter of every such livery, badge, token, or sign, to forfeit and pay for every such livery and sign, badge or token, so accepted, 100s ...[9]

Which sounds very firm and severe, as though the government was determined to eradicate a pressing social evil. In fact the evil remained and prosecutions under the livery statutes were rare. Even the Tudors could not by royal fiat change overnight the established pattern of decades. Livery and maintenance did dwindle during the first half of the sixteenth century but not because of a deliberate campaign waged against it by the sovereign. The forces of change were more fundamental: economic pressures militated against large households; royal power became more of a reality in the remoter areas; trade, maritime expansion and new business ventures provided potentially more profitable outlets for capital, labour and enterprise; the consolidation of land holdings reduced the need for landlords to keep bodies of armed retainers to guard their interests in different places. But the pace of change was very slow and even the mighty Tudors knew that it was wise to accept the fact that there were parts of the land where the great men and their liveried retainers held more sway than the representatives of the crown. On 13 January 1524 Lord Dacre wrote from Morpeth to report on the continued feuding between the Horsleys, the Claverings and the Carrs. There had recently been two murders and this had led to fresh outbreaks of violence. The JPs had been called in to compel the contending parties to keep the peace. The magistrates had summoned all parties before them, heard evidence and made awards to those who could prove loss or injury. They had done their best to impress on the sullen defendants the need for peace and harmony. Solemnly, they had extended the king's pardon for all previous crimes and abjured the troublesome borderers to refrain from further violence. It was no use; the Carrs and the Claverings refused to abide by the justices' decision. What could the royal representative do? Dacre lacked the resources to deal with the many outbreaks of petty violence throughout his extensive territory. All he could do was appeal to the king to send a special letter obliging the feuders to keep the peace.[10]

The system of patronage did not by any means cease at the outermost fringe of the extended household or 'affinity' as it was called. It was the accepted custom for those who could afford it to buy the support of any who could be useful to them. Religious houses paid local magnates to act as 'stewards'. Thus Sir William Ayscough was steward of the Stallingborough estates of Thornton and Selby abbeys, steward of Nun Cotham Priory and chief steward of Newsome Abbey. His emoluments from these posts amounted to £6 6s 8d a year.[11] For his money Sir William rarely had much to do but his patronage was valuable to the monks and nuns. The support of a powerful man discouraged neighbours who might be tempted to interfere with their interests, and when serious disputes arose involving the king or his ministers they had a champion to plead their cause. Such stewards never found their friendship put severely to the test, until 1536–40 when the dissolution of the monasteries presented them with a not insignificant dilemma.

In the same spirit, noblemen and substantial gentlemen paid underlings (and sometimes each other) to represent them at court and in other places of influence. Members of the House of Commons drew pensions from magnates and business cartels. The Earl of Northumberland paid £10 a year to Mr Heneage, 'gentleman usher to my lord cardinal' and £5 to Wolsey's chamberlain.[12] At the same time the earl was receiving £20 a year as steward of Holderness for the Duke of Buckingham.[13] In such lawless times landowners whose estates were scattered throughout the realm needed alliances with powerful men able to protect their interests.

Where the great men led lesser men followed.

Your lordship's [Thomas Cromwell's] humble beadsman Edward Boughton earnestly desires your lordship to be good lord to my niece Anne Banastre and order her husband to give her an honest living out of her own. I cannot, being but a poor man, make your lordship payment but will give your lordship fine timber to the new parlour.[14]

I [Sir William Parr] make suit to your lordship [Lord Dacre] on behalf of my poor tenant John Warrener of Kendal whose farmland is claimed by his brother. Your lordship helped him before but now his brother is reclaiming the land and he has the help of Sir Roger Bellingham. I would take it in friendly part if you would write to the judges at Appleby on Warrener's behalf . . .[15]

At every level of society the poorer were dependent on the richer, the impotent on the powerful. Whatever a man wanted – a job, land, a benefice, help with a lawsuit, even support against troublesome relatives or neighbours – his first concern was to find some exalted champion who, for a consideration, would be his 'especial good lord'. It was a state of affairs accepted by both sides: the lower orders did not resent the paternalism of their superiors; the powerful were not aggravated by the importunity of their many suitors. Only in an age like our own which makes an elaborate pretence of social equality are the bonds holding society together relaxed. In the sixteenth century men knew that their status carried responsibilities. By and large, they were prepared to discharge those responsibilities.

For any man close to the king this meant that petitioners and place-seekers were daily presenting themselves at his door. Young hopefuls whose families could scrape up the most distant relationship sought a place in the great man's household. Some were successful; others had to be firmly discouraged from returning. It must have been difficult for servants to know who might be admitted to the household and who might not. Thomas Cromwell had to make a list for his steward. The names were under three heads: 'Gentlemen not to be allowed in my Lord's household aforesaid but when they have commandment or cause necessary to repair thither'; 'Gentlemen most meet to be daily waiters upon my said Lord'; and 'Gentlemen meet to be preferred unto the King's Majesty's service.[16]

It was a system, if such a hotch-potch of casual relationships can be so called, based on mutual advantage. It was not perfect. It encouraged lawlessness; it did not prevent exploitation; it might even add to the problems of unemployment and vagabondage which were the dominant social diseases of the day, for many retainers,

> ... never learned any craft wherby to gette their livynges. These men as sone as their mayster is dead, or be sicke themselfes, be incontinent thrust out of dores. For gentlemen hadde rather keepe idle persones, then sicke men, and many times the dead man's heyre is not hable to mainteine so great a house, and kepe so many serving men as his father dyd. Then in the meane season they that be thus destitute of service, either starve for honger, or manfullye playe the theves ...[7]

Nevertheless the system had the advantage of being understood and accepted by all.

At no time was the dependence of the commons on the great men more clearly seen than during the rare outbreak of rebellion. In 1497 the men of Cornwall marched northwards. They were for the most part tin miners, peasants and ill-educated yeomen. Leaders of a sort they had – a blacksmith and a lawyer – but they needed more prestigious generalship so they opened secret negotiations with James, Lord Audley, a nobleman known to be discontented with the new regime, who joined the host at Wells. The northern and Midlands rebellion of 1536 was a more serious affair. In Lincolnshire the insurgents made it their first objective to lay hands on as many of the gentry as possible. They apprehended a band of royal commissioners and '... they did swear us first to be true to your Grace and to take their parts in maintaining of the commonwealth and so conveyed us with them from the said Caistor unto the town of Louth ...'[18]

Among other leaders pressed into service by the rebels were the sheriff and the lord lieutenant, the latter of whom was to pay with his head. In Yorkshire the situation was even worse: Lord Darcy, the Archbishop of York and most of the local gentry fell into the rebels' hands. Some readily accepted the leadership of the 'Pilgrimage of Grace' (see pp. 89–91); others had to be coerced. It was not an easy decision for any of them. If their loyalty to the king was in question, so also was their position in local society.

But the patronage system in normal times worked for the king rather than against him. He was, after all, the fount of all patronage – the man best able to grant boons and reward service. Appeals for aid came in a constant stream to him and to the men and women of his entourage, who were deliberately placed at court by their families in order to secure royal favour. If gained, royal favour could be gratifyingly abundant in its expression – and as capricious as it was abundant.

Thomas Boleyn was, by all accounts, an unremarkable man. The second son of a Norfolk gentleman, he served the king as a soldier and local administrator and, during the early years of Henry VIII's reign, he achieved acceptance at court and was employed on occasional foreign embassies. An unremarkable man, but he had remarkable daughters – remarkable, at any rate, for their beauty – and it was they who were to unlock the royal favour for Thomas Boleyn. Mary took the king's fancy some time in 1518 or 1519. In 1520 she became pregnant and Henry married her off to William Carey. Within a couple of years the king's dishonourable intentions were turned towards the younger daughter, Anne. The story of the protracted wooing is well known. For some years Anne held out against her royal suitor, which only increased his determination to have her. At length she became his mistress but only after he had set in hand the ponderous machinery for the annulment of his marriage to Catherine of Aragon.

The byproduct of these Henrician infatuations was for Thomas Boleyn an enormous increase in wealth and social status. He received considerable grants of land, while titles and offices flowed in a gratifying stream – Treasurer of the Household, Knight of the Garter, Keeper of Beskwood Park, Keeper of Thundersley Park, Steward of Swaffham, Viscount Rochford, Earl of Wiltshire and Ormonde, Lord Privy Seal. In 1525 his income was assessed at £800 per year, equivalent to something in the region of half a million in modern terms. It was more than adequate reward for producing pretty daughters.

It was the dream of every ambitious father that one of his sons or daughters might somehow find the king's favour and thus establish the family fortunes. There was little room for subtlety. The clamorous

Anne Boleyn, by
Holbein

Collection the Earl of Bradford

competition at court was too great. Some young people found it difficult to sustain the role imposed upon them by their 'pushing' relatives.
We cannot but feel for Anne Bosset who wrote to her mother, Lady
Lisle: 'I have presented your quince marmalade to the King's
Highness, and his Grace does like it wondrous well and gave your
ladyship hearty thanks for it. And whereas I perceived by your ladyship's letter, that when the King's Highness had tasted of your marmalade, you would have me to move his Grace for to send you some
token of rememberance . . . I durst not be so bold.'[19]

Doubtless, Lady Lisle fretted and fumed over this lost opportunity.
Now she would have to find some other means of gaining that manor,
that position at court for her cousin, that royal support in her King's
Bench suit, or whatever 'token' she was seeking.

The first section of a son's journey on the road to favour and fortune
was a sound education. That meant, first and foremost, a firm grasp of
Latin. During Thomas More's lifetime written English was asserting
itself. Increasingly, books, administrative documents, wills and contracts were written in the vernacular but, as Caxton complained, there

was as yet no precise, reliable and standardised form of written English. Thus, for some decades, Latin would remain the language of scholarship, the law and the church. (To some extent Latin shared a place with French as the language of diplomacy. This was the last refuge of French which, in Chaucer's day, had been the language of polite society and commerce but which had been gradually ousted by the vernacular.)

St Anthony's in Threadneedle Street where Thomas More received his basic education was the City's leading grammar school. Founded some 250 years previously, it provided the sons of merchants and lawyers with a basic training in Latin. Not only were pupils expected to read and write in Latin and to know by heart many passages from the Classical authors, they were also expected to be able to dispute in Latin. Schools with such a high reputation as St Anthony's were always crowded, and the young More would often have found space to sit only on the floor. From this position he would listen to the master slowly intoning the texts which were to be written down or committed to memory by the boys. Later in life More remembered ruefully the beatings with which lessons were driven home and tardiness punished.

Few boys were fortunate enough to enjoy a standard of teaching comparable to that at St Anthony's but the pattern of school life was much the same whether the instructor was a poor chantry priest with little grasp of Latin or a university-trained specialist teaching choirboys and local children in one of the great Benedictine abbeys. This aspect of education was very largely in the hands of the church. It reflected the, by now, antiquated belief that boys who received a grammar school education were destined for an ecclesiastical career. There were other kinds of education for the young and all of them were career-oriented. The sons of gentlemen and noblemen were farmed out to other great households to imbibe the etiquette and the skills that were deemed necessary for their future station in life. Other lads underwent the long and exacting apprenticeships laid down by the masters of the various trade guilds. In the same way the universities were geared to the production of theologians, physicians, lawyers and administrators.

But this pattern of education and the assumptions underlying it were soon to be called in question and More himself would be among the principal critics. The outer ripples of Renaissance humanism had been lapping at the walls of English universities for some decades but the first breach was made by John Colet and his circle in the 1490s. These were, indeed, men of the 'new learning'. They campaigned for new curricula, new methods of study and new assumptions as to the pur-

'Learning' embraced an ever-widening area. In the grammar school the basic education comprised reading, writing and disputing in Latin. At the universities courses were extended to include arithmetic, geometry, cosmography, medicine, Greek, Hebrew and Arabic

pose of study. For them the aim of education was not the training of men for their chosen station in life; it was to make better men, men morally and intellectually equipped to lead virtuous lives of service to God and the king.

The new momentum in school education began when Colet left Oxford to take up the post of Dean of St Paul's Cathedral. In 1508 he founded St Paul's school and there put into practice his radical ideals. It must have been with an excitement bordering on intoxication that Colet and his friends saw the first children arrive and begin to imbibe the learning and attitudes that were to equip them as pioneers of a new, enlightened age. The complaints of establishment men about the dangers of the revolutionary St Paul's experiment can only have heightened that excitement. Arid texts and teaching methods were cast aside. New grammars and textbooks were written which would engage the interest of the boys and make them want to learn. The curriculum was widened to include classical authors of which the church distinctly disapproved. Meaningless conning of texts was replaced by deep study of the authors' meaning and by a new breadth of approach to know-

A scholar might make a career in any of the emerging sciences, might even aspire, like Nicholas Krantzer, to the post of royal astronomer (portrait by Holbein)

It took medical men a long time to get the dignity and importance of their craft recognised. An important step was the acquiring by the Barber Surgeons of their charter from Henry VIII, commemorated in this painting by Holbein (destined to remain unfinished at the artist's death)

Collection Dowager Viscountess Galway

Royal College of Surgeons

ledge. The study of pagan poets, for example, might lead on to a knowledge

> first of the names ancient and modern, of mountains, rivers, cities; secondly, of names of trees, plants, animals, of dress, appliances, precious stones, in which the average writer today shows a strange ignorance. Here we gain help from the works which have come down to us upon agriculture, architecture, the art of war, cookery, precious stones and natural history. We can make good use in the same subject of etymology ... We can trace word change in names through modern Greek, or Italian and Spanish.[20]

It is significant that Colet chose for the governors of his school not a religious institution but the Worshipful Company of Mercers, and that the first high master of St Paul's was not a cleric but the layman and humanist William Lily.

Reactionary churchmen might grumble but St Paul's school was a manifestation of a new learning which was very fashionable in high circles. Prominent statesmen and courtiers sent their sons there. The king himself maintained pupils there. St Paul's boys were not infrequently summoned to perform plays at court. Other schools, such as Magdalen College school, Oxford, and Berkhamsted school, were founded with charters similar to Colet's.

Many schools were established in this period and the majority of them were conceived on purely traditional lines. Increasingly, wealthy merchants, lawyers and courtiers founded or endowed grammar schools or made provision in their wills for such foundations or endowments. Most of these institutions were not devoted to the inculcation of humanism but the fact that they existed at all owed much to the passion for education engendered by the men of the new learning. This passion was much in evidence at the time of the dissolution of the religious houses. One of the reasons urged by Protestant preachers for the royal appropriation of abbey lands and buildings was so that they might be used to endow much needed new schools, providing education for rich and poor alike. Some schools were, indeed, founded or refounded after the dissolution but by and large the government failed to give the hoped-for lead, and school buildings were sold off to clamouring buyers along with churches, barns, conventual buildings and farms. At this juncture many local corporations and private benefactors intervened to save old schools or establish new ones. At Sherborne, for example, the town bought the abbey church from the grantee, Sir John Hersey, and rented the schoolhouse so that the master could continue teaching there.

The next phase of Thomas More's education, as we have seen, was spent in the household of John Morton. He joined the archbishop's retinue in about 1490 and served as a page while learning the etiquette of high society and continuing his education at the hands of scholars employed by the archbishop. Probably Thomas's father had had to wait for a suitable vacancy to occur in Morton's entourage, for boys and girls were usually 'farmed out' at a somewhat earlier age. This custom, of long standing in England and apparently peculiar to this island, was one which intrigued and appalled foreign observers, including the Venetian diplomat who observed,

> The want of affection in the English is strongly manifested towards their children, for . . . they put them out, both males and females, to hard service in the houses of other people . . . And few are born who are exempted from this fate, for every one, however rich he may be, sends away his children into the houses of others, whilst he, in return, receives those of strangers into his own.[21]

Morton quickly fell a prey to the lad's charm, and Thomas became a favourite of the old man (as More senior must have hoped he would). If we are to believe William Roper, More's son-in-law and biographer, the archbishop prophesied, 'This child here waiting at the table, whosoever shall live to see it, will prove a marvellous man.'[22] For about two years Thomas More attended Morton and his guests – setting up the trestle tables in the great hall, serving wine from the ewers ranged on the buffets, ensuring that the oak livery cupboards in the sleeping chambers were charged with fresh food, packing the archbishop's silver and gilt plate into the great iron-bound coffers when he travelled from one palace to another.

In about 1492 Archbishop Morton sent his precocious young protégé on to Oxford, where for two years More lived the traditional life of a poor student, dividing his time between serious study and riotous living. The new arrival may have been entered at Canterbury College. Most students in fifteenth-century Oxford lived in hostels. Colleges existed largely for the benefit of poor scholars who could not afford such lodgings and it seems that More fell into this category. An early biographer tells us that More, 'in his youth . . . did not know the meaning of extravagance or luxury, could not put money to evil uses, seeing that he had no money to put to any uses at all, and, in short, had nothing to think about except his studies.'[23] It may be that Judge

More was scarcely in favour of his son's Oxford studies. He had already decided that the lad was to follow a legal profession and may well have considered futile Thomas's refinement of an already more than adequate Latin style and his attendance at theology and philosophy lectures.

Thomas, however, was in his element. The blend of scholarship and devotion he found at university was entirely to his taste. Had he followed his own inclination he might well have taken monastic vows, studied for his doctorate in theology and played a very different role in the turbulent history of the Reformation. It was only a decade later that another young man forsook his legal training to espouse the religious life. That man's name was Martin Luther. It is astonishing that in two brief years the teenage More, who never studied for a degree, should have been completely won over to the Renaissance humanism which was only just making itself felt at Oxford and, moreover, that he should have been recognised as an accomplished exponent of the new learning.

William Grocyn had recently returned from Italy and begun public lectures on the Greek language. Thomas Linacre also came back to his university about this time, bringing with him the influences he had imbibed during several years' study at Florence, Venice and Padua. These pioneers were in close contact with foreign scholars and, doubtless, with Colet, who was still on his Italian tour. These international humanists had all drunk at the clear, sparkling rivulets of new thought and could no longer be satisfied with the stagnant pools of medieval scholasticism. They challenged the old curricula and the established teaching methods. Further than that, they wanted to bring their new knowledge to the long overdue task of reform in church and state. In the event they had to be patient for a few more years before they saw the humanist movement begin to gather momentum in England.

Very occasionally, perhaps once in three or four generations, the medieval university was taken by the ears. Abelard did it at Paris in the early 1100s. Roger Bacon did it at Oxford around 1250. Duns Scotus did it in both universities at the turn of the fourteenth century as did John Wycliffe ninety years later. In 1497 it was the spare, eloquent John Colet who excited the student body and packed the schools to the door with his lectures on Paul's Epistle to the Romans. The thirty-year-old scholar, newly returned to his university from a long stay in Italy, interpreted the scriptures with a vividness and a directness altogether unprecedented. He brought the epistle to life and actually

presented Paul before his enthralled students as a real person. He set
the apostle in his historical setting and then expounded the plain words
of the text, applying them to contemporary life. That may not seem
very remarkable, but consider for a moment the type of biblical
exegesis to which fifteenth-century minds were accustomed. The following extract from a medieval textbook showing how the building of
Noah's ark should be understood is typical.

> Now the fact that the ark is six times as long as it is broad and ten
> times as long as it is deep presents an exact likeness with the human
> body in which Christ was made manifest. For the length of a body
> from the crown of the head to the sole of the foot is six times the
> breadth, that is to say from one side to the other, and it is ten times
> its height, that is the measurement from the back to the belly, etc,
> etc.[24]

Theological students were supposed to stuff into their heads meaningless statistics and heavy spiritualised glosses such as this throughout
the eight years they spent studying for their master's degree.

John Colet's lectures were vivid, fresh and unorthodox but there was
another reason why the undergraduates loved them – they were anti-
establishment. Paul, the lecturer pointed out, earned his living as a
tentmaker: he did not take alms from the poor like 'our monks and
friars'. Paul made a voluntary collection for saints at Jerusalem whereas
now the church 'extorted money by bitter exactions under the names of
tithes and oblations'. With the apostle, Colet affirmed that only faith
availed for salvation; 'rites and ceremonies neither purify the spirit nor
justify the man'. The earnest little Oxford don was standing on the
authority of the Bible to challenge the church, something which had
not been done outside Lollard conventicles since the time of Wycliffe.

An excited group of humanist scholars gathered round Colet and for
a few brief months (1499–1500) Eramus, the Dutch scholar, was drawn
to Oxford by Colet's reputation, and was there turned from the
thickets of dilettante scholarship into the broad meadow of theology.
The thirty-three-year-old monk and wandering academic was already
beginning to win a reputation as a *savant*, famous for his deep learning, devastating wit, elegant written style and cynical contempt for
much that passed for piety and education in fifteenth-century Europe.
More than any other man Erasmus made the new learning fashionable.
His brilliant irreverence won the devotion of a generation of young
students. His clear exposure of hypocrisy and decadence struck a chord
even among older conservatives, many of whom were aware that spiri-

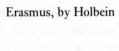

Erasmus, by Holbein

Louvre, Paris;
Cliché des Musées Nationaux, Paris

tual life and vitality had forsaken the old institutions but had not been able to diagnose the malaise. Yet, until his meeting with Colet Erasmus had been little more than a *littérateur*, a stylish cynic. From 1499 onwards he turned increasingly towards positive theology and, though the two sides of his nature would ever remain in conflict, he would eventually give the world such revolutionary books as the *Enchiridion Militi Christi* (*The Weapon of the Christian Knight*) and the *Novum Instrumentum* (a new Latin translation of the New Testament). One day it would be possible for Catholic critics to complain that 'Erasmus laid the egg that Luther hatched'.

Although More had left Oxford by the time these exciting events took place he was very much a leading member of the humanist brother-hood. He met and entertained Erasmus during his visit and a close friendship was forged between the two men which was to last until More's death. Colet's influence widened considerably in 1504 when he was appointed Dean of St Paul's. Now a large group of disciples, including the young lawyer Thomas More, gathered round him. They met in Colet's house in the close or strolled along the river bank excitedly discussing the meaning of Bible passages, the importance of

Greek and Hebrew studies, and ecclesiastical abuses. They were a self-conscious *avant-garde* clique who believed themselves to be leading a liberated generation of scholars against an oppressive and outdated establishment.

St Paul's Cross, which Colet now had free access to, was the most famous pulpit in the land and the new dean used it fearlessly. While thousands of Londoners and visitors gathered to hear him he launched a vigorous assault on the twin citadels of ignorance and decadence. He was appalled as much at superstitious pseudo-Christianity which passed for faith among the masses as at the inability or unwillingness of the clergy to instruct them. Nor did his impassioned, elegant oratory fall on deaf ears. Educated clergy and laymen became devotees of the new learning – gentlemen and lawyers, abbots and friars, courtiers and those employed as tutors in the households of kings and nobles. The Bishop of London was wrong when he denounced Colet as a heretic but the reformer's teachings were, as Fitzjames accurately sensed, dissolving the mortar which held medieval Christendom together.

It was at the universities and particularly at Cambridge that new ideas advanced most rapidly. This was a period of considerable change, new building and expansion at the ancient centres of learning. It saw the establishment of the collegiate system. Royal patronage gave a boost to this development. King's and Queens' Colleges were founded at Cambridge in the mid-fifteenth century. Christ's and John's were established at the same university during the early 1500s by Henry VII's mother, Margaret Beaufort. The first two Tudors made bequests for the completion of Henry VI's chapel at King's, which has ever remained Cambridge's most famous building, and Henry VIII took over Wolsey's Cardinal College at Oxford to create the new foundation of Christ Church. Between 1441 and 1546 a total of eight colleges at Cambridge and five at Oxford were founded or refounded. Teaching was now centred on the colleges. The dissolution of the monasteries involved the disappearance of many hostels and a change of emphasis in the pattern of university membership but both these developments were already well under way before 1536. It is significant that in 1517 Bishop Oldham, co-founder of Corpus Christi, Oxford, dissuaded his colleague from making the new house a monastic institution: 'What, my lord, shall we build houses and provide livelihoods for a company of buzzing monks, whose end and fall we ourselves may live to see; no, no, it is more meet a great deal that we should have a care to provide for the increase of learning and for such as by their learning shall do good in church and commonwealth.'[25]

In 1495 Lady Margaret Beaufort met at Greenwich the ascetic and scholarly John Fisher, Master of Michaelhouse, Cambridge. It was to prove a pregnant encounter. The king's mother appointed Fisher as her confessor and, under his influence, devoted a considerable amount of her fortune to the cause of university education. As well as the two new Cambridge colleges, she founded divinity professorships at both universities so that students could receive free theological instruction. She provided for sermons to be preached at appointed centres by well-qualified preachers. The stress on public preaching in an age when very few parish priests were able or inclined to deliver sermons was an important plank in the humanist platform. The statutes of Lady Margaret's colleges also showed the influence of the new learning. Regular lectures on Greek and Hebrew were to be delivered and there was provision for the teaching of arithmetic, geometry, perspective, cosmography, Arabic and Chaldaic.

Fisher remained a devoted son of the old church, and died for it two weeks before the execution of his friend Thomas More, but the Cambridge he largely shaped was the home of the Reformation. He was succeeded as Lady Margaret Professor of Divinity by no less a person than Erasmus (1511–14). Among the Dutchman's eager students were Thomas Cranmer and Hugh Latimer. The 1520s saw gathered with them at Cambridge many of the men whose endeavours and sacrifice would carry England firmly into the Protestant camp – Thomas Bilney, William Tyndale, Miles Coverdale, John Frith and Robert Barnes to mention but a few. In their rooms and inns they studied the works of Luther and other forbidden books, then went out to spread the new heresies in their own sermons and books. No official support for religious radicalism came from the authorities at either university. From time to time town and gown were entertained by public bonfires of banned books. Yet official commitment to the new learning steadily increased. Chairs in Greek, Hebrew, Civil Law and Physic were established; after 1536 men proceeding to degrees were required to renounce the 'pretended authority' of the Bishop of Rome; theology came to be based on the study of the Bible rather than on medieval commentaries and glosses. Of the thousands of students who passed through Cambridge and Oxford in the first half of the sixteenth century, the majority, for all their eager reading of forbidden books, never ventured beyond the Catholic humanism of More and Erasmus, but a minority espoused Lutheranism – and that minority was a large one.

The situation was similar at the inns of court, whither More was installed about 1494 by an impatient father anxious to see his son embarked on his professional training. The inns, which dotted the fields now known as Holborn, had been devised as the common law training ground as distinct from the universities which were for men bent on an ecclesiastical career. This was still their principal function but an increasing number of gentlemen and noblemen were sending their sons to the inns to gain a general education and a smattering of law which would be valuable to them in the administration of their estates.

> . . . ther is in these greater Innes, yea and in the lesser to, beside the study of the laws as it were an university or schoole of all commendable qualities requisite for Noblemen [and gentlemen]. There they learn to sing and to exercise themselves in all kinde of harmony. There also they practise dauncing and other Noblemen's pastimes as they use to doe which are brought up in the king's house. On the working daies most of them apply themselves to the studie of the Lawe and on the holy daies to the studie of Holy Scripture; and out of the time of Divine Service to the reading of Chronicles. For there indeede are vertues studied and vices exiled.[26]

Young Thomas followed the accepted pattern among legal students: he went first to one of the inns of Chancery – New Inn – and, having there received a grounding in the mechanics of the judicial system, he went to one of the greater inns – Lincoln's Inn. At both establishments More listened to the lecturers, or readers, expounding from the great standard works and took part in the 'moots' where points of law and their application were debated in Latin. The new century found the young lawyer sufficiently well versed in his profession to be serving as a reader at Furnival's Inn, one of the inns of Chancery.

But the law by no means filled his life, any more than it filled the life of any other young legal student. London had many other distractions to offer. Apart from the obvious pleasures of the town there were stirring sermons and stimulating lectures to hear. More learned Greek from Grocyn who had been appointed vicar of St Lawrence Jewry and was giving lectures on the church fathers at St Paul's. More himself was invited to expound Augustine's *De Civitate Dei* in Grocyn's church. There was among students of all kinds a keen appetite for learning, an appetite stimulated but not satisfied by new ideas and the printed books in which those ideas were served. The young gentlemen of the inns of court flocked to hear Colet, More and Grocyn as they would later flock to hear such Protestant champions as Hugh Latimer and Edward Crome. They avidly read Erasmus just as they would later avidly read Tyndale's New Testament and the works of Luther.

The spread of humanist and heretical beliefs among the men of the civil law was to prove a particularly significant characteristic of the early sixteenth century. There was a long-standing rivalry between canon lawyers and civil lawyers, one which brought sharply into focus the more fundamental rivalry between church and state. Anti-clericalism was a potent force among those who were contending for the supremacy of statute law and who resented the fact that most suits concerning church personnel and property were reserved to the ecclesiastical courts.

The civil lawyers were a formidable group in Tudor society, as Erasmus complained: 'The study of English law is as far removed as can be from true learning but in England those who succeed in it are highly thought of. And there is no better way to eminence there; for the nobility [the leading men of the realm] are mostly recruited from the law.'[27] The civil law was now, literally, the royal road to high office in the state and even in the church, for many bishops received their preferments as rewards for services rendered to the crown as experts in statute law. This goes a long way towards explaining the ease with which most of the Reformation legislation passed through Council and parliament. Not only were many of the king's advisers and members of the Commons men trained in the civil law; those who might have been expected to defend papal supremacy had a similar background and were more aware of legal arguments than theological implications.

It was not so for Thomas More. Theology was his greatest love and he was a devoted son of the church. His years at the inns of court must have been years of anxious self-examination and intellectual questioning. He was a civil lawyer, yet he believed firmly in the rights and privileges of the church. He was an emancipated critic of ecclesiastical abuses, yet he adhered firmly to Catholic doctrine and could never take the path which led via anti-clericalism to heresy. Genuine piety made a deep impression on him and he spent four of his student years as a lodger in the nearby Charterhouse. He shared the simple fare and the daily routine of the Carthusians and seriously considered taking vows himself. But he was a young man of normal passions, and a series of sexual adventures convinced him that the celibate life was not for him. To be sure, such scruples did not trouble many of More's contemporaries but the young lawyer must have felt that anyone who was as outspoken as himself about moral laxity among the clergy could not join the company of priests who openly or secretly kept mistresses.

Denied, or denying himself, both the cloister and the scholar's ivory tower, More now committed himself to the legal profession. He also took a wife and committed himself to the maintenance and upbringing of a family. By devoting his brilliant intellect to his chosen vocation and by contriving to seek the patronage of important men in court and city he advanced rapidly along the road to royal service.

4

'The King is in the room of God'

Court and Parliament

IN 1504 Thomas More was elected as a burgess to represent the city of London in the House of Commons. It was the beginning of a quarter of a century of public and royal service which would lead him to the highest lay office in the land. It would also lead him to a traitor's death. For all his radical ideas, he was no revolutionary and it was his misfortune to be part of a regime dedicated to revolution.

The revolution which raged in England during More's lifetime and finally bore him away was the most far-reaching social upheaval in England's history. It was at once more devastating and creative than the industrial and agrarian revolutions of three centuries later. Those movements changed the face of England and made the majority of its people into scurrying, confined town-dwellers. The decades which launched the Renaissance and the Reformation upon England inseminated radical changes of thought, attitude and belief deep in the minds of the people. Like all revolutions this one was violent and bloody. Buildings were destroyed and the executioners were busy. Change left the people confused and at variance with each other.

Yet, paradoxically, one of the major changes that came over English society at this time was a new stability. Basic to this stability was the establishment of the Tudor monarchy. From 1425 to 1485 the crown was like a quoit tossed on to the green by competing noble factions. The Battle of Bosworth, in the latter year, was the last conflict in which the occupancy of the throne was decided by alliances between leading families. It took Henry Tudor the whole of his twenty-four-year reign to establish the right of his dynasty to rule and the administrative machinery to make it possible, but he succeeded.

He succeeded in large measure because the mass of the people willed him to succeed. They were tired of the foreign armies that trampled the crops, looted the farms and fought through the streets in the name of the white rose or the red. They wanted strong government and assured succession. Even if strong government degenerated into tyranny, that was preferable to anarchy.

> It is better to suffer oon tyrant then many, and to suffer wronge of oon than of every man. Yea, and it is better to haue a tyrant unto thy kinge then a shadoo... For a tyrant, though he do wronge unto the goode, yet he punisheth the evil and maketh all men obey... A kinge that is as softe as silk and effeminate ... shall be more grievous unto the realme then a right tyrant.[1]

The words were not those of Machiavelli, the apostle of despotism, but of William Tyndale, the Protestant martyr, and they found an echo in the hearts of many Englishmen who could never have articulated their feelings. The struggles between the Yorkist and Lancastrian factions were only an extension of the running private wars fought by the great landowners over the fields and pastures of their tenants. In the decade in which Thomas More was born the Commons had petitioned the king:

> ... sovereign Lord, it is so that in divers parts of this realme, greet abominable mudres, robberies, extortions, oppressions and othyr manifolde maintainances, misgovernances, forcible entrys, as well upon them being in by judgemente as ootherwise, affrais, assaultes, be committed and doon by soch persones as either bee of greate might, or els favoured under persones of great pouer, in soch wise that their outrageous demerits as yet remain unpunished, insomuch that of late divers persones haue been slain, som in Southwark, and hir nigh about the City, and som here at Westminister Gate, no consideracion taken ... that your presence is hade hir at your Palace of Westminister, nor that your high court of Parliament is hir sitting ... to the great discouraging of your well ruled and true begemen [beadsmen], and to the great emboldning of all rioters and mis-gouerned persones.[2]

Some political theorists lifted the whole issue of law and order on to a higher plane. Its preservation was not only a practical necessity; it was a divine charge. Edmund Dudley served Henry VII well as a justice and financial administrator. He spent his last days in the Tower of London – a not unusual reward for faithful service to the Tudors – and while there wrote a treatise, *The Tree of Commonwealth*, for the guidance of the young Henry VIII. Having given the new monarch the benefit of his sage advice, the ex-minister ends with a long monologue ascribed to the Deity in which he indicates the eternal rewards attendant on Henry's acting on that advice.

> Thou hast kept the temporall subiectes in a loving drede, and hast not sufferyd them, nor the mightest of them, to oppresse the poore, nor yet woldes not suffer thyn owne seruantes to extort or wring any other of my people, thy subiectes, nor hast not sufferid the nobles of thy realme, nor any other of thei subiectes [so] to rune at riot as to ponisshe or reuenge there owne quarelles... Thou hast kept them all, from the highest degre to the lowest, in a good concord and vnytie emongist them selves, and hast also kept them by thy greate studdie, wisdom and pollicie, in good peace, withowt warr... Wherfore come now to me and reigne with me as my glorious knight and Christen king, my dere sonne, my good and singuler belovid brother in manhode, my verie felloo in creacion of thy soule. I shall annoynte the a king eternall with the holie oyle that issuith owt of the bosome of my father, and crowne the with the crowne of myn owne immortall glorie and honour.[3]

Nor was this the unsupported opinion of a flattering courtier desperately trying to escape the axe. More reputable theologians also believed in a prototype of the divine right of kings. For Archbishop Thomas Cranmer it was a cardinal article of faith that,

> All Christian princes have committed unto them immediately of God the whole cure of all their subjects, as well concerning the administration of God's Word for the cure of souls, as concerning the ministration of things political and civil governance...

> Though the magistrates [rulers] be evil, and very tyrants against the commonwealth, and enemies to Christ's religion; yet the subjects must obey in all worldly things, as the Christians do under the Turk, and ought so to do, so long as he commandeth them not to do against God.[4]

But the writings of the political and theological theorists (and they reflected, more or less accurately, the assumptions of the populace) did not constitute a blueprint for the worst kind of dictatorship. If one ingredient in the mortar of society was obedience, another was service. The 'haves' of the Christian commonwealth were expected to minister to the needs of the 'have nots'. This was the very essence of the idea of the 'common weal' or 'commonwealth', that harmonious ordering of society which all men desired.

> The end of all politic rule is to induce the multitude to virtuous living ... To the aid and setting forward [of a true commonwealth] every man for his part, by the law and order of nature, is bounden; which hath brought forth man for this purpose and this end: that after such manner he might live a civil life, ever having before his eyes the common weal, without regard of his own vain pleasures, frail fantasies and singular profit.[5]

In the well-ordered commonwealth the greatest responsibility lay with him who had the greatest authority – the king. A high sense of duty in the discharge of his divine vocation was the principal safeguard against tyranny. More was quite clear about this:

> But let him rather amende his owne lyfe, renounce unhonest pleasures, and forsake pride. For these be the chief vices that cause hym to runne in the contempte or hatred of his people. Let him lyve of his owne, hurtinge no man. Let him doe cost not above his power. Let him restreyne wyckednes. Let him prevente vices, and take away the occasions of offenses by well orderynge his subjectes, and not by sufferynge wickednes to increase afterward to be punyshed. Let hym not be to hastie in callynge agayne lawes, whyche a custome hathe abrogated: specially suche as have bene longe forgotten, and never lacked nor neaded. And let him never under the cloke and pretence of transgression take such fynes and forfaytes, as no Judge wyll suffre a private persone to take, as unjuste and ful of gile.[6]

The longest treatment of this theme was Dudley's *The Tree of Commonwealth*. In this the king is urged to espouse the virtues of a saint, the strength and valour of a crusader and the wisdom of Solomon.

There is yet another strand in the exalted concept of kingship which dominated sixteenth-century minds. It is not entirely coincidental that the summer which saw the establishment of the Tudor dynasty saw also the printing, by Caxton, of the first and finest English version of the Arthurian legend. Malory's *Morte d'Arthur* was, for years, one of the most popular books in the language and its concept of chivalrous Christian kingship added a flavour of romantic idealism to royal government, a flavour Henry VII was only too pleased to make use of when he christened his first son – the promised heir in whom Yorkist and Lancastrian blood was mingled – Arthur. It was a master stroke.

With a godly prince at the helm, controlling the material and spiritual destinies of his subjects and with the response of humble obedience from the populace, peace, stability and prosperity must, according to the political theorists, ensue. There would be no need for any of the disturbing factors which tended to break down society. The rapacity of the nobles, the ambition of the merchants, the restlessness of the peasants would all be quelled. The hierarchy would be intact; all men would be content in the station in which God had placed them. 'Standeth it with any reason,' asked Cranmer, 'to turn upside down the good order of the whole world, that is everywhere and hath ever been, that is to say the commoners to be governed by the nobles and the servants by their masters?' 'Take away gentlemen and rulers,' he asserted, 'and straightway all other falleth clearly away and followeth barbarical confusion.'[7]

If the lower orders feared a return to aristocratic anarchy, their superiors were uneasy at the prospect of popular revolt. They had an object lesson in the horrors of jacquerie in 1524–5 when the peasants of Germany rose against their masters in a holocaust of looting, arson and massacre. The governing classes watched anxiously, as their descendants were to watch the events in France two and a half centuries later, and expressed themselves vigorously on the subject of civil disorder. Stephen Gardiner, Bishop of Winchester, was unequivocal: 'The contempt of human law, made by rightful authority, is to be punished more heavily and more seriously than any transgression of the divine law.'[8]

The most execrated and feared group in society was not the Lutherans or the practitioners of black arts, but the Anabaptists, those heretics on the very fringe of the reform movement. And what made them so objectionable was not so much their religious views as their rejection of usury, oath-taking, military service, distinctions of wealth and class and the conventions of commerce – their rejection, in fact, of contemporary society. Such creatures, in the public imagination, were capable of any crime. They were anarchists, men with no moral code and no loyalty to God or king. Henry VIII certainly thought so when he disposed of fourteen of them in one *auto da fé* in 1535. (Anabaptism was never a strong force in England but this did not prevent the authorities feeling nervous of extreme religious radicalism.)

Of course, all the scholarly debate about the godly prince and the true commonwealth was only so much talk, and ink on paper. The reality was very different:

Is not this an unjust and an unkynde publyque weale, whyche gyveth great fees and rewardes to gentlemen, as they call them, and to goldsmythes, and to suche other, whiche be either ydle persones, or els onlye flaterers, and devysers of vayne pleasures: And of the contrary parte maketh no gentle provision for poore plowmen, coliars, laborers, carters, yronsmythes, and carpenters: without whome no commen wealthe can continewe? But after it hath abused the labours of theire lusty and flowring age, at the laste when they be oppressed with olde age and syckenes, being nedye, poore, and indigent of all thinges, then forgettyng their so manye paynefull watchinges, not remembring their so manye and so great benefites, recompenseth and acquyteth them moste unkyndly with myserable death. And yet besides this the riche men not only by private fraud but also by commen lawes do every day pluck and snatche awaye from the poore some parte of their daily living . . . so god helpe me, I can perceave nothing but a certein conspiracy of riche men procuringe their owne commodities under the name and title of the commen wealth.[9]

When More spoke in the passage we have already quoted of kings who revise antiquated statutes, devise new taxes to wring money from their subjects and use justice to their own ends, he was not speaking hypothetically; Henry VII of blessed memory had displayed all these vices. Indeed, as More observed sadly, 'it is not possible for al thinges to be well, onles all men were good'.[10]

Neither the Tudor kings nor their people were particularly good. Henry VII made his rule absolute, broke the power of the territorial nobility and used the nation as a milch cow to fill the churns of the royal treasurer. His son deliberately shattered the myth of united Christendom, confiscated the enormous wealth of the English church and attempted to dictate to his people what they should believe. Lawlessness, especially in the remoter areas, did not noticeably abate. Indeed, conflict between the old religion and the new increased the quota of national violence. There was at least one serious popular revolt.

Yet despite their grievances, despite the many symptoms of grave maladies in the body politic, despite the confusing blasts of new ideas, men clung on to their basic beliefs about society. In 1536, as we have seen, the men of Lincolnshire rose in revolt and this had scarcely been crushed before the more serious 'Pilgrimage of Grace' broke out in Yorkshire. The rebels' complaints were against economic exploitation and religious change. Not a few were openly hostile to the Tudor regime but the more responsible leaders were most concerned to show that they were not rebelling against their king. They were, they said, convinced that Henry was being guided by evil ministers. They petitioned for these men to be removed and certain grievances to be redressed. When their leader, Robert Aske, summoned the host to assemble he ordered them to 'make your proclymacion every man to be trewe to the kings issue, and the noble blode, and preserve the churche of god frome spolyng; and to be trewe to the comens and ther wel-this. . .'[11] The rude shiremen responsible for the revolt were too sensible of their own humble station to lead the rebellion. Their first task was to capture as many as possible of the leading gentlemen of the area and force them to be their figureheads. Aske's loyalty to the king led him to make the foolish error of trusting the king's word. When Henry offered him a pardon and promised to give the rebels' petition serious consideration Aske believed him. He paid for the mistake with his life. It was a mistake many of his contemporaries would have made; in an age of revolutionary change men need to believe in changeless conventions.

There was one convention Henry himself believed in and was determined to impress upon his disaffected subjects – his own sovereignty and power. He ordered the Duke of Norfolk:

> Before you close up our said banner again you shall in any wise cause such dreadful execution to be done upon a good number of every town, village and hamlet that have offended in this rebellion, as well by the hanging them up in trees, as by the quartering them, and the setting up of their heads and quarters in every town, great and small, and in all such other places, as they may be a fearful spectacle to all other hereafter that would practice in any like manner.[12]

Harsh measures, but measures accepted and understood by a people who needed the security of despotic government. Thomas More was a remarkable man; he faced death with a serenity and confidence rarely paralleled in any age. Yet he was totally a man of his age in his attitude towards the king's rightful authority. When, after months in prison, he was told that the day of his execution had arrived he replied to the messenger:

> I have been always much bounden to the King's Highness for the benefits and honours that he hath still from time to time most

bountifully heaped upon me; and yet more bound am I to his Grace for putting me into this place, where I have had convenient time and space to have remembrance of my end. And, so help me God, most of all, Master Pope, am I bound to his Highness that it pleaseth him so shortly to rid me out of the miseries of this wretched world. And therefore will I not fail earnestly to pray for his Grace, both here and also in another world.[13]

The Tudors worked hard to instil awe into their people and extract obedience from them. One method they used to put themselves beyond the reach of ordinary mortals was their careful contrivance and exploitation of all the external trappings of monarchy. No one before or since has accused Henry VII of being a lavish spender but he never begrudged money expended on displays which would impress his own people and foreign visitors with the splendour of his court.

In the first year of his reign alone Henry VII found three major occasions to impress the people with his magnificence. The coronation ceremonies extended from 27 October to 13 November 1485. They had to be lavish. It was little more than two years since Richard III had proudly processed before his cheering commons and submitted himself in the Abbey to all the ancient ceremonies. At every point Henry surpassed his Yorkist predecessor. The feasting was longer, the pageantry more elaborate, the clothes and hangings more costly. For example, at Richard III's coronation the horse of the king's champion had been covered in a mantle of 'whyt sylke and red'. When the same champion, Sir Robert Dymock, entered the banqueting hall of the Tower on 30 October 1485 his charger was decked in a 'riche trapper of Cadewaladras armes', of which the embroidery alone had cost 66s 8d.

The court was sumptuously entertained for Christmas and the festivities of the holy season were scarcely over before the realm was celebrating the union of the two roses on Henry's marriage to Elizabeth of York (18 January 1486). In every village masses were said and feasts made as men and women gave unrestrained expression to their relief and their hope. But in London the magnificence and the rejoicing were at a level never seen before.

Henry knew that it was not enough to impress the capital. Two months later he set out with his bride, his court and an armed retinue on a progress to the North. It was both a display of force intended to dispel any lingering Yorkist pretensions and a display of regality designed to inspire awe, respect and affection. The king and queen were personally attended by a newly raised corps of two hundred royal bowmen, brilliantly equipped and meticulously drilled. They did not fail in their effect. Nor did the fine clothes of the royal party or Henry's ostentatious distribution of alms along the route.

As he began so did Henry VII continue. In the display of sovereignty he established a tradition which was to be followed by his great son and his greater granddaughter. The Tudor rulers all proved themselves masters of royal theatricality. With a show of splendour and a carefully worded speech they could move a thousand hearts to loyalty or dread, joy or shame. In 1501 a marriage alliance with Spain provided an excellent opportunity for more costly celebrations.

> This year was sent into England the King of Spain's third daughter, Catherine, to be married to the Prince Arthur, and she landed at Plymouth the eighth day of October, and was received into London in the most royal wise the twelfth day of November, then Friday. And the Sunday following she was married at St Paul's Church. . . And the feast was held in the Bishop of London's palace. And the day of her receiving into London were made many rich pageants; first at the bridge, at the conduit in Gracechurch Street, the conduit in Cornhill, the standard in Cheapside (the cross newly gilded), at the little conduit; and at St Paul's west door there was running wine – red claret and white – all the day of the marriage. And at the same marriage the king made fifty-seven knights.[14]

What Henry VII did as a matter of policy his seventeen-year-old successor did as an expression of youthful exuberance. The reign of 'young King Hal' was another fresh start for England. The enthusiastic athlete who occupied the throne was taken to the hearts of the people. In his extravagance and his love of tournaments, feasting, public festivities and other costly diversions he embodied the popular idea of what a king should be. Indeed, he devoted himself almost exclusively to this aspect of the royal task, having found in Thomas Wolsey an able and willing packhorse on to whom he could load the tedious routine trivia of day-to-day government. Wolsey was also a born organiser of lavish spectacles. When the king went on campaign in France in 1513, the expedition which wound its way to Dover was not just an army; it was a display. Henry's personal entourage consisted of 600 armed men, secretaries, clerks, sewers (servers), grooms, gentlemen and pages of the chamber, chapel priests and choir to the number of 115, his lutanist, his master of the jewel house, 14 horses 'with housings of the richest cloth of gold and crimson velvet with silver gilt bells of great

This portrait of Henry VIII at the age of about twenty-seven reveals a sensitivity which vanished with the increase of age and the exercise of power

National Portrait Gallery

value', numerous carts carrying clothes, armour and plate and a wooden house in prefabricated sections carried in fourteen waggons. And where the sovereign led, others were obliged, by royal decree, to follow. The dress and equipage permitted to each member of the expedition was nicely specified. Each duke, earl, baron and knight had to be turned out 'as to your degree, the honour of us and this our reame it apperteineth'.[15]

The most preposterously extravagant of all Tudor spectacles was the one stage-managed by Wolsey in June 1520 for a diplomatic meeting between Henry and his French counterpart and rival Francis I on the border of the pale of Calais. The chronicler Du Bellay called it 'le camp du drap d'or', the Field of Cloth of Gold, because of the acreages of that rich material used for clothes, horse trappings, tent and pavilion hangings. The English king was accompanied by the papal legate (Wolsey), one archbishop, two dukes, one marquis, ten earls, five bishops, 20 barons, four Knights of the Garter, 70 knights, 200 members of the king's guard, and 569 assorted household servants and attendants. Each member of the entourage whose status merited it was allowed his own servants so that the total personnel was 3997 persons (and 2087 horses). The queen was equipped with a further 1175 persons and 778 horses. Once again precise regulations and high standards were laid down for every member of the entourage, so much so that many knights and barons virtually impoverished themselves by selling lands and manors in order to buy fine clothes, tournament armour, harness and victuals. Yet places in the royal party were so greatly coveted that for months before the embarkation Wolsey was pestered with requests and bribes from peers, barons and knights who wanted to be included.

The activities varied from solemn masses performed by the bejewelled Cardinal, served by England's premier peers, to feasts featuring every delicacy known to the culinary art, and mummings or 'disguisings' at which several companies of actors kept their audience entertained for hours with their mimes and antics. But all the activities had one thing in common – extravagance. The Field of Cloth of Gold was a special occasion with a high diplomatic purpose but it reflected a style of monarchy to which Henry VIII and his court were well accustomed. In 1527 a new temporary structure was erected at Greenwich for the sole purpose of housing the royal entertainments of that summer and autumn. Work began in early January and was brought to a successful conclusion only by artisans and craftsmen working day and night shifts for four months. Among the staff were Italian painters brought over especially for the job and paid 20s a week. The building was a twofold structure; a banqueting hall and a 'disguising house'.

The hall was about a hundred feet in length and thirty feet in breadth. Its ceiling was covered with crimson brocatel of little value but beautiful to see . . . and decorated with roses and pomegranates. A short distance below the roof were set windows 'all clere stories with curious monneles strangely wrought, the lawe peces and crestes were karued wyth Vinettes and trailes of savage worke, and richely gilted with gold and Bise'. To this extravagant wall decoration were affixed candlesticks of 'antyke woorke' casting a flood of light upon the hall. The preparation of the roof and the lighting had been entrusted to Clement Urmeston, whose account covers ironwork for the candlesticks, red buckram for the roof, and other necessaries. In addition to the lights set into the sides of the building there were also branches of hanging lights, so that, in all, there were prepared some 230 'antique cuppis' with a hundred 'antique knoppis pomander ffacion for garnyshing the shanks of the hanging lights'. The beams supporting these lights were further adorned with four hundred 'Litell Rosis of Leade' and five hundred 'Litell antique Levis of lead', and gilded with party gold and fine gold. . .

The walls of the banquet hall were decorated with costly tapestries representing the history of David, a favourite character of Henry VIII's; and on each side, near tables arranged in a horseshoe, was an immense cupboard, reaching from floor to ceiling, filled with golden vessels. At the far end of the chamber, leading out to the disguising house, was a lofty triumphal arch . . . with three entrances – the two outer ones for the passage of dishes for the tables. The great central span was flanked on either side by a cupboard bearing wine for the feast, and the whole structure was surmounted by a balcony for musicians. The decoration of this arch, according to Hall, was full of 'Gargills and Serpentes' and armorials, surmounted by 'sondri Antikes and diuises'. Spinelli, the Venetian observer, is more specific and mentions the royal arms, the motto *Dieu et Mon Droit*, certain Greek words; and busts of Emperors. The last item is probably to be identified with the 'vj antique hedds gilt silueryd and paintyd at xxvjs viijd the pece' provided by Giovanni Da Maiano who executed similar decorations for the arch in the disguising house.[16]

Such lavish spectacle at the royal palaces and repeated every summer when the king went on progress pleased Henry and by and large it pleased his people. Then, as now, Englishmen liked their sovereign to make a 'show'. But then, as now, there were dissentient voices. The poet, John Skelton, thought little of the Field of Cloth of Gold:

> There hath ben moche excesse
> With banketynge braynlesse,
> With ryotynge rechelesses
> With jambaudynge thryflesse,
> With spende and wast witlesse,
> Treatinge of trewse restlesse,
> Pratynge for peace peaslesse,
> The countryng at Cales [Calais]
> Wrang us on the males [purses].[17]

Erasmus was openly contemptuous of the life-style espoused by Henry VIII and his brother monarchs. Folly, the hero and narrator of his satire, *In Praise of Folly*, asserted:

Kings are baited with so many temptations and opportunities to vice and immorality, such as are high feeding, liberty, flattery, luxury, and the like, that they must stand perpetually on their guard, to fence off those assaults that are always ready to be made upon them. In fine . . . after their reign here they must appear before a supremer judge, and there be called to an exact account for the discharge of that great stewardship which was committed to their trust. If princes did but seriously consider (and consider they would if they were but wise) these many hardships of a royal life, they would be so perplexed in the result of their thoughts thereupon, as scarce to eat or sleep in quiet. But now by my assistance they leave all these cares to the gods, and mind only their own ease and pleasure, and therefore will admit none to their attendance but who will divert them with sport and mirth, lest they should otherwise be seized and damped with the surprisal of sober thoughts. They think they have sufficiently acquitted themselves in the duty of governing, if they do but ride constantly a-hunting, breed up good race-horses, sell places and offices to those of the courtiers that will give most for them, and find out new ways for invading of their people's property, and hooking in a larger revenue to their own exchequer.[18]

More himself made the point with a greater economy of words: 'And verelye one man to live in pleasure and wealth, whyles all other wepe and smarte for it, that is the parte, not of a kynge, but of a jayler.'[19]

In breaking the political power of the nobility the Tudors were fortunate in that destiny had done part of the job for them. Neither Henry VII nor his son had royal brothers who might become legitimate figureheads for disaffected noble factions. Some of the leading magnates who, during the fifteenth century, had worn the power if not the purple, had destroyed themselves and dissipated their fortunes in the York versus Lancaster struggle. Other ancient houses had faded through failure of the main line. In 1450 there were twenty-eight members of the senior nobility (dukes, earls and marquesses). Twelve titles were created or re-created by the Yorkist kings before 1485. Of those forty, only twelve continued without a break and were still thriving in 1550. Twenty-four lines had failed and four were deliberately curtailed by Henry VII and his son. The first two Tudors created or revived nineteen, so that by the death of Henry VIII there were thirty-one senior nobles.

At the outset of his reign Henry VII had no Machiavellian scheme in mind for the calculated destruction of the nobility as a class. The idea would never have occurred to him; the peers had a place in society and were vital administrative agents in the pseudo-feudal politico-economic system. It was their ability to form powerful factions bidding for power that he was determined to remove. Those who had selected the wrong side in 1485 were automatically attainted and their lands confiscated. Throughout the reign disaffected magnates made sporadic attempts at organised rebellion and paid the same penalty. The king hesitated to wield the executioner's axe – a clemency dictated as much by policy as squeamishness. It was his concern to establish peace and strong government, not to indulge in a personal war against over-mighty subjects. His ends were sometimes established by removing his enemies; more often they were served better by clemency or contempt – as when he employed the impostor and pretender Lambert Simnel in the royal kitchens. Richard III had lost a large measure of public support because it was noised abroad that he was a man of blood. Henry had no desire to make the same mistake.

A policy of decisive military action coupled with leniency towards the lives (though not the lands) of vanquished enemies paid handsome dividends. Though there were sporadic attempts at rebellion throughout the reign, none of them had much popular support. None of them stood serious chance of success. In 1509 the crown passed peacefully to a seventeen-year-old boy. There was no attempt by a faction of nobles to exercise power on behalf of or through the young king. Henry VIII had no need to be cautious nor had he any inclination to be squeamish. He removed the last members of the Yorkist line whose royal blood – however dilute – was a remote threat to the Tudor regime. In this way perished the Duke of Buckingham, the Earl of Suffolk, Lord Montague and the Countess of Salisbury. It was ruthless action but it probably saved the realm from further abortive rebellions. The redistribution of wealth did more than anything else to secure the power of the new dynasty. Bacon said of Henry VII, 'the less blood he drew the more he took of treasure', and the financial measures the king employed were certainly effective in sapping that economic strength of which independence and rebellion can spring. There is more than a little truth in the traditional picture of Henry as the miser-king. The Spanish ambassador informed his master that the King of England 'spends all the time he is not in public or in his Council in writing the accounts of his expenses with his own hand'. Apart from irregular taxes the crown had four sources of revenue – customs duties, income from royal estates, the exploitation of feudal and prerogative rights and the profits of justice. It was the latter two which bore most heavily upon the wealthier section of society. Henry VII and his ministers breathed new life

Revenues

into an old word – 'prerogative'. This never-defined but oft-employed term was used to justify and excuse a series of exactions and imposi- tions which enriched the crown and helped to control the wealthier sections of the 'common weal'. He did not do anything which con- travened law or custom; rather he employed the best legal brains – men like Morton, Empson and Dudley – to exploit to the uttermost the traditional rights of the crown, many of which had been lost sight of during the decades of weak monarchy and powerful baronial factions.

Four centuries of economic and social development had resulted in a system known to historians as 'bastard feudalism'. Once, the mortar which bonded each layer of the feudal pyramid to the layers above and below had been service. The peasant rendered so many days' labour on the lord's demesne; the tenant pledged his knight service to the tenant- in-chief; the tenant-in-chief provided knights for the king's army. By 1495 all that had changed; the mortar of society was no longer service but money. At all levels service was commuted and virtually every feudal obligation could be excused on consideration of a fee. Landhold- ing became a complex system of financial transactions, entrusted to stewards, bailiffs and treasurers. The king, of course, had many more feudal rights than anyone else and royal agents had a difficult task collecting all that was due to the crown. This situation was, as a matter of course, exploited by tenants-in-chief and other major landowners. Throughout the troubled decades of the fifteenth century men wishing to defraud the government had largely got away with it. Inevitably, when Henry VII set about closing all the loopholes the resentment was enormous.

The frequent exactions of an efficient administration were irksome in the extreme to the landed classes. A man paid for the privilege of entering his inheritance (*relief*). He paid for the privilege of marrying an heiress. He paid for a royal licence to sell (*alienate*) any of his manors. Even piety was chargeable, for the granting of lands to the church (*mortmain*) was also subject to a royal fee. Landlords had to pay for rights of hunting, hawking, coursing, grazing and turbary in the royal forests. Henry VII also managed to discover special occasions on which the payment of feudal 'aids' was appropriate. Such occasions were the knighting of Prince Arthur and the marriage of Princess Margaret. These levies were barely tolerable when succession to titles and lands passed smoothly from father to son. In those uncertain times few families could expect the normal process of primogeniture to sur- vive more than two or three generations. When there was no heir at all, lands reverted (*escheated*) to the crown. When a woman inherited, her marriage was at her feudal lord's disposal; which meant that it would be sold to the highest bidder. When the heir was a minor he became a royal ward, his lands being administered by the crown until his coming of age, at which time he had to pay his livery, the fee due for the privilege of entering on his own inheritance. Under the Tudor regime wardships were usually sold by the crown and were an extremely lucrative source of revenue. Henry VII issued commissions for the seeking out of concealed wards' lands and appointed officers at central and local level for the scrupulous exploitation of this source of revenue. Competition for wardships through the Court of Wards was keen, for the purchase of a wardship usually led to the marriage of the heir (or heiress) to a member of the purchaser's family and was, therefore, a recognised way of building up estates or providing for one's children.

Stated baldly, these administrative facts give no impression of the fears, tensions, griefs, greed and ambition which lay behind the fossilised legal wording of royal grants and charters. Land meant everything to the Englishman of yeoman status and above. It was vital to a family that its estates should be kept secure for future generations and, if possible, extended. Land was a man's heritage from the past, his trust for the future.

How these hopes and responsibilities might be frustrated is illustrated by the story of the Hansard family of South Kelsey on the edge of the Lincolnshire wolds. The Hansards had been a prominent gentry family for generations and seemed as permanent as their square, moated manor house, looming protectively over the small village.[20] The Hansard estates in Lincolnshire and the neighbouring counties were extensive. Sir William Hansard was an able local justice, who frequently served on royal commissions, and was sometimes 'pricked' (the term derives from the custom of the king's pricking a written short list with a golden pin to indicate the man of his choice) as sheriff. He served in the king's French wars and was knighted for his service. He attended Henry VIII to the Field of Cloth of Gold. Of the many children borne by his wife, Elizabeth, only three reached maturity – a son, William, and two daughters. On 11 January 1522 Sir William Hansard died of the sweating sickness at the age of forty-three.

The family grieved but there was no cause for undue alarm as young William, newly married to Agnes Tyrrwhit, entered his inheritance. What was alarming was the persistence of the sweating sickness. This disease which struck without warning and killed swiftly was the Tudors' most unwelcome gift to England. Brought over in 1485 in Henry of Richmond's baggage train it stayed to torment the land ruled over by his dynasty, then disappeared late in the sixteenth century as abruptly as it had come. It was usually at its most virulent in the summer months but in this mild winter of 1522 it hovered over the Midland counties, claiming shepherd, steward and squire in its sinister disregard of social distinction. On 15 April the new lord of South Kelsey manor felt the terrifying stiffness in his limbs, the headache and the feverish heat. Within hours he was dead.

There was yet a slender chance that the direct male line of the Hansards would not die out; at the time of her husband's death Agnes was four months pregnant. The household of women at South Kelsey waited with anxiety the outcome of her confinement. So did other interested parties. There were many wealthy and influential neighbours interested in gaining control of the Hansard estates. Prominent among them were Sir Robert Tyrrwhit, Agnes's father, and Sir William Ayscough of Nuttall, Nottinghamshire, who held considerable property in the two counties. In October the baby was born. It was a girl and it survived the first crucial weeks. The race was now on. Tyrrwhit and Ayscough both made suits to the master of the wards, Thomas Wolsey. No documents survive but we may be sure that as well as their direct applications both parties urged friends and relations at court to make representations and offer bribes to Wolsey, beseeching him to be their 'especial good lord'.

In the end it was Ayscough who won. He took over the wardship of the infant Elizabeth. The child was betrothed to his own eldest son Francis. In the fulness of time the two were wed and the Hansard lands passed permanently into the Ayscough family. But Sir William did not wait for the fulness of time; he treated the Hansard acres as if they were already his. Being himself a widower, he married Sir William Hansard's relict and moved into South Kelsey Hall which now became the centre of his augmented estates.[21]

Such domestic dramas were commonplace; they were the stuff of life for the landed classes. It is not difficult to imagine how much the intrusion of royal agents demanding their feudal pounds of flesh was resented in these local rivalries and territorial manoeuvrings. The tightening up of feudal controls begun by Henry VII was continued by his son. But not without difficulty: no single piece of legislation roused more opposition than the Statute of Uses. It took Henry's ministers five years to force this measure through the Commons (a body which represented exclusively the gentry and mercantile classes). The object of the statute was to prevent men who held land in chief from the crown providing, by will, rent payments for the benefit of younger sons and other dependants. Long usage had accustomed the nobility and gentry to regard the testamentary disposal of their estates as a private family concern. Now the law flexed its feudal muscles and deprived younger sons, widows and unmarried daughters of their security. The Act was bitterly resented. Adam Fermour, a Sussex yeoman, returned home from a visit to London incensed at the news of the new Act: 'the King will make such laws that if a man die his wife and his children shall go a-begging. He fell but lately and brake one of his ribs, and if he make such laws it were a pity but he should break his neck.'[22] In 1536 many otherwise loyal gentlemen were driven to supporting the Pilgrimage of Grace solely in opposition to this single piece of legislation.

In following up the implications of the Tudor extension of their prerogative rights we have wandered slightly from our theme of the humbling of England's great men, the potential 'over-mighty subjects'. As well as the humdrum routine of feudal law, the king had other means of dealing with the nobility. Yorkist purses felt very severely the cost of involvement in the abortive rebellions during the first half of Henry VII's reign. The king confiscated the lands of those most heavily involved and imposed large fines or bonds on others. Bonds were deposits of cash held by the exchequer against good behaviour. Fines and bonds proved so effective that they were increasingly employed by Tudor ministers. There were between 1485 and 1509 about sixty-two families at all levels of nobility. Forty-seven of them were at one time or another at the king's mercy. Some were under attainder, some heavily fined, and some had to provide bonds and recognisances. All in all, the ancient families were under debilitating restraints and anxieties.[23]

Pressure on the temporal lords was slightly relaxed by Henry VIII, particularly after he transferred attention to their spiritual counterparts, but by 1509 the ability and will of the nobles to combine against the crown had been sapped. This financial weapon wielded so effectively against the magnates clearly served a double purpose for the Tudors. It had yet another advantage: skilfully used it could keep the crown relatively independent of parliament.

Parliament was by now fully recognised as an essential part of government but it was only an occasional part. The Lords and Commons were summoned at the discretion of the monarch, discussed business, most of which was originated by the crown, and were dismissed as soon as that business was concluded. This is not to say that parliament was a rubber stamp for royal and ministerial decisions – far from it. Indeed, the only information we have of Thomas More's behaviour as a burgess underlines the independence exercised by individual members and, sometimes, by the Commons as a whole.

In 1504, so the story goes, Henry VII asked parliament for three-fifteenths (most taxes on property were either 'tenths' or 'fifteenths') by way of a feudal aid on the marriage of Princess Margaret to the Scottish king. This would have produced about £90,000 in revenue but the motion ran into difficulties in the Commons. The most persuasive opposition speech was made by the twenty-six-year-old Thomas More, and a royal servant had to report to his chagrined master that it was a mere 'beardless boy' who had 'disappointed all his purpose'.[24] The outcome was that Henry received a grant of only £40,000 and Thomas's father was clapped in the Tower for a few days.

It is difficult to know whether we can believe this story in all its details but it certainly reflects accurately the relationship between king and parliament. Members enjoyed considerable freedom of debate (which explains why Henry could not vent his wrath directly on Thomas). Even though many members of parliament were royal servants and supporters the king could not be sure of controlling either house (particularly the Commons), but he had many ways of overawing the two assemblies. Both Tudors made a point of addressing parliament on important matters. Henry VII, within weeks of his accession, asserted his right to the crown before the assembled lords, knights and burgesses. Sixty years later his son, illness-aged and with little more than a year to live, made his last visit to the parliament house to make a plea for religious unity. And there were many other royal speeches heard in parliament between 1485 and 1545. In 1539, for example, the king intervened in the upper chamber to ensure the passage of the Act of Six Articles, which caused Archbishop Cranmer to complain 'if the King's Majesty himself had not come personally into the Parliament house, those laws had never passed'.[25]

The first two Tudors, however, had sufficient political acumen to realise that personal appearances should be kept for special occasions. The glitter of monarchy should not be tarnished by over-exposure. More often than not, therefore, royal admonitions were delivered by ministers. Sometimes delegations were summoned to court to be told that the king was 'amazed' at the reaction of parliament to the latest measures proposed by their 'loving sovereign'. The Tudors had no reason to fear parliament and every reason to respect it. Not only was it an occasional necessity; it could also be extremely useful in moulding public opinion and obtaining support for official policy. The crown, like other interested parties in town and country, tried to influence Commons elections but there was never a concentrated effort to 'pack' parliament with royal nominees; or if there was it was unsuccessful. The king could usually count on the support of the upper house where the majority of court officials, councillors and prominent ecclesiastical and civil lords reliant on royal favour had their seats. It was in the Lords that most legislation was introduced (with the striking exception of the Reformation Parliament – see below). With the Commons a varied technique had to be employed, composed of flattery, threats, impressive displays of royal magnificence and occasional gracious submission to their will.

As in so many other spheres, the 1530s mark a watershed in the history of parliament. In the summer of 1529 writs went out for the summoning of the estates of the realm to what would be one of the longest lived and one of the three most important parliaments in English history (the other two being the Long Parliament of 1640–47 and the parliament which passed the Reform Act of 1832). When its members were finally dismissed in the spring of 1536 many of them had sat through seven long sessions, had created well over a hundred statutes covering a wide range of topics, had severed their country from papal allegiance and created a national church, and, though they probably did not realise it at the time, had established for parliament (and especially for the Commons) a new and permanent importance in the government of England. Most of the business was managed by Thomas Cromwell and his agents from the lower house, a procedure deliberately adopted because of the widespread anti-clericalism among the merchants, knights and lawyers of the realm.

Those merchants, knights and lawyers were elected on a very restricted franchise and by no means represented the mass of the people. They were at Westminster to speak for the class of substantial landowners and local administrators. There were 310 of them:[26] seventy-four knights of the shire, selected by the major landowners in each of the English counties (the Welsh were not enfranchised until 1536), 232 burgesses elected by the senior members of 116 double-member parliamentary borough constituencies and four London members.

Whether he was an ambitious courtier striving to prove his loyalty to the king or an alderman of some distant borough, a member of the House of Commons was a prey to many concerns and anxieties. He no doubt wished to give his attention conscientiously to the sundry bills brought before the assembly but he also had to consider the interests of his community, his patron and his king. He was worried about his prolonged absence from his estates or place of business. He was bothered at the cost of his enforced stay in the capital. Always he was pestered by relatives, friends and acquaintances wanting him to use his influence on their behalf.

The *ad hoc* nature of parliament is clearly illustrated by the arrangements made to house it. There were no special buildings set aside for the purpose. The medieval idea of the Great Council in Parliament persisted into the Tudor era. According to this idea the king summoned the peers of the realm to join with him and his Council for discussion of important matters. They met in one of the larger rooms of whatever palace the court happened to be occupying. By 1485 the summons to the Commons had become automatic but they still met in another place. Usually in the early Tudor period they borrowed the chapter house of Westminster Abbey. Indeed, if any single event can be said to mark the turning-point in the long career of the House of Commons it was their acquisition of a permanent meeting-place of their own in 1549. They were granted the use of St Stephen's Chapel, an ancient building and one of the few on the Westminster Palace complex not to be destroyed by fire in 1512. When King, Lords and Commons had to meet together, special arrangements had to be made to find a chamber large enough to house all the members of the parliament as well as the royal retinue. In 1529, for instance, parliament was ceremonially opened at the great London monastery of Blackfriars which adjoined the royal palace of Bridewell.

If the most significant changes occurred in the Commons, the most obvious transformed the Lords. At Henry VII's accession the upper house consisted of forty-nine spiritual lords and twenty-nine temporal lords. Reinstatement of some noble families to royal favour, and new creations established a more even balance after a few years. But the dissolution of the monasteries removed thirty abbots and priors from the Lords and, though five new bishoprics were created, the secular dominance of the assembly was thus ensured.

Henry VIII had considerable power. He often ruled tyrannically. He appeared to be a despot. But the appearance is deceptive, owing more to the force of his personality than to legal reality. By 1547 the position of parliament had changed dramatically. The supremacy of statute law over royal and papal edict had been established. England experienced a new kind of sovereignty – the sovereignty of king in parliament. It would take a long and troubled century before the full implications of the Tudor revolution in government were fully apprehended. Then it

would be seen that that revolution had made England a constitutional
monarchy.

The trend towards parliamentary democracy and limited royal
power was far from clear to contemporary observers, especially when
they felt in their purses the authority of the crown. To establish peace,
internal stability and sound government cost Henry VII money. To
maintain these blessings cost Henry VIII much more money because
he was hampered by two disadvantages: inflation and his own extravagance. Ultimately, that money had to come from the people. It
mattered little to them that the taxes and other exactions levied by
royal agents had been granted by parliament.

Henry VII was sparing in his approach to parliament for money. He
obtained grants of customs duty and a subsidy on wool for life. He was
granted additional taxes in 1487 (after the battle of Stoke), in 1489 (for
war with France), 1491, 1496 (for an ultimately aborted war with
Scotland) and 1504. Opposition was, however, vociferous and effective.
In 1497 the poor men of Cornwall rose in revolt when asked to contribute to a war with Scotland. Armed 'with bows and arrows and bills,
and such other weapons of rude and country folk',[27] they marched
through the southern counties to within sight of the capital before the
inevitable slaughter took place. It was not a challenge to Henry's security but it made its point.

Henry VII left his successor a full coffer but it did not long survive
the wars and the expensive style of Henry VIII and Wolsey. The
government was forced to borrow heavily from international banks and
to rely more on direct taxation. Wolsey demanded money from parliament in 1513, 1515, 1522, 1523 and 1524. Each turn of the screw
increased the pressure of resentment building up throughout the
country. Magistrates in several areas found themselves hearing cases
such as that of Peter Wilkyson, presented to the Norfolk JPs in June
1523. It was deposed that Wilkyson had said he heard it reported that
every man of the value of forty shillings should pay twenty to the king;
every man of twenty shillings should pay ten; and every man of ten
shillings should pay five. The accused had then become violent. 'If
every man would do as I would do, we would take him by the head and
pull him down,' he swore. Asked whom he would 'pull down', he
replied 'Harry with the crown'.[28]

It is scarcely surprising that rumours were spreading of the king's
intention to take half of every man's goods. By 1525 there were three
sets of commissioners out assessing and trying to collect taxes: those
appointed to raise the 1524 'Amicable Grant' (as Wolsey euphemis-

tically described the forced loan he was levying) were treading on the
heels of others still vainly trying to complete the collection of the 1522
and 1523 subsidies. It was an impossible task.

> Those of your Grace's subjects who have been before us seem well
> minded to accomplish your Grace's demands, and would make no
> demur if their goods were sufficient; but there is great poverty,
> especially of money, here in Kent. At several fairs men having their
> wares and cattle to sell have departed without selling anything,
> unless they would have sold them at less than half their values.
> Landed men can get little or nothing of their farmers, who say they
> can get no money for their corn and cattle.[29]

In Suffolk the situation was more serious. An angry crowd of a
thousand men gathered on the border at Stanstead, declaring that they
would not pay and threatening their more timorous neighbours that
they would be 'hewn in pieces if they make any grant'.[30] Henry accurately gauged the temper of the people and called off the collection. Had
he not done so he might have had another Cornish rebellion on his
hands but this time it would have been not only Cornwall that raised
the standard of revolt.

For several years government finances were in dire straits. Then
Thomas Cromwell hit upon the scheme of enriching the crown at the
expense of the church. The land and possessions of the monasteries
should have put Henry's exchequer on a permanently sound footing
but royal extravagance and inflation frittered away this enormous bon-
anza. Instead of providing a steady source of income, most of the
monastic lands were sold off and by the end of the reign the government was again bankrupt. Lord Chancellor Wriothesley's panic-
stricken account of the situation in 1545 speaks for itself:

> ... touching the Mint we be now so far out with that, if you take
> any penny more from it these three months ... you shall utterly
> destroy the trade of it ... as to the Augmentations it shall not be
> able to pay the £5000 ... yet these six days... And of the revenue
> ... there is yet to come in ... £15,000 or £16,000, but when we
> shall have it, God knoweth. As to the Tenth and Firstfruits [the
> tenth was a direct tax granted by parliament; firstfruits was a tax
> levied on the church], there remains not due above £10–12,000,
> which is not payable till after Christmas... The Exchequer shall
> not be able to minister above £10,000 (and that at Candlemass) of
> the remainder of the subsidy. The Surveyors Court owes so much

that when all shall be come in that is due to it . . . they shall not be able to render up . . . more than £5000 or £6000; and when that shall be, God knoweth. . . I assure you, Master Secretary, I am at my wits' end how we shall possibly shift for three months following, and especially for the next two. For I see not any great likelihood, that any good sum will come in till after Christmas. . .[31]

Government finance was thus in as parlous a state at the end of the period as it had been at the beginning. In fact, England in 1547 was on the brink of bankruptcy. Few people realised this but everyone had to shoulder his part of the national burden. The Tudors, father and son, bullied the church, exploited the gentry and the burgesses, and drove desperate peasants and artisans to seditious talk and to the brink of revolt. Yet most of them did not revolt; most of the king's subjects remained loyal. There are many reasons: the landed classes had a community of interest with the crown; the Tudors created efficient policing and propaganda systems; they projected well the image of kingship. But all this would not have been enough to hold down a disgruntled populace. No, if most Englishmen were unwilling to relinquish their hold of the firm, guiding hand of the Tudors it was, to use Hilaire Belloc's words, 'for fear of finding something worse'. The new regime had delivered England from anarchy, had given security, firm government, peace and a feeling of national identity. For such benefits the people were prepared to forgive their rulers much. Back in 1486 Henry Tudor had married Elizabeth of York and all war-weary England had gone wild with joy, for 'By reason of [this] mariage peace was thought to discende oute of heauen into England, consideryng that the lynes of Lancastre and Yorke . . . were now brought into one knot and connexed together, of whose two bodyes one heyre might succede, which after their tyme should peaceably rule and enioye the whole monarchy and realme of England.'[32] The euphoria lingered for a very long time.

At first sight it is not easy to see why Thomas More entered the service of the Tudors. He frequently declared himself indifferent to royal favour and unwilling to be sucked into the vicious whirlpool of court politics. Like Sir Thomas Wyatt he knew how insecure were the lives and fortunes of those whose ambition carried them into Henry VIII's claustrophobic chambers.

> Who list his wealth and ease retain,
> Himself let him unknown contain;

Press not too fast in at that gate
Where the return stands by disdain:
  For sure, *circa Regna tonat.*

The high mountains are blasted oft
When the low valley is mild and soft;
Fortune with health stands at debate,
The fall is grievous from aloft,
  And sure, *circa Regna tonat.*

These bloody days have broken my heart:
My lust, my youth did them depart,
And blind desire of estate,
Who hastes to climb seeks to revert:
  Of truth, *circa Regna tonat.*[33]

In More's, scarcely concealed, opinion Henry VII had been an avaricious tyrant who had made damaging inroads on the liberty and wealth of his subjects.

> Suppose that some kyng and his counsel were together whettinge their wittes and devisinge, what subtell crafte they myght invente to enryche the kinge with great treasures of money. First one counselleth to rayse and enhaunce the valuation of money... Another counselleth to fayne warre, that when under this coloure and pretence the kyng hath gathered greate aboundaunce of money, he maye, when it shall please him, make peace with greate solemnitie and holye ceremonies, to blinde the eyes of the poor communaltie. ... Another putteth the kynge in remembraunce of certeine olde and moughteeaten lawes, that of longe tyme have not bene put in execution, whych because no man can remember that they were made, everie man hath transgressed. The fynes of these lawes he counselleth the kynge to require: for there is no waye so proffitable, nor more honourable, as the whyche hathe a shewe and coloure of justice ...[34]

Henry VIII, for all his love of music and his ability in theological and philosophical debate, was, the young lawyer soon concluded, potentially more wilful than his father. A few years later, after he had embarked on a career of royal service, he wrote to Erasmus expressing his misgivings quite clearly: 'You are a wise man in keeping yourself from being mixed up in the busy trifles of princes; and it shows your love for me that you wish me rid of them; you would hardly believe how unwilling I am. Nothing could be more hateful to me than this mission.'[35]

Yet More's scepticism about courts and kings did not prevent his commending himself to the new monarch with an epithalamium on Henry's marriage to Catherine of Aragon. He saw no contradiction in winning the patronage and friendship of Archbishop Warham, Morton's successor at Canterbury. His reputation as a wit and scholar won him many friends at court and we know that during Henry VII's reign he had access to the household of the royal children. There is no evidence that he deliberately shunned the limelight or declined the opportunities which his contacts brought him. He may have entertained doubts about the wisdom of entering the royal service but he kept those doubts for his private correspondence. In his public life he was completely involved in the system of patronage. He sought it and accepted it. Henery VIII

Even if he had seriously tried to escape from that system it is doubtful whether he would have succeeded. For patronage worked two ways: if poor men sought the aid of kings and nobles, kings and nobles also sought out the talented from among the lower orders to serve them. Wolsey heard of the silver-tongued lawyer with a reputation for wisdom and scrupulous honesty. In 1514 he appointed More a member of a commercial mission to Flanders. It was a test he passed with flying colours for, on his return, the king offered to retain him on a yearly pension. At first More declined the offer, much to his wife's disgust. But it was as difficult to resist Henry VIII's generosity as it was to escape his malice. Slowly, steadily, Thomas More was drawn into the royal service to become one of the many ministers from whom Henry sucked the genius and devotion before discarding them like empty oranges.

Even so it must again be stressed that More was not drawn into the life of court and Council chamber entirely against his will. It was during these crucial years that he was writing his most famous book, *Utopia*. In it there appears what may well have been an attempt at self-justification. He was debating the duty of philosophers. Should they, he asked, shun royal courts, where their counsel would inevitably be ignored? He concluded that such action was indefensible.

Yf evel opinions and noughty persuasions can not be utterly quyte plucked out of their hartes, if you can not even as you wolde remedy vices, which use and custome hath confirmed: yet for this cause you

must not leave and forsake the common wealthe: you must not forsake
the shippe in a tempeste, because you can not rule and keepe downe
the wyndes. No nor you must not laboure to dryve into their heades
newe and straunge informations, whyche you knowe wel shall be
nothinge regarded wyth them that be of cleane contrary mindes. But
you must with a crafty wile and a subtell trayne studye and
endeavoure youre selfe, as muche as in you lyethe, to handel the matter
wyttelye and handesomelye for the purpose, and that whyche you can
not turne to good, so to order it that it be not verye badde. For it is not
possible for al thinges to be well, onles all men were good.[36]

Of all the positions that More held we may well believe that he
found the Mastership of Requests the most congenial. The Court of
Requests was sometimes called the court for 'poor men's causes', and
that is largely what it was. It began life as a department of the royal
household and was staffed by members of the Council and household
lawyers to consider the plethora of pleas presented to the crown by
those who could not afford the process of litigation in the prerogative
and common law courts. For many years it met wherever the king was,
but Wolsey gave it a permanent base in the White Hall at Westminster
where, it was promised 'poor suitors . . . shall have hearing with expedition'.[37] The sittings of the Court of Requests were not limited to
the legal terms and it carried quite a large personnel, so it seems that
the Cardinal's intentions were to a considerable extent realised.

More and his subordinates found themselves adjudicating on a wide
variety of cases. William Burgess, a chaplain, wishes to leave the employ of Mistress Lacy whom he has served, as per prior agreement, for
one year, but the lady will not release him. Some brewers of Holborn
complain that William Bobye is preventing them from drawing water
at the well on his land, a right established by long custom. Cornelius
Peterson declares he has been unlawfully expelled from the guild of St
Barbara. John Amadas bought a new silver cross worth £62 0s 4d for
the parish church of Tavistock but the churchwardens refuse to reim-
burse him. Disputes between neighbours, disagreements over debts
and obligations: these were the meat and drink of the Court of
Requests.[38] For the most part they were issues demanding common
sense, diplomacy and tact rather than a knowledge of legal niceties. But
there can be no doubt that the court was very necessary. In an age
when the scales of justice were heavily weighted against the poor, the
government did recognise its obligation to care for the less favoured
members of the commonwealth.

The court in which More affected to be so reluctant a prisoner* was a complex living organism and one which was, superficially at least, very attractive. It was a crowded, intimate, claustrophobic world where there was little privacy and where tiny indiscretions were common property. Young courtiers slept two or more to a bed, as did the ladies of the queen's side. The young Earl of Surrey found it an enchanting world

> The large green courts where we were wont to hove
> With eyes cast up into the maiden's tower
> And easy sighs such as folk draw in love . . .
> The secret thought imparted with such trust
> The wanton talk, the divers change of play
> The friendship sworn, and promise kept so just
> Wherewith we passed the winter nights away.

But Surrey's mentor, Thomas Wyatt, had long since seen through the gay façade. He despised the qualities required of the successful courtier:

> With the nearest virtue to cloak alway the vice, . . .
> To press the virtue that it may not rise,
> As drunkenness good fellowship to call,
> The friendly foe with his double face
> Say he is gentle, and courteous therewithal,
> And say that favel [flattery] hath a goodly grace
> In eloquence, and cruelty to name
> Zeal of justice and change in time and place,
> And he that sufferth offence without blame
> Call him pitiful, and him true and plain
> That raileth reckless to every man's shame,
> Say he is rude that cannot lie and feign,
> The lecher a lover, and tyranny
> To be the right of a prince's reign . . .[40]

---

* More to Fisher: 'It was with the greatest unwillingness that I came to court, as everyone knows, and as the King in joke often throws up in my face. I am as uncomfortable there as a bad rider is in the saddle. I am far from enjoying the special favour of the King, but he is so courteous and kindly to all that everyone who is in any way hopeful finds a ground for imagining that he is in the King's good graces ... the King has virtue and learning, and makes great progress in both with daily renewed zeal, so that the more I see His Majesty advance in all the qualities that befit a good monarch, the less burdensome do I feel this life of the Court.'[39]

Of course both poets were right. The court was a place of shimmering splendour where all the arts and civilised accomplishments were encouraged, where a galaxy of suitors and hangers-on clustered to gaze at and admire the beautiful men and women of the privileged solar system. But the court was no place for those who lacked the stamina for ruthless place-seeking and no-holds-barred rivalry. That rivalry could be bitter unto death. Every leading councillor and courtier had his paid dependants who spied on their master's enemies, started rumours and were prepared to perjure themselves before the royal judges. The court of the capricious and ruthless Henry VIII was particularly vicious. Thomas More was not deceived into false security by the king's friendship. As he told young Roper, 'if my head could win the king one castle in France it should not fail to go'. When gifted and loyal servants like Empson, Dudley, Wolsey and Cromwell could be disgraced and destroyed on blatantly unjust charges and royal wives cast aside because they had incurred the king's displeasure it was obvious that no one was safe. Those devoted to intrigue had every encouragement to spin their sinister webs. But Henry was always the master, and devious ministers had always to take care lest they should run their plans on to the solid rock of the king's stubborn loyalty to his friends.

In 1543 the Catholic faction on the Council tried, not for the first time, to bring down Thomas Cranmer. Henry agreed to allow his archbishop to be examined on a charge of heresy but on the night before the confrontation he had Cranmer brought secretly across the water from Lambeth and in private he disclosed the plot. Cranmer thanked his master and declared himself ready to submit his opinions to scrutiny.

> 'O Lord God!' cried Henry. 'What fond simplicity you have, to let yourself be imprisoned, so that every enemy of yours may take advantage against you. Do you not know, that when they have you once in prison, three or four false knaves will soon be procured to witness against you, and condemn you . . . No, not so, my Lord, I have better regard unto you, than to permit your enemies so to overthrow you.'[41]

Taking a ring from his finger he told Cranmer to show it to his accusers on the morrow as a sign that he had resumed the case into his own hands. Cranmer triumphed. His enemies were put to confusion. Not all the members of the king's inner circle were so fortunate.

But we must not fail to give due prominence to the other side of the coin. The English royal household lacked some of the graces and

National Monuments Record

The Henry VII Chapel at Westminster Abbey represents the summit achieved by the Gothic style in England. This ultimate development, known as the Perpendicular, was marked by such features as slender and graceful columns, wide windows and intricate fan vaulting

achievements of the courts of Lorenzo the Magnificent or Pope Julius II but Renaissance influences were beginning to show themselves. Henry of Richmond knew from his years of exile that there were fine craftsmen to be found on the continent and he began the custom of seducing some of the best foreign talent across the Channel. Unfortunately the king's love of fine work and his determination to get value for money sometimes cancelled each other out and Pagenino, the first sculptor to be brought over from Italy, left in a huff after arguments about his fee. Negotiations soon began with the Florentine Pietro Torrigiano who subsequently designed Henry's magnificent tomb in the new chapel at Westminster Abbey and that of his mother, the Lady Margaret, before returning home to boast 'every day about his gallant feats among those beasts of Englishmen'. Well might he boast; the tomb of Henry VII and his queen is justly regarded as one of the noblest monuments in northern Europe.

After Torrigiano many Italian sculptors came to serve the Tudor sovereigns and the members of their court. Benedetto da Rovezzano worked for years on a tomb of unparalleled magnificence for Cardinal Wolsey. It was too magnificent; after the minister's fall Henry VIII appropriated the unfinished monument for himself but it was still incomplete when da Rovezzano returned to Italy in 1540. After many vicissitudes the tomb was broken up and only the sarcophagus survived to provide a suitable, and still impressive, memorial to Horatio Nelson in the crypt of St Paul's. Henry VIII tried in vain to attract the incomparable Benvenuto Cellini to England after he had quarrelled with Torrigiano (neither of the Tudor kings seems to have been prepared to make any allowance for artistic temperament). Wolsey was more successful in his overtures to Giovanni di Majano, who carried out much of the decorative work at Hampton Court.

But we have yet to mention the greatest genius the Tudors ever employed. When we look at the personnel of Henry VIII's court and, indeed at Henry himself, we look at them, inevitably, through the eyes of one man – Hans Holbein the younger. For the first time in history the English court was preserved for posterity in the paintings and drawings of one supreme master, and for that fact we largely have Thomas More to thank. It was Erasmus who recognised the worth of the struggling young painter in Basle and sent him to More with a letter of introduction.

'Your painter, dearest Erasmus,' More wrote in December 1526, 'is a wonderful man but I fear he will not find England as fruitful as he had hoped. Yet I will do my best to see that he does not find it absolutely barren.'[42] As well as commissioning Holbein to paint his own portrait and those of other members of his family, More introduced the young Swabian to many of his friends and, apparently, to the king, for Holbein was soon working on the decoration of Greenwich Palace preparatory to a reception for some envoys from France. The commissions steadily increased from members of the court and the London merchant community, though his first portrait of the king was not begun until 1537. Thus, thanks to Hans Holbein's sensitive brush, we know what they looked like, those men and women with whom Thomas More and Henry VIII walked in the gardens at Westminster, played *primero*, hunted in Greenwich park.

And it is important that we should know; it saves us from relying solely on the written word. Take, for instance, this description of a lady of the court: 'not one of the handsomest women in the world. . . Of middling stature, swarthy complexion, long neck, wide mouth, bosom not much raised, and in fact has nothing but the king's great appetite, and her eyes, which are black and beautiful.'[43] If that were all we had to go on we should be hard put to understand why the king, who could have had any woman who took his fancy, had to have this particular woman. But when we look at Holbein's sketch of Anne Boleyn the mystery evaporates (see p. 70).

The father of English portraiture was more than just a recorder of faces. His patrons called upon him to perform a variety of jobs. A gateway to be designed for the new Westminster Palace; a moulded and painted ceiling for St James's; a title-page for Miles Coverdale's English Bible; the court painter took on a variety of commissions. Henry VIII was a generous patron and, though Holbein's home town of Basle made repeated attempts to win him back, the painter was too much of a success in England to contemplate going elsewhere. And thus we have the pictures of a wilful, middle-aged king in his immovable stance, feet apart, elbows bent, staring defiantly straight from the canvas; the touching sketch for Thomas More's family group; the monumental *Henry VIII and the Barber Surgeons*; and the splendid collection of drawings (now at Windsor) of court personalities.

High fashion for the young bucks and ladies of the court meant French (or perhaps Italian) fashion. We have only to consider the names of the popular dances of the day – coranto, gigue, pavan, galliard – to realise their continental origin. In 1512 a new kind of court entertainment had its début in England 'the kyng with xi other wer disguised after the maner of Italie, called a mask a thing not seen afore in England.'[44] The extravagant elegance of clothes is seen at its most dazzlingly arrogant in Guillim Scrot's portrait of the Earl of Surrey. This 'foolish proud boy' whose egotism wrought his own destruction was famous for his expensively fashionable dress. His taste for foreign styles was even seriously urged as one of the charges against him at his trial for high treason in 1546. All courtiers and ministers were throwing off their insularity and embellishing their fine houses with exquisite French furniture, Flemish tapestries and oriental carpets (used principally as tablecloths rather than floor coverings). Even the stolid Cromwell (who must always have had before him the fate of his old master Wolsey as a warning of what may happen to a subject who aspires to too great personal glorification) liked beautiful things and commissioned his agents to seek them out for him. In 1529 Stephen Vaughan reported from Antwerp that he was sending home ten ells of linen by his 'brother Johnson' to make shirts for Cromwell. He was also about to buy a dining table. 'It hath about it a border superficially made, wherein is set out certain Scripture in Greek, Hebrew and Latin, the neatest piece of work that I have ever seen. It cost 40 crowns.'[45] For the young men of Henry's court these outward trappings were all a part of the desire to be 'new', 'different', 'progressive'. They were men of the new

Fashionable dress among ladies and gentlemen of Henry VIII's court was meant to emphasise the wealth and importance of the wearers. Long trains of expensive material, deep sleeves and exaggerated shoulders all helped towards the desired effect. Costume sketch by Holbein

Thomas Howard, Earl of Surrey, the 'foolish, proud boy' whose talk of achieving power after Henry VIII's death brought him to the block in 1547. Poet, soldier, courtier and patron of the arts, Howard was to the fore in adopting French styles of dress and introducing Renaissance influences into England

learning and were as delighted to discuss the deliciously radical doctrines of the reformers as they were to learn the latest song or argue about the fashionable length for hose. It is no surprise to learn that the elegant Surrey was once examined by the Council for dabbling in Lutheranism.

This passion for foreign styles and the assumption of Renaissance styles was not without its critics. The chronicler, Hall, complained of the fashionable, slavish imitation of things Gallic. Nothing would satisfy that was not 'all French, in eating, drinking and apparel, yea, and in French vices and bragges . . . so that nothing by them was praised, but if it were after the French turn.'[46] If sophisticated Italian and French visitors are to be believed, ordinary Englishmen, unblessed by court influence, were possessed by a paranoid chauvinism. 'When they see a foreigner they become so many wolves and bears, by the Lord; they put on the malevolent look of a pig when you take away his trough.'[47] This was not a universal opinion and there were some continentals (notably Erasmus) who had pleasant things to say about the English, but the belief that the English were culturally backward was widespread among the international intelligentsia. It was a belief shared by many English members of that cultural élite. The patron of the Beauchamp Chapel at Warwick, for example, left instructions that the builders were 'not to use any glass of England'.

It was unfortunate and not altogether fair that the leaders of society should have sold English craftsmanship short. Native artists and technicians excelled in many fields. London's goldsmiths were famous. The development of English music between 1450 and 1550 was dominated by an almost unbroken sequence of brilliant exponents – Dunstable, Fayrfax, Cornysh, Taverner, Tye, Tallis – and the Chapel Royal under the active patronage of the first Tudors became a gushing fountain of composition. English carpenters created such masterpieces as the font cover of Ufford church, and the widely famed Devon rood screens. Increasingly they were directing their controlled exuberance to domestic buildings (e.g. Hampton Court great hall) and furniture (e.g. the richly carved bed originally at Lovely Hall, Blackburn). Architects, sculptors and masons were developing that uniquely English consummation of the Gothic style – Perpendicular – seen at its best in Bath Abbey, King's College Chapel, Magdalen Tower and Henry VII's chapel at Westminster. Despite the opinion quoted above, England could boast good glaziers in this period. Although most of their work did not outlast the Reformation, surviving windows such as those at York Minster and Tatteshall, Lincs, prove that fastidious patrons did not have to seek their artists abroad. Exponents of many crafts

Pietro Torrigiano was brought over from Italy by Henry VII but he left after a comparatively short stay, complaining that the English were mean patrons. The superb funeral effigies of the King and his wife Elizabeth (shown here) and of his mother, Margaret Beaufort, are all that survive of the great sculptor's English period

Warburg Institute

possessed both skill and imagination. Examine, for example, the very English grill enclosing Torrigiano's tomb for Henry VII at Westminster.

Yet, when all this has been said it must be admitted that English artists were slow, uncertain, in their response to Renaissance influences. They were not unique in this; throughout northern Europe the challenge of new ideas from Italy was evoking consternation and resentment as well as uncritical enthusiasm among artists and patrons. Very slowly English craftsmen experimented with these new ideas. Many decades would pass before they were absorbed into the English style. Holbein, for example, left no 'English school' of court painters to continue his work. Meanwhile, kings and nobles wishing to grace their homes with the finest examples of the decorative arts continued to employ foreigners.

The glittering, cruel world of the court moved with its furniture and tapestries, its chests of clothes and plate from one to another of the royal manors in and near London throughout the year. The first Tudors were great builders and they increased the number of their homes within a day's ride from London from seven to sixteen. Henry VII's favourite residence was Richmond Palace, a monumental Gothic edifice built in the amazingly short time of two years to replace Sheen Manor which was burned down at Christmas 1498. Within the City Henry enlarged, modernised and embellished Baynards Castle, and downriver he similarly improved the sprawling, red-bricked mass of Greenwich. Further out lay Eltham, Windsor and Woodstock. More himself made allusion to Henry VII's building projects in an early elegiac poem on the death of Queen Elizabeth (Elizabeth of York), when he put these words in the dying woman's mouth:

Where are our castles? Now where are our towers?
Goodly Richmond, soon art thou gone from me,
At Westminster, that costly work of yours,
Mine own dear Lord, now shall I never see.
Almighty God vouchsafe to grant that ye
For you and your children well may edify.
My palace builded is; and lo! now here I lie.

It might have been considered that, with Westminster and the Tower as well, the Tudor monarchs had enough homes but Henry VIII – egged on by a desire to impress foreign visitors and to rival the accomplishments of Francis I of France whose palaces at Fontainebleau and along the Loire valley excited universal admiration – was always building or planning new mansions. Beside London's Fleet ditch he built Bridewell, at a cost of £14,000. From the fallen Wolsey he acquired the magnificent residences of York Place and Hampton Court. He bought Oatlands in Surrey from Archbishop Cranmer. He acquired the Bishop of Ely's palace at Hatfield, Herts, and used it as a country home for his children.

Then there was Nonsuch, an extravaganza built with the first inrush of funds from the confiscated monasteries. Consciously designed to surpass Francis I's château of Chambord, it remained unrivalled as a concept of wild and unrestrained imagination until the Prince Regent built his Pavilion at Brighton. The village of Cuddington was swept away and an army of brickmakers, masons, carpenters, glaziers and slaters moved in, accompanied by the best foreign artists and crafts-men Henry could obtain. Cartloads of stone – broken angels and frag-mented saints – were trundled to the site from nearby Merton Priory and were tipped into the foundations. And upon those foundations arose a

Henry VIII's taste for extravagant and lavish display was given full rein in the building of Nonsuch Palace. Determined to outdo the châteaux of his rival, Francis I of France, Henry added towers, pinnacles, cupolas, domes and a wealth of bizarre decoration

Subjects who wanted to emulate the royal exuberance had to be content with such objects as 'Nonsuch' chests. Inlay of holly, bog oak and various coloured woods was used to represent buildings very similar to the new royal palace

Gothic–Renaissance phantasmagoria as outsize and exuberant as its royal architect.

Nonsuch might have been the purest architectural expression of Henry's personality but Westminster remained the centre of his life and the seat of his government, as it had been for his father. Henry VII liked sprawling, old-fashioned Westminster and in its great abbey he carried out, heedless of expense, the crowning achievement of his reign. The Henry VII Chapel stands in the same rank as the chapels of King's, Cambridge, and St George's, Windsor. If England's craftsmen generally lagged behind their continental counterparts, her ecclesiastical architects and masons were without peer. Henry might bring in Italian sculptors to add the embellishments to his chapel but the soaring structure itself and William Vertue's ethereal fan tracery were products of pure English genius. The medieval palace of Westminster was outmoded and crowded. Its buildings had to house parliament and law courts as well as the royal household. Therefore it cannot have been felt as an unmitigated disaster when almost the whole site was gutted by fire in April 1512. Baynards Castle, Bridewell and the Tower had to suffice for the court and government officials for some years. But in 1529 Henry VIII took over Wolsey's sumptuous palace of York Place and installed Anne Boleyn there. So popular was the house with Henry's second queen that he decided to make it the centre of a vast new complex. Once again hordes of workmen were recruited and an area of twenty-three acres was ruthlessly cleared of all existing buildings. Whitehall, as the new palace was called, extended from the Thames to where Downing Street now stands. Its state rooms and privy chambers were designed for the comfort and convenience of a busy, pleasure-loving court. As well as a banqueting hall and miles of rooms providing a suitable setting for lavish royal hospitality, there were five tennis courts, a tilt yard and a cockpit. As if all this were not enough, Henry acquired in 1532 the nearby site of St James's hospital and built himself another palace there.

It should not be thought that the life of the Tudor court was moulded to a fixed, unchanging pattern. On the contrary, it reflected directly the mood and predilections of the king. Henry VII, for all his financial caution, loved pleasure and was prepared to pay for it. His meticulous account book records frequent small sums paid to lords of misrule, musicians and jesters and even quite generous donations such as 'To the young damsel that daunceth £30'.[48] The royal menagerie housed in the Lion Tower of the Tower of London was a particular source of delight to him and he was always prepared to buy exotic new

Whether in public or in private, the Tudor rulers were sur-
rounded by ceremonial. Henry VIII walking in procession to the
opening of parliament in 1512

Henry VIII at dinner (after Holbein)

specimens for the collection. He played cards, dice and tennis; he competed with his close companions at the butts; but his first love was the chase.

Unlike his subjects who sometimes had to content themselves with lesser game the king's wardens, foresters and huntsmen could always assure him of a supply of red deer or roe deer at Windsor, Richmond, Greenwich or wherever his majesty was staying. The hunt might take various forms. It might be a simple *chasse* involving the king and a few close friends. This was the purest kind of sport and the one which both Tudors, father and son, loved best. It took them away from the squabbles of the court and affairs of state into God's clean country air. With a few hand-picked male companions they could become one with nature in all its grandeur and cruelty.

The thrill of the chase lay (as it still does today) in watching hounds (who might be a motley collection of greyhounds, mastiffs and harriers) at work, seeking and finding a scent, then following this at full cry over ground strewn with a variety of natural hazards – ditches, bog, pot-holes, fallen trees. When the beast was finally brought to bay the king or some favoured friend took his hunting sword and delivered the *coup de grâce*.

The hunt might also take the form of a *battue*, a much more lavish affair, lasting for several days and involving the whole court. Such entertainments were frequently laid on for visiting ambassadors and foreign dignitaries. Variety was the keynote of these splendid occasions. There would be mounted pursuits of various game, contests of falconry, shooting at birds using special, blunt arrows, and the drive. The latter involved a group of beaters driving the game past stands where the leaders of the court stood ready with bows and arrows or cross-bows. There would be feasting at tables laid out in sylvan glades or within large silk-hung pavilions.

Royalty and nobility alike were jealous of their hunting rights which constituted a mark of social difference. These rights were coming under serious attack. The growing number of free landowners – lesser gentry, yeomen and merchants – was swelling the ranks of those able to practise the ancient art of venery. The disorder of the fifteenth century had made the forest laws difficult to enforce and had given consider-able encouragement to poachers, and the invention of firearms made this ancient pastime much easier. Both Tudor kings found it necessary to legislate against the extension of legal and illegal hunting. From the wording of these statutes it is obvious that 'common folk' were using 'guns, bows, greyhounds, or other dogs, ferrets, tramels [nets for birds], lowbells [bells set close to the ground to drive game into nets], or harepipes . . . deer hayes [nets] or buck stalls [traps], or other snares or engines to take game, crossbows, handguns, hakebuts and demi-hakes'.

When Henry VIII became king in 1509 he was the first ruler for almost a century who had been groomed for the job. Not since Henry V's accession in 1413 had a royal prince of mature years entered peacefully upon his inheritance, an inheritance he had had plenty of time to contemplate. The pampered young king resolved to deny himself nothing and to spare no expense to make his court one of the most brilliant in Europe. As he expressed it in one of his songs:

> Pastyme w^t good companye
> I love and shall vntyll I dye
> Grudge who list but none denye
> So God be plesyd and live wyll I
> For my pastance [diversion]
> Hunt, synge and dance
> My hart is sett
> All goodly sport
> For my comfort
> Who shall me let.

Life at court in the early years of the reign was a virtually unending cycle of entertainments. If special state occasions and the annual festivals of Christmas, New Year, Easter, May Day and Midsummer did not provide sufficient occasions for diversion, occasions were invented. There were disguisings, maskings, plays, dances and banquets – but, above all, there were tournaments.

The period 1510–30 was the golden age of the tournament, a sport at which England's athletic young king excelled. These events, which usually lasted three or four days, were staged with the utmost splendour. The tilt yard would, with the aid of timber and painted canvas, be transformed into a wonderland – Camelot, perhaps, or an enchanted forest – and the actual contests were interspersed with pageants and allegorical scenes. Consider, for example, the tournament of February 1511 to celebrate the birth of the Prince of Wales (who died a few days later). The festivities began when a gigantic pageant car was drawn into the Westminster tilt yard, disguised as a forest,

> with rockes, hilles and dales, with divers sundrie tree, flowers, ha-thornes, ferne and grasse, with six forsters, standynge within the same

forrest, garnyshed in cotes and hodes of grene Veluet, by whome lay a great number of speres, all the trees, herbes and floures, of the same forrest were made of grene Veluet, grene Damaske, and silke of divers colours, Satyn and Sercenet. In the middes of this forrest was a castell standing, made of golde and before the Castel gate sat a gentleman freshly appareiled, makynge a garlande of Roses for the pryce. This forrest was drawen, as it were by strength of twoo great beastes, a Lyon and an Antelop, the Lyon floryshed all ouer with Damaske golde, the Antelop was wrought all ouer with siluer of Damaske, his beames or hornes and tuskes of golde: these beastes were led with certayne men appareiled like wilde men or wood-houses, their bodies, hedes, faces, handes, and legges, couered with grene Sylke flosshed: On either of the saide Antelop and Lyon, sate a ladye richely appareiled, the beastes were tyed to the pageant with greate chaynes of golde, as horses be in the carte. When the pageant rested before the Quene, the forenamed forsters blew their hornes, then the deuise or pageant opened on all sides, and out issued ... foure knyghtes, armed at all peces, euery of them a spere in his hande on horsebacke with great plumes on their heddes, their basses and trappers of clothe of gold, euery of them his name embroudered on his basse and trapper.[49]

Such spectacles, and, of course, feasting, were interspersed with the sport. This comprised jousts royal in which mounted knights separated by a barrier ran at each other with lances; tourneying, mounted combat with swords; foot combat with axes or swords; and running at large or jousting without a barrier.

Many of these lavish entertainments were open to the public. When king and court celebrated May Day 1515 in the woods near Greenwich a large crowd (though the contemporary estimate of 25,000 is an exaggeration) watched their sovereign and his queen served at a banquet by 'Robin Hood and his men', and, afterwards, entertained by 'Lady May' and 'Dame Flora'. Henry liked to show himself to his cheering people and his court was by no means closed. Indeed, the new palace at Westminster was designed on a very 'open plan' and members of the public could walk through it.

In the 1530s a change came over the atmosphere of the court. The struggle for the divorce and the conflict with the pope occupied much of the king's time. Though Wolsey was succeeded by the even more able Cromwell, Henry took more interest in routine government than he had done during the Cardinal's great days. Life was more serious

during the Reformation; pageants and spectacles had a propaganda
objective now. In 1538, for example, the bogus rood of grace from Boxley
Abbey was publicly exposed. It was borne in procession through London
and on to Westminster. At court a large crowd gathered to watch as the
mechanism which made the statue's lips and eyes move was demonstrated
before the king. Then the Bishop of Rochester preached a sermon against
the image before handing it over to the mob, who cheerfully smashed it and
made a bonfire of the pieces.

But the main reason for the duller life of the court was that Henry
was getting older and had lost his youthful vigour and health. In 1528
his leg ulcers had begun to trouble him and his appearances in the lists
ceased. Since Henry was little interested in pastimes in which he could
not play the central role, the number of tournaments dwindled. Almost
to the end of his days the king went hunting. Once his massive bulk
was hoisted into the saddle it stayed there all day and Henry often wore
out courtiers half his age. Occasionally there were flashes of the days of
'Bluff King Hal' when the king married another wife, for instance, or when
there were foreign dignitaries to be impressed. But more and more Henry
preferred the company of a small group of friends with whom he played
cards late into the sleepless, pain-racked nights, or talked theology in the
palace gardens.

When we consider how appallingly wasteful of talent the Tudor
court was, it is difficult to imagine how career-minded courtiers could
survive and even prosper. Men of such considerable and varied gifts as
Thomas More, the Earl of Surrey, Edmund Dudley, Bishop Fisher,
Thomas Cromwell and Cardinal Wolsey were wantonly destroyed as
though their rare talents were in plentiful supply. The answer is that
the patronage system inevitably brought gifted men to the surface and
although the Tudor tyrants got many of the mediocre time-servers they
deserved there were always sufficient men of real worth to give their
court a Renaissance refinement and their government a keen cutting
edge.

When all that has been said it must be admitted that the Mores and
the Surreys were not typical of the men who served the first two
Tudors. Such a distinction (if so it may be called) belongs more to
Richard Rich. Some twenty years More's junior, Rich was also born in
the city of London; the two families were, in fact, close neighbours in
the parish of St Lawrence Jewry, and Rich followed the older man by
becoming a student of law at the Middle Temple. He, naturally, used
his acquaintance with More in an attempt to further his career but
More had a poor opinion of the young man as he was to declare years

later: 'you were always esteemed very light of your tongue, a great
dicer and gamester, and not of any commendable fame either there [at
home] or at your house in the Temple.'[50] It seems very likely that
young Richard did, indeed, live the dissolute life of a student whose
father could afford to finance his excesses, for Richard Rich the elder
was a prominent London draper. Petitions to Wolsey and other
prominent men at court brought no preferment and Rich was well into
his thirties before he attained any prominence. In 1529 he was elected
member of parliament for Colchester. In that 'Reformation Parliament'
he took every opportunity of loudly supporting government policy and
of commending himself to Cromwell who was always on the lookout
for ambitious men who could be useful to him.

The patronage of Master Secretary improved Rich's position out of
all recognition. Small government appointments came his way and, in
1533, he was knighted and appointed Solicitor-General. In this position
he developed a penchant for interrogating political prisoners. He
visited John Fisher in the Tower and, under pretence of coming from
the king who desired to know in secret the bishop's views on the royal
supremacy, he tricked the prisoner into a damning statement in support of papal authority – a statement Rich did not hesitate to reproduce
in court.

A few weeks later Rich was back in the Tower visiting his 'old friend
and neighbour' Thomas More. He tried the same tactics but he was
dealing with a much more wily protagonist – a cautious lawyer and a
far finer one than Rich would ever be. But the fact that More made no
statement was no deterrent to the Solicitor-General. When the ex-
Chancellor came to trial Rich unequivocally stated that More had
denied that parliament could appoint anyone head of the English
church and it was on this uncorroborated evidence that Thomas More
was to be sent to his death.

As the Reformation advanced so did Richard Rich. He became
chancellor of the Court of Augmentations and naturally used the position to accumulate considerable wealth. As Speaker of the House of
Commons in 1536 he opened the session with a speech of odious
adulation in which he opined that King Henry combined all the gifts of
Solomon, Samson and Absalom. He was now a member of the Council
and the owner of vast estates in Essex and he owed everything to
Thomas Cromwell. But in 1540 Cromwell fell, suddenly and finally. It
is no surprise to find Richard Rich among those who gave evidence at
the minister's attainder for treason.

Rich now sought new allies and, considering Gardiner and Norfolk,

Richard Rich, by
Holbein

leaders of the conservative faction, to be stronger than their rivals, he now became a persecutor of heretics. It was he, with Chancellor Wriothesley, who examined the age's most celebrated Protestant martyr in the Tower. In their determination to obtain evidence against Queen Catherine Parr the conservatives arrested Anne Askew, a Lincolnshire gentlewoman who was well known at court through her friends and relatives. But Anne refused to be cajoled or browbeaten into disclosing anything against the queen. In exasperation Wriothesley and Rich had her put on the rack and, when the lieutenant of the Tower refused to apply pressure to the wheel, they doffed their gowns and did the job themselves.

Such a man was Richard Rich. He went on to serve under Protestant Edward and Catholic Mary, to become a baron, Lord Chancellor of England and to die full of years – in his own bed. To be a successful politician under the Tudors it was not necessary to be amoral and ruthless – but it certainly helped.

5

'Unsatiable Cormorant'

Landlords, Tenants and Inflation

. . . your shepe that were wont to be so meke and tame, and so smal eaters, now, as I heare saye, be become so great devowerers and so wylde, that they eate up, and swallow downe the very men them selfes. They consume, destroye and devoure whole fieldes, howses and cities. For looke in what partes of the realme doth growe the fynest, and therfore dearest woll, there noblemen, and gentlemen: yea and certeyn Abbottes, holy men no doubt, not contenting them selfes with the yearely revenues and profytes, that were wont to grow to theyr forefathers and predecessours of their landes, nor beynge content that they live in rest and pleasure nothinge profiting, yea much noyinge the weale publique: leave no grounde for tillage, thei inclose al into pastures: thei throw doune houses: they plucke downe townes, and leave nothing standynge, but only the churche to be made a shepe-howse. And as thoughe you loste no small quantity of grounde by forestes, chases, laundes, and parkes, those good holy men turne all dwellinge places and all glebeland into desolation and wildernes. Therfore that on covetous and unsatiable cormaraunte and very plage of his natyve contrey naye compasse aboute and inclose many thousand akers of grounde together within one pale or hedge, the husbandmen be thrust owte of their owne, or els either by coveyne and fraude, or by violent oppression they be put besydes it, that they be compelled to sell all: by one meanes therfore or by other, either by hooke or crooke they muste needes departe awaye, poore, selye, wretched soules, men, women, husbands, wives, father-lesse children, widowes, wofull mothers, with their yonge babes, and their whole houshold smal in substance, and muche in numbre, as husbandrye requireth manye handes. Awaye thei trudge, I say, out of their knowen and accustomed houses, fyndynge no place to reste in. All their householdestuffe, whiche is verye little woorthe, thoughe it myght well abide the sale: yet beeynge sodainely thruste oute, they be constrayned to sell it for a thing of nought. And when they have wandered abrode tyll that be spent, what can they then els doo but steale, and then justly pardy be hanged, or els go about a beggyng. And yet then also they be caste in prison as vagaboundes, because they go aboute and worke not: whom no man wyl set a worke, though they never so willyngly profre themselves therto. For one Shephearde or Heardman is ynoughe to eate up that grounde with cattel, to the occupying wherof aboute husbandrye manye handes were requisite.[1]

It is a forlorn story, the telling of which shows More in a moving and indignant vein. No one could possibly be unaware of the problems of depopulation and vagrancy (or, to give it its true name, unemployment) but as a lawyer he was closer to them than many. He had seen the distressing cases pass through the courts – appeals against landlords for unjustly raising rents; thefts of sheep and poultry; desperate, hollow-cheeked men accused of breaking down hedges and drawing the plough across pasture; cottages broken into by wandering desperadoes; innocent townsmen 'mugged' in broad daylight. He saw the endless stream of those condemned to the gallows and he knew that for most of them their only crime was poverty. In his outrage he turned, like many of his contemporaries, on the greedy landlord, who was 'contented for to pull down houses of husbandry so that he may stuff his bags full of money'.[2]

In fact, the causes of poverty and unemployment were far more complex. They resulted from the uncontrolled interplay of economic factors which sixteenth-century writers and politicians imperfectly understood. Fundamental to the problem was the rise in population. Between 1495 and 1545 it increased from 2·2 million to 2·8 million after having remained virtually static for more than a century. As families increased in size, peasant and yeoman holdings were less able to support them. Younger sons could no longer depend on finding employment on the manor or the family farm. They were forced to hire themselves out as labourers to other landowners or tenants. More often than not there were simply no vacancies locally. Farmers either could not afford to employ more hands or were, for sound economic reasons, laying men off.

Many landlords were, in their way, in as dire straits as the labouring class. The cost of food, and therefore the level of wages, and con-

Scenes from rural life. Peasants lived in very simple thatched, windowless hovels very much at the mercy of the elements. Whether they farmed land in the common fields or plots around their dwellings they seldom managed to keep themselves above subsistence level

All the village was involved in the harvest on the feudal demesne. But by the sixteenth century most people had commuted their feudal service, and landlords had to hire extra labourers at harvest time

An old obligation villagers could not escape was the annual payment of tithes in money or kind to the parish priest. Such dues became a cause of bitter conflict between clergy and laity

There were, of course, opportunities to relax and enjoy, for example, a friendly (or sometimes not so friendly) game of skittles

sequently the cost of most manufactured items increased in a way which, to any age other than our own, would appear alarming. An index has been compiled which shows the rise in the cost of a 'basket' of food items including grain, malt, butter, cheese, meat and fish, part of which is reproduced here:[3]

(The figure of 100, based on an average of prices 1451–75, is taken as the basis)

1490–1500	100
1501–1510	106
1511–1520	109
1521–1530	159
1531–1540	161
1541–1550	217

It is generally true that the burden of inflation falls most heavily upon the poor who have no economic staff on which to lean. This proposition is, however, an over-simplification as far as the sixteenth century is concerned. The rural peasantry lived on the edge of a money economy. They were accustomed to bartering goods and services and were therefore partly protected from dramatic price rises. Landlords, whose incomes derived largely from rents, felt the bite of inflation most sharply. Most tenancies were copyhold and ran for several years. Some covered the lifespan of the tenant. Some agreements even included clauses covering the taking over of the tenancy by the present incumbent's heirs. Throughout the period of the agreement the rent remained static. It is little wonder, therefore, that when the opportunity to increase the rent did occur many landlords grabbed it. This led to cries of rack renting and some tenants were forced to leave the houses and the lands their fathers had inhabited for generations.

Of course, there were always good landlords. Sir John Gostwick advised the heirs to his estates in Bedfordshire always to value highly the goodwill of their tenants and neighbours. They should 'take not above one year's rent for a fine' and 'heighten no rent unless your farmers have heightened theirs to sub-tenants'.[4] Was Gostwick an example of exception or norm? The very nature of the evidence makes it difficult to answer that question. The written records fall largely into two categories: works by More and other humanist reformers who were appalled by the problem of vagrancy and who cannot be regarded as objective reporters of the contemporary scene; and court records which are, of course, concerned with cases of real or alleged injustice.

Nor should we forget that the landlord was as much bound by local custom as his tenants. In some areas, such as parts of Devon, ninety-nine-year leases (i.e. three-generation leases) had been secured. Such agreements amounted virtually to freehold tenancies. The moral and social pressures on the landlord not to terminate or alter drastically such long-standing arrangements were considerable. Local traditions concerning inheritance frequently created more hardship than hard-pressed landlords. A cottager with just enough land to feed his family (and that might be as little as one or two acres in some areas) either had to pass on his holding intact to his eldest son, which left his other children unprovided for, or divide the land equally between his heirs, which would leave none of them enough to live on.

While our sympathy is, rightly, engaged on behalf of the poor dispossessed, we should spare a thought for the class of gentlemen who found themselves in the position described by the imaginary knight in *A Discourse of the Common Weal*. As he explained to a representative of the lower orders:

Sir, I knowe it is true ye complayne not with oute a cause. So it is as true that I and my sorte, I meane all gentlemen, haue as greate, yea a far greater, cause to complayne then anie of youe haue; for as I said nowe that the price of thinges weare risen of all handes, youe may better live after youre degree then we, for youe may and doe raise the price of youre wares, as the price of victualles and other neces-saries doo rise. And so can not we so muche; for thoughe it be true that of suche landes as come to oure handes, either by purchace or by determination and ending of suche termes of yeares or other estates that I or my auncestor had graunted thearin in times past, I doe either receive fyne than of old was vsed, or enhaunce the rent thereof, beinge forced thereto for the chardge of my howshold that is increased over that it was, yet in all my life time I looke not that the thirde parte of my lande shall come to my dispocition, that I maye enhaunce the rent of the same; but it shalbe in men's holdinges, either by lease or by copie, graunted before my time, and still conty-nuinge, and yet likely to continewe in the same estate, for the most parte duringe my life, an perchaunce my sonnes; so as we can not rayse all our wares, as youe maye yours, and me thinkes yt were reason we did. And by reason we can not, so many of vs as haue departed . . . oute of the Countrie [out of the rural areas] of late, haue bene driven to give over oure houshold, and to kepe either a chambere in London, or to waight on the courte uncalled, with a

man and a lacky after him, wheare he was wonte to kepe halfe a score
cleane men in his house, and xxtie or xxxtie other persone besides,
everie day in the weke.[5]

Hardship among the employing classes was, thus, inevitably passed on
immediately to their economic dependants. Cutting staff was one of the
easiest ways of saving money. There were other, perfectly legal, means
of achieving the same objective.

Many landowners deliberately forced their tenants out in order to
engross their holdings and farm their estates themselves. Over a wide
area of England the traditional life of the manor was steadily changing
as more and more of the field strips came directly into the lord's hands.
It was obviously more economical to farm the manor as a unit, to
remove the banks of earth between the old holdings, to plough and
harrow with fewer teams, to utilise every inch of land and to ensure
that it was all farmed with equal efficiency.

It was not only the big landowners who saw the sense of this arrange-
ment. A villager of the 1540s explained how he and his neighbours
had faced the threats and opportunities presented by economic change:

Manie of vs saw, xij yere ago, that oure proffittes was but small by
the plows; and therefore divers of my neighboures that had in times
past, some two, some thre, some fowre plowes of theire owne, have
laid downe, some of them parte, and som of theym all theire teames,
and turned ether part or all theire arable grounde into pasture, and
thereby haue wexed verie Rich men. And everie day some of vs
encloseth a plote of his ground to pasture; and weare it not that oure
grounde lieth in the common feildes had bene enclosed, of a common agreament of all the townshippe, longe ere this time. And to
saie the truthe, I, that haue enclosed little or nothinge of my
grownd, could never be able to make vp my lordes rent weare it not
for a little brede of neate [oxen], shepe, swine, gese, and hens that I
doe rere vpon my ground; whearof, because the price is sumwhat
round, I make more cleare proffitt then I doe of all my corne; and
yet I haue but a bare liuinge, by reason that manye thinges doe
belonge to husbandrie which now be exceadinge chargeable, over
they weare in times past.[6]

Which brings us to the subject of enclosing arable land and turning
it over to sheep pasture. We have already seen that the cost of all
agricultural produce was high. On the face of it, therefore, it is difficult
to see why estate owners should quit arable for sheep farming. A letter

written in November 1532 provides us with a number of clues. It was
sent to Thomas Cromwell by the mayor of Norwich, Reynold
Lytylprow. Like many civic leaders he was under constant pressure
from the poor of his town and the surrounding area. There was little he
could do for them. In a year of bad harvests when the price of corn was
even higher than usual, the charitable funds at his disposal were swiftly
exhausted. He frequently wrote to the Council to make them aware of
the situation only to be met by the haughty regrets and statements of
lofty policy with which local government workers of all epochs are only
too familiar. At last, he decided to despatch a more eloquent missive.
He sent one of the ragged wretches who habitually haunted his door to
the king's secretary with this note:

> The bearer is in suit for grain, as are many more, and he desires your
> favour as he is very poor. I never saw these parts in so much poverty
> and idleness. People can get no wool, and all commodities made of it
> are decayed in these parts. I doubt not that you will be able to find a
> remedy[!]. Corn is dear in these parts, wheat being 10s a quarter and
> barley 6s 8d, owing only to the regraters, who are great farmers, and
> others who have corn to sell. Some remedy must be provided . . .[7]

At ten shillings a quarter corn certainly was dear but its price was
being artificially boosted by racketeers who bought up stocks and controlled the market. It was, thus, not the producer who benefited from
the high price of grain. Moreover, the farmer's own costs were high
and his profit margin was scarcely sufficient to compensate him for his
battle of wits with the elements. He needed little temptation to turn to
an alternative if such could be found. And in early Tudor England it
could be found. The woollen cloth industry was booming. The spinners
and weavers who worked in their own homes simply could not get
enough wool. The local clothiers who controlled the industry were
prepared to pay almost any price for their raw material.
    It was during the fourteenth century that England began the change
from a wool-exporting to cloth-manufacturing country. Between 1350
and 1400, encouraged by heavy duties on the export of wool, sales of
cloth abroad trebled, a trend which continued, if less dramatically,
throughout the Hundred Years War and civil wars. The coming of
peace and commercial stability in 1485 soon produced another rapid
rise in the number of cloths of assize shipped across the Channel. From
50,000 in the year of Bosworth, exports rose to 140,000 by 1540. The
demand for the raw material was thus insatiable and the price corre-
spondingly high. At the same time the input costs of animal husbandry

were comparatively low. The perpetual labour cycle of planting, hoeing, reaping, threshing, storing, ploughing, harrowing and sowing in the open fields kept every member of the manor occupied. Sheep farming involved the enclosing with fence or hedge of as large an area as possible and the placing of one shepherd in charge of each flock. Casual labour could be taken on to help with shearing and lambing. Apart from that the scraggy animals with their thin, but valuable, fleeces ($1\frac{1}{2}$–2 lb per sheep was an average yield from the best native strains) could largely be left to fend for themselves.

Under this stimulus every rural landholder who could do so raised sheep either exclusively or on the common pasture to which he had access. The wealthy built up enormous flocks. Sir William Fermour, a London merchant, bought many scattered manors in Norfolk and built, between 1520 and 1530, a magnificent house at East Barsham which still stands as a memorial to the enormous wealth derived from England's golden fleece. On his own lands and on rented pastures Fermour kept a total of 17,000 sheep. A statute of 1533 complained of 'covetous sheep-farmers', some of whom had flocks of 24,000 animals.

The temptations for landlords to increase their pasturage by fair means or foul were legion. Peasant holdings were taken over on points of dubious legality. Manorial lords 'swamped' the common pasture with their own sheep. The most frequent complaint was the enclosing of common land. The villagers who had grazed their own animals on the common from time out of mind had no legal claim to the pasture. Many of them had long since sold their rights in the open fields to the lord or ambitious neighbours and their animals provided their only livelihood. When the common was enclosed they lost everything. It was not only the big landlords who were to blame. Enterprising yeoman farmers took ruthless advantage of their neighbours' financial difficulties to add to their own holdings.

The end result of this unbridled interplay of market forces was a widening gulf between the 'haves' and 'have-nots'. Villages dwindled and disappeared. The dispossessed moved to other villages where, if they were not driven off by the local people, they hurriedly threw up single-roomed thatched huts. By completing the building of a dwelling between sunrise and sunset they established squatters' rights. These rural slums were as welcome to respectable sixteenth-century villagers as gypsy sites in modern suburbia but, by and large, they were tolerated.

Distressing as this phenomenon was we should be wrong if we thought of Tudor rural society as a society in decline largely because of the ruthless exploitation of the poor by the wealthy and enterprising. For one thing, society was much more flexible in the early sixteenth century than it had been in the heyday of the feudal system. The growth of trade and industry provided new opportunities for young men in the towns. The unmarried and those with young families might become vagabonds as they toured the country seeking employment, charity or patronage, but that does not mean that they were condemned to a life of perpetual wandering and beggary. Suffering there certainly was and in large measure but the hard core of the vagrancy problem was, then as in other ages, the men and women who had no love of honest labour and preferred the easier life of begging and larceny (see below, pp. 156–61).

The enclosure movement was neither new nor extensive. It had its origins in the fourteenth and fifteenth centuries and it was largely over by the time Henry VII came to the throne. Enclosing for pasture only made sense in areas where soil and climate were right and where there was reasonable access to the major textile centres of East Anglia and the Cotswolds. This principally meant the Midland counties of Bedfordshire, Leicestershire, Oxfordshire, Berkshire, Northamptonshire and Warwickshire. In other sheep-rearing counties such as Suffolk and Gloucestershire the open-field system had never been extensive, for the independent yeoman farmer had always been a significant element in society there. Of the 1200 or so square miles enclosed between 1455 and 1637 the greater part was fenced before 1485. Moreover, the textile industry which caused the rural depopulation also provided job opportunities for at least some of the dispossessed.[8] In some areas, notably those serving London, Bristol and the other major population centres, arable farming was still more profitable than rearing sheep.

What was happening in the English Midlands was so distressing that it demanded the sympathy and dominated the vision of writers, legislators and magistrates. We can scarcely blame them for presenting a very unbalanced impression of the contemporary scene but we should be careful not to follow them. What was happening was the completing, the 'tidying up' of an enclosure movement of ancient origin. Villages were not swept away overnight; they dwindled. Tenants were forced out or paid off a few at a time, as occasion arose. Landlords who thought they could get away with it (as many certainly could) used strong-arm methods to evict peasants and yeomen whose lands and houses stood in the way of improvement. Such a one was John Palmer, Lord of Westangmering in Sussex, who 'spoiled, destroyed and pulled down' some of the houses of his tenants and forced them 'to take other lands, being none of his own, in other places farther off at his pleasure'. Most Tudor enclosures were of small areas, between ten and twenty acres, and the tenacious villagers held on as long as possible to their dwellings and manorial rights. At Stretton Baskerville, Warwickshire, seven houses disappeared between 1485 and 1488 and sixteen between 1488 and 1517. Chelmscote, in the same county, was reported as being considerably decayed in 1517. Two more houses had been vacated by 1547 but it was the end of the century before Chelmscote ceased to exist.[9] Sixteenth-century English travellers saw the poignant memorials of an outdated socio-economic system – cottages turned into byres, roofless and slow-crumbling homesteads through which the sheep roamed free, untenanted villages and deserted churches standing alone among the new-hedged fields – and they were moved to sorrow and anger. What they failed to record for us on the other side of the balance sheet was the augmented villages, the wool centres like Lavenham, the wealth of whose inhabitants increased enormously during the period, and the growing towns.

The new rural situation was not without its apologists – the disciples of progress.

> The country enclosed I praise
> T'other delighteth not me
> For nothing the wealth it does raise
> To such as inferior be.

So wrote Thomas Tusser in *A Hundred Good Points of Husbandry*, which was to become one of the best-sellers of the sixteenth century. His reasons?

> More plenty of money and beef,
> Corn butter and cheese of the best,
> More wealth anywhere (to be brief)
> More people, more handsome and prest [mentally alert],
> Where find ye (go search any coast)
> Than there where enclosures are most?

Tusser was writing in 1557 but he was preceded thirty years earlier by Sir Anthony Fitzherbert, one of the leading justices of the day, who turned his trained mind to the problems of agriculture in his earnest treatise, *The Book of Husbandry*. Fitzherbert advocated mixed farming on enclosed fields where crops could be grown most economically and maximum manuring of the ground would be achieved. He dismissed as wasteful the open-field system and the driving of flocks and herds on to the common pasture.

The importance of Fitzherbert, Tusser and other writers was not the changes they advocated, but their popularity. England would have to wait another two hundred years before revolutionary techniques appeared which made a significant difference to yields from the land and from farm animals, and, despite what the Tudor experts advocated, the open-field system would remain the dominant feature of large areas of rural England for many decades. What is significant is the extent to which these books were read. The *Book of Husbandry* went through eight editions and many printings between 1523 and the end of the century. All manner of educated landholders – magnates, gentlemen, merchants buying into rural society, and yeomen – were reading these books. Under inflationary pressures and faced by the opportunities of growing demand, a new breed of landlord was emerging; one who was not content to regard his estates as static capital producing income in the form of rents and dues but was increasingly involved in their exploitation as economic units. 'The gentlemen which were wont to addict themselves to the warres, are nowe for the most part growen to become good husbandes [husbandmen] and knowe well how to improve their lands to the uttermost as the farmer or countryman, so that they take their fermes into their handes as the leases expire, and eyther till themselves, or else lett them out to those who will give most.'[10]

Land *was* wealth and, in an inflationary age, the only secure form of wealth. The rise of prices and the debasement of the coinage meant that precious metal could no longer be regarded as the measure of a man's financial standing. The debasement process was begun by Wolsey in 1526 when he increased the price of gold from 40s to 45s an ounce and issued new, lighter coins. From the government's point of view the experiment was successful and tampering with the coinage became a disastrously simple method of increasing revenue. The worst period was the 1540s. During this decade the value of the pound at Antwerp was halved. This situation led William Cecil (the future Lord Burghley) to define, perhaps for the first time, the 'inflationary spiral'.

The fall of the exchange within thys iiii dayse hathe cawsyd and wyll cause to be boughte clothes at lvi li the packe wyche before wold not have byn bowghte for lii li the packe; so that yow may perseve that the exchange doth ingender dere clothe, and dere clothe doth engendar dere wolle, and dere wolle doth ingendar many scheppe, and many scheppe doth ingendar myche pastor and dere, and myche pastor ys the dekaye of tyllage, and owte of the dekaye of tyllage spryngethe ii evylls, skarsyte of korne and the pepull unwroghte, and consequently the darthe of all thynges.[11]

The decline in the value of money and the increasing demand for arable and pasture pushed up land prices. Farmland which had been already enclosed commanded a price thirty per cent or more above that of 'champain'. Competition for land was intense. Richard Carew (who wrote later in the century but who makes it clear that the situation he describes has been in existence throughout living memory) reported that in Cornwall 'a farm . . . can no sooner fall in hand, than the survey court shall be waited on with many officers, vying and revying each on other; nay, they are mostly taken at a ground-hop, for fear of coming too late'.[12] As the attitude to land changed so, gradually, were more and more landholders caught up in the race to acquire acreage. The enterprising yeoman worked hard to produce a few extra bushels for sale at market or drove a keen bargain over the sale of his few fleece and all the time in his mind's eye he saw the field of his neighbour who, he knew, was deeply in debt and would soon be forced to sell. Robert Furse, an Elizabethan gentleman, boasted that his Devonshire ancestors were men 'of smalle possessyon and hablyte, yt have theye by lytell and lytell . . . so run ther corse . . . that by these menes we ar com to myche more possessyones, credett and reputasyion than ever anye of them hadde.'[13]

In those uncertain times property might suddenly and unexpectedly come on to the market for a variety of reasons – bankruptcy, sudden death by plague or affray, failure of inheritance, illegal dispossession. Sometimes a land title lapsed because the deeds had been carelessly or fraudulently drawn up (see below, pp. 143–5). Then it was the man who could step in quickly with ready cash (usually raised by pawning his other lands) who gained the prize.

As well as enterprising and ambitious gentlemen and yeomen there were always newcomers competing for the fairest estates; merchants who, having made their fortunes in trade, now aspired to the status of country gentlemen. They were buying permanence, translating part of their assets out of the uncertainty of commerce into the enduring reality of plough and pasture and firm-rooted rural society. They envisaged the building of impressive new houses set about with the gardens and farmlands which would support the household and pay for its continued magnificence. Set about also with parkland where they and their influential friends could enjoy the pleasures of hawking, coursing and the chase. They saw also the enormous polychrome marble tomb they would raise in the parish church as a reminder to future generations of their wealth and power and a link between time and eternity. In mid-Suffolk there stood, about 1550, two fine, newly built mansions. Their stories and the stories of the men who built them show us clearly the sort of people who were changing the face of England.

Thomas Kytson was born in 1485 at Werton on the Lancashire coast. His father was a farmer but his contacts were not circumscribed by the local agricultural community. Friends of his, the Glasyers, had a relative who had done very well for himself in London. It was to this mercer, Richard Glasyer, that young Thomas was sent as an apprentice. The mercers' guild was the wealthiest of all the London merchant guilds and offered excellent opportunities for young men of enterprise and industry. He became a freeman of his guild, joined the Company of Merchant Adventurers and participated in many lucrative trading voyages to Flanders. By the time he was thirty-six he had amassed a considerable fortune, so much so that he was able to approach the Duke of Buckingham with an offer for estates the nobleman was selling. Buckingham was the most notorious encloser of the day and in 1521 he needed money for his castle and estates in Gloucestershire. It was a sign of the times that a *nouveau-riche* cloth merchant could pay £2340 to a prince of the blood royal for lands in Suffolk and Nottinghamshire. In the former county Kytson spent a further £3000 building at Hengrave a moated house on the medieval plan but exuberant with towers, finials, orioles and gatehouse of ostentatious splendour. It was thirteen years in the building and by 1538 stood proudly and possessively amid the even fields ready to receive its master on his rare holidays from pressing commitments in London and Antwerp.

The builder of Redgrave Hall was a local boy. The Bacons had for generations been yeomen farmers at Drinkstone and Hessett, near Bury St Edmunds. Robert Bacon served the great Benedictine abbey there as a sheep reeve. He prospered, gradually increasing his property and income. He was able to send his eldest son, Nicholas, to Cambridge and thence to Gray's Inn. Completing his legal studies with some distinction, the young man sought a patron and was fortunate in catching the attention of Thomas Cromwell, who needed clever lawyers to assist in the task of dismantling the English branch of medieval Christendom. In 1537 Nicholas Bacon was appointed to the Court of Augmentations, the legal body set up to receive and dispose of the confiscated monastic lands. It was the ideal position for an ambitious young man. He was able to enrich himself with the bribes pressed upon him by eager suiters and disburse his income on some of the best bargains coming on to the property market. Within three or four years he had acquired Redgrave and other adjoining manors and the hospital of St Saviour's in Bury St Edmunds. The former provided the site for a new estate and the latter the necessary stone and timber to erect a suitable house upon it. Redgrave Hall was scarcely less splendid than Hengrave though, thanks to the large amount of building material at his disposal, it cost only £1300. It was certainly proof positive that the Bacons had arrived. Though Nicholas went on to become Lord Keeper of the Great Seal to Elizabeth and though he built other and more splendid houses, nothing can have given him as much satisfaction as the creation of his first great house in his own county.

In choosing to study at the inns of court Nicholas Bacon was typical of every up and coming young gentleman. Not only was the civil law an excellent qualification for government service, it was essential equipment for any landlord who was to compete successfully in the property race. The market place was full of unscrupulous speculators and the unwary purchaser could find himself saddled with a conveyance or lease which was deliberately ambiguous. He might find himself buying a parcel of land from a vendor whose title to the property in question later turned out to be at best dubious. The function of land was changing: once the adhesive of feudal society, it was becoming a highly desirable commodity to be bought, sold and bargained for like barley or worsted. It took the law a long time to catch up with this change. Land titles and conditions attaching to ownership were sometimes recorded on manorial rolls, sometimes registered in the royal courts, sometimes they rested on nothing more substantial than local custom. Daily, through every legal term, the justices were sitting upon disputed land title suits arising from misunderstanding or plain fraud. Nor were all the cases involved by any means small. In 1545

A great suit was tried . . . at Nottingham, in which George Lascelles Esq., claimed against Richard Townby Esq. the manors of Gateford, Everton, and Haworth, with the appurtenances, and one hundred and twenty messuages, forty tofts, one dovecote, one hundred and twenty gardens, one hundred and twenty orchards, two thousand acres of arable land, two hundred of meadow, one thousand of pasture, two hundred and fifty of wood, one hundred of moor, forty of turbary [land affording turf or peat for fuel] and forty shillings rent in Gateford, Everton, Haworth, Worksop, Groingely, Wellow, Bole, Babworth, Ordsall, Sturton, Eaton, W. Markham, Blyth, and several other places.[14]

The Tudor landlord had to be an opportunist if he was to augment his estates. He had to be ruthlessly efficient if he was to make them pay. He also had to be highly litigious if he was to hold on to them.

Henry VIII's government was so worried about 'the great strifes, debates and variances' over real property that it tried to overhaul the entire land law. In the end it succeeded only in bringing in some minor reforms. Cromwell attempted to induce parliament to create a central land registry but he was defeated by powerful legal and financial interests in both houses. It is at first sight surprising that those closely involved in property negotiations should not have welcomed a move to put the market on a sound and fair footing. What we have to remember is that the wealthy buyer who might welcome government control of unscrupulous vendors was sometimes a vendor himself.

When John Palmer, a Sussex landlord, was reproached by his tenants for ruthless enclosure he replied, angrily: 'Do ye not know that the King's grace, hath put down all the houses of monks, friars and nuns? Therefore now is the time come that we gentlemen will pull down the houses of such poor knaves as ye be.' The response is highly significant. It goes to the heart of the Tudor despotism. The king was deliberately breaking old customs, sweeping away ancient institutions, challenging orthodox beliefs, upsetting the whole balance of society. Lesser mortals could survive only by accommodating themselves to the changes – or, to use a modern idiom 'if you can't beat him, join him'. The equation also worked in reverse. It was precisely because the fabric of society was weakening, loosening, that the Tudor monarchs could tear holes in it. Certainly it was the frantic competition for land that paved the way for Henry VIII's appropriation of the monastic estates. His action outraged Catholic opinion throughout England and the rest of Europe but by selling and granting the bulk of the newly acquired lands to suitors he neatly involved almost every member of the ruling classes in his act of spoliation. As England's largest ever land deal got under way the most ardent supporters of the old religion did not dare allow themselves to be left behind. This was the opportunity of a millennium to acquire property of all kinds – vast acreages of pasture, buildings which could be converted into dwellings or used as a supply of stone, timber and lead, small plots of land which would enable a gentleman or yeoman to consolidate existing holdings.

There was nothing new about dissolving religious houses which had outlived their usefulness. Spiritual and temporal leaders had always been ready to close down houses where the monastic rule was flagrantly and consistently violated or where the personnel had dwindled to a mere handful of aged people. What was new was the implication that monasticism as an institution had outlived its usefulness. It seemed that the king had now been won over to a viewpoint previously held only by heretics and the wilder anti-clericals.

Thomas Cromwell, the agent behind this movement, proceeded with all the caution of which his energetic soul was capable. The dissolution was spread over a period of five years. In 1535 the Vicar-General exercised his new role by sending out agents to compile a complete record of all the church's income. This *Valor Ecclesiasticus* is a remarkably detailed account, a considerable bureaucratic achievement for a government relying completely on amateur administrators. These commissioners (men like Sir John Markham and Sir William Ayscough) went into every parish church, cathedral and abbey demanding to see account books and the contents of multi-locked coffers. A year later another set of commissioners was out making a lightning tour of the religious houses.

It was a wet, heavy and oppressive summer and, as the little groups of London officials (this time Cromwell used men he knew well, men who clearly understood the real purpose of the visitation) moved around the countryside with ostentatious pomp, they found the people apprehensive and sullen because of the changes already made and those that, it was feared, were soon to come. 'It is long of the King that this weather is so troublous and unstable. There was never good weather since the King began this business . . . it maketh no matter if he were knocked or patted on the head.'[15] So concluded one old man in Worcestershire. The investigators clattered up to the portals of abbeys and nunneries, making a brave show with their armed escorts. They bullied the superiors, mocked at the objects of superstition in the churches, and cajoled the inmates into informing against each other. Relays of messengers were kept in a constant flurry, galloping back and forth between the itinerant visitors and the itinerant royal court with highly colourful reports. The abbot of Battle is 'the veriest hayne [wretch], beetle [blockhead] and buserde [idiot], and the arentest chorle that ever I see'[16] and the abbey – 'so beggary a house I never see, nor so filthy stuff . . . the stuff is like the person.'[17] Durford had 'better be called Dirtford'.[18] From Sopham they sent Cromwell a love letter confiscated from the prioress, 'to make you laugh'.[19]

When the visitors concentrated on being more informative than witty their reports were of greater value to Cromwell (and also to the historian).

> We have visited Bath, and found the prior a very virtuous man, but his monks more corrupt than any others in vices with both sexes . . . the house well repaired but £400 in debt . . . I send you *vincula* [finger ligaments] *S. Petri*, which women put about them at the time of their delivery. . . I send you also a great comb called Mary Magdalen's comb, and St Dorothy's and St Margaret's combs. They cannot tell how they came by them. . . I send you a book of Our Lady's miracles, well able to match the Canterbury Tales, which I found in the library.[20]

> As for the abbot [of Bury St Edmunds] we found nothing suspect as touching his lyving, but it was detected that he laye moche forth in his granges, that he delited moche in playing at dice and cardes, and therin spent moche money. . . As touching the convent, we coulde geate little or no reportes amonge theym, although we did use moche diligence in the examination. . . And yet it was confessed and proved, that there was here suche frequence of women commyng and reassorting to this monastery as to no place more. Amongst the reliques we founde moche vanitee and superstition, as the coles that St Laurence was toasted withall, the paring of St Edmundes naylles, St Thomas of Canterbury penneknyff and his bootes, and divers skulles for the hedache, etc.[21]

There were two common faults which rendered many of the monasteries unacceptable to the Cromwellian regime. They perpetuated the worse kinds of superstition, now frowned on by men of the new learning. They were pockets of resistance to the royal supremacy.

More fundamental, though, was the fact that monasticism in its existing form was an anachronism. The great and lesser houses had become fully secular institutions yet they continued to enjoy spiritual privilege and immunities. They had to administer large estates and pay for the upkeep of expensive buildings just like any temporal lord, and they adopted the same measures. They were not conspicuously better landlords than their lay contemporaries. They, too, resorted to enclosures and rack-renting. They consistently resisted the pleas of borough tenants for privileges. At Bury St Edmunds, for instance, the abbot appointed court officials and aldermen, confirmed the election of bailiffs, taxed the town's merchandise, controlled the market, levying tolls on stallholders and keeping the best sites for the abbey produce. Not for the burgesses of Bury the freedom won long since by many other boroughs. As times grew harder the monks had to devote more and more of their time to the material problems of keeping up the fabric and exploiting the estates efficiently. For the poorer houses the struggle was too great; thus the filth and dilapidation discovered by Cromwell's visitors. Even many larger monasteries met their obligations only by running into debt, like Bath Abbey.

Oppressed with these burdens, the dwindling numbers of religious had less time and energy to devote to their social role as providers of hospitality, charity, education, and care for the sick and aged. As early as 1545 writers were gazing on the pre-dissolution era through rose-tinted spectacles: 'For although the sturdy beggers [monks] gat all the deuotion of the good charitable people from them, yet had the pore impotent creatures some relefe of theyr scrappes, where as nowe they haue nothyng. Then had they hospitals, and almshouses to be lodged in, but nowe they lye and starue in the stretes. Then was ther number great, but nowe much greater.'[22] The truth was less simple. The degree of charity offered by any house was directly related to its wealth and the policy laid down by its superior. Some foundations were too poor or too concerned with making ends meet to take seriously their obligations to the poor. Some disbursed faithfully the endowments left them for the specific purpose of almsgiving but these amounted to some two and a half per cent of the total of all monastic income. Some houses gave generously in the form of alms on specific saints' days and the regular doles from the refectory. The trouble with monastic charity was that it was haphazard and undiscriminating. The Duke of Norfolk, who was by no means an enemy of the religious, was among many contemporaries who believed that monastic charity actually encouraged idleness.

I do understand his maiestie hath now sent lettres to thiese parties concernyng vacabonds, your good lordships shall perceyve by copies of lettres which I have a good tyme past sent to all justice of pease and religiouse houses in theis parties, that I haue not neglected that matier; surely I neuer sawe so many as be in thiese cuntrees. And the almes that they haue in religious houses is the great occasion thereof, and also the slackenes of the Justice of peace, for not doying ther dewties. I haue and shall so order thiese cuntrees under my rewle that I thinke ye shall shortely here of no small nomber of them that shall drawe Southeward.[23]

Similarly the record of the monks as educators has been exaggerated. Many houses took in the children of noblemen and gentlemen and some provided teachers to almshouses where the destitute children received instruction. Major abbeys such as Reading and Evesham had fine schools and a long record as educators. But as with charity so with education the service provided by the religious was a very hit-and-miss affair. It was Cromwell's declared aim and the pious hope of all the reformers who actively supported him that some of the proceeds of the dissolution would be used to establish an extensive system of state education. This intention even found its way into official print: the preamble of the Bishoprics Act, 1539, runs:

> Forasmuch as it is not unknown the slothful and ungodly life which hath been used amongst all those sort which have born the name of religious folk, and to the intent that from henceforth many of them might be turned to better use as hereafter shall follow, whereby God's word might the better be set forth, children brought up in learning, clerks nourished in the universities, old servants decayed to have livings, almshouses for poor folk to be sustained in, Readers of Greek, Hebrew, and Latin to have good stipend, daily alms to be administered, mending of highways, exhibitions [maintenance grants] for ministers of the church; It is thought therefore unto the King's highness most expedient and necessary that more bishoprics, collegiate and cathedral churches shall be established. . .[24]

Obviously the monastic system was long overdue for a drastic pruning – a pruning which should bring new vigour to the plant. When the first Dissolution Act was passed in 1536 this was all the government envisaged: 376 religious foundations whose annual value was less than £200 were closed. The dispossessed were provided with benefices or pensions or were found places in other houses. The plate, vestments and other movable wealth came to the exchequer. The real estate was disposed of by the specially formed Court of Augmentations.

Yet more commissioners were therefore launched upon the nation to attend to the valuation and dismantling of monastic property and to deal with the human and administrative problems raised by the dispossession of the monks and nuns. The problems were varied, vast and daunting. What was to be done with the elderly and infirm who had nowhere else to go? Was all stone, glass, slate and tile to be stored securely for the king's use or could it be given to local people who continually pestered the commissioners? Did the king wish to retain any of the monastic servants? How were priests to be appointed to parishes which had been served by members of the religious communities? What personal effects should the deprived inmates be allowed to keep? Membership of a dissolution commission was certainly no sinecure. The work was demanding and often distressing, though, of course, the royal agents were well placed to request considerable perks from the property they were handling.

As the commissioners moved from abbey to nunnery crowds of local people gathered to gape at the cowled figures who emerged leading the pack animals which carried their few belongings. Some bystanders wept, others jeered, most cast speculative eyes around the empty cloisters to see what pickings there would be. But even the heartless were gripped by the all-pervading atmosphere of insecurity and anxiety. Royal power was reaching into their lives in a quite unprecedented way. Through the villages travelled a succession of tax commissioners, *Valor* commissioners, official preachers and dissolution commissioners. Royal injunctions urged them to forsake 'superstition' and informed them that by the new system of parish registers every baptism, marriage and death must be recorded. This basic pattern of bureaucratic activity was soon embellished by exuberant rumours: more taxes were imminent; all church property would be confiscated; parishes were to be united and the superfluous churches pulled down; poor men would not be allowed to eat white bread, goose or chicken without paying a fee to the king; every man would be obliged to render an annual account of property and income; the remaining abbeys would soon go the way of the smaller houses.

The last rumour would soon prove to be justified, and many religious superiors anticipated the coming closures. They hid or gave away jewels and plate. They granted long leases to friends and relatives. They applied to Cromwell for fat pensions in return for voluntary surrender. This frenzied activity was one reason which induced the government to move into the next phase of dissolution. Monasteries and nunneries were encouraged, bribed or bullied into voluntary surrender. More visitors went round to enquire into the state of the contemplative life in the larger houses and to destroy all shrines and objects of superstition. So began in earnest the destructive aspect of the Reformation which was to continue sporadically for over a century. For generations pilgrims had travelled hundreds of miles to gaze in awe on the gorgeous, haphazardly heaped altars and shrines glowing with gold and silver, the sparkling, jewel-encrusted reliquaries, the gilded statues of the virgin draped with gems. Now gangs of workmen armed with picks and crowbars moved into the great abbey churches and, in the name of a king who claimed to have the most pious motives, took away these priceless objects of ancient devotion by the sackful. At Bury St Edmunds 'We found a rich shrine which was very cumbrous to deface. We have taken in the said monastery in gold and silver 5000 marks and above, over and besides a good and rich cross with emeralds, as also divers and sundry stones of great value, and yet we have left the church, abbot and convent very well furnished with plate of silver necessary for the same.'[25] From the shrine of St Hugh at Lincoln 2621 ounces of gold and 4285 ounces of silver were removed but Henry was not satisfied. When he visited Lincoln himself in 1541 he gave orders that the tomb of the saint was to be 'taken away until there remain no memory of it'.[26] The common criticism was obvious and the less thick-skinned commissioners tried to draw a veil of secrecy over their doings. At Winchester St Swithun's shrine was dismantled under cover of darkness. That done, the iconoclasts decided to 'sweep away al the rotten bones', lest it should be thought 'we came more for the treasure than for avoiding of the abomination of idolatry'.[27]

For some of Henry's subjects the changes, the spoliations, the visitations and the rumours of worse things to come proved too much. In the autumn of 1536 Lincolnshire and the North rose in a revolt which came nearer than any other event in the whole of our period to toppling the Tudor throne.

'Mouldwarp be come', so grew the conviction as men and women in the remote, introspective parts of the realm smarted under real and imaginary grievances. Mouldwarp, the evil king prophesied by Merlin, the man accursed of God with coarse hide, rough as goat's skin, who should spoil the land until the Dragon, the Wolf and the Lion rose up to drive him into the sea. These were the old prophesies the northerners were reminding each other of and convincing themselves that the evil Mouldwarp and Henry Tudor were one and the same. They looked to their old leaders the Percies, Dacres, Husseys and Darcys to take up the banner against upstarts like Cromwell, heretical bishops such as Cranmer and Latimer and all the king's other evil advisers. They looked for champions in a holy cause – the full restoration of the old religion with all its institutions and the condemnation of the divorce and the dissolution. They wanted to put the clock back by having obnoxious legislation repealed, taxes cancelled, holy days restored. In the words of Professor Scarisbrick, 'The Pilgrimage must stand as a large-scale, spontaneous, authentic indictment of all that Henry most obviously stood for; and it passed judgement against him as surely and comprehensively as *Magna Carta* condemned King John or the Grand Remonstrance the government of Charles I.'[28]

It began in Lincolnshire in October. The church bells were rung in Louth, Caistor and Horncastle and the men of the fenland answered the summons of their peasant leaders, Nicholas Melton, alias Captain Cobbler, and William Morland, an ex-monk. They raided the houses of the gentry, forcing a number of them to join their cause. Growing in number, hour by hour, as contingents arrived from all over the county, the host made its way to Lincoln. From there they sent their demands to the king and there they received his answer. If the Tudor tyrant was shaken by the rebellion he certainly did not show it. His reply castigated 'the rude commons of one shire, and that one of the most brute and beastly of the whole realm'. How dare they find fault with their prince and 'take upon you, contrary to God's law, and man's law, to rule your prince, whom ye are bound by all laws to obey, and serve, with ... your lives, lands, and goods'. The king 'marvelled' at his subjects' 'treachery', 'unkindness', 'unnaturalness', 'madness' and 'rebellious demeanour'. If they did not submit immediately and deliver up a hundred hostages they would be putting their 'lives, wives, children, lands, goods, and chattels, besides the indignation of God, in the utter adventure of total destruction, and utter ruin by force and violence of the sword.'[29] Within days of the receipt of this broadside the Lincolnshire host had dissolved.

The propaganda of Tudor despotism had done its work well. The rebels had numerical strength, determination and a deep sense of grievance. They even had the leadership of the gentlemen, some of whom, at least, were fully sympathetic to their cause. But when it came to pitting themselves unequivocally against their lawful king, and loosing anarchy and disorder, they hesitated and their hesitation was fatal.

Ultimately it was the same in the North where the much more dangerous Pilgrimage of Grace was already under way. For a start the natural leader, Henry Percy Earl of Northumberland, pleaded illness and refused to place himself at the pilgrims' head. (Percy, one time fiancé of Anne Boleyn, was in truth a sick young man, in both mind and body. His tenants and relatives were all solidly behind the revolt and when persuasion failed they used threats until the earl 'fell in weeping, ever wishing himself out of the world'. Eventually, he had to retreat to York for his own safety.) The movement did, however, have excellent leadership in the lawyer Robert Aske and Lord Darcy. By the end of the year most of the country north of a line from the Humber to the Mersey was in open revolt. A vast army of malcontents might have marched southwards and the levies sent to meet them under the dukes of Suffolk and Norfolk would have been powerless to control them. In fact, it was Aske, Darcy and the other leaders who held them in check. Insisting that they were pilgrims presenting a peaceful petition, and not revolutionaries seeking to overthrow lawful authority, they took the momentum out of the movement. The rebel captains believed that they could trust their king to give them a fair hearing and to honour his word.

They would have done better to try the fortunes of war than the virtue of Henry VIII. The king, his back firmly to the wall, instructed his lieutenants to promise free pardons, a new parliament to discuss their grievances, anything to stay the pilgrimage. Aske was summoned to court and returned again to the north with a pardon for his associates and assurance that their demands would be considered. The rebel camps were broken up and the king's aggrieved subjects went home. That was the signal for fresh instructions to be sent to Henry's commanders in the field.

> Our pleasure is, that, before you shall close upp our said Baner again, you shal, in any wise, cause suche dredfull execution to be doon upon a good nombre of the inhabitauntes of every towne, village, and hamlet, that have offended in this rebellion, as well by the hanging of them uppe in trees, as by the quartering of them, and the setting of their heddes and quarters in every towne, greate and small, and in al suche other places, as they may be a ferefull spectacle to all other herafter, that wold practise any like mater: whiche We requyre you to doo, without pitie or respecte ... remembring that it shalbe moche better, that these traitours shulde perishe in their wilfull, unkynde, and traitorous folyes, thenne that so slendre punishment shuld be doon upon them, as the dredde therof shuld not be a warning to others: wherof shall ensue the preservation of a greate multitude; whiche, if the terrour of this execution shuld not lye in the eye of their remembraunce, might percase, upon light rumours, tales, and suggestions of evyll personnes, fall into the pytte of like mischief.[30]

Pour encourager les autres Henry exacted the lives of some two hundred of his subjects[31] as well as Aske, Darcy and the other leaders of the Pilgrimage of Grace. The clenched fist of Tudor despotism had been clearly seen and the sight was long remembered.

The experience of 1536–7 only determined Henry to press on more rapidly and thoroughly with the dissolution of the monasteries. The trickle of 'voluntary' surrenders became a flood. The orders of friars were disbanded and in 1539 the Second Dissolution Act was passed which gave Henry the property of all the remaining monasteries and nunneries.

'I pray Jesu send you shortly an abbey.'[32] So wrote Lord Lisle's steward to his master in January 1538. Lisle was a courtier of long standing and was fairly confident of benefiting from the dissolution. It was those well placed at court who were most successful in the great land grab. Others thronged the antechambers of Cromwell and fellow councillors or made representations through relatives and friends in the royal household. For several months, until it had established a procedure and acquired adequate personnel, the Court of Augmentations was choked with applications. Gradually, however, the log-jam shifted and the flow of grants and leases began.

The principle adopted seems to have been 'to him who has shall more be given'. The main beneficiaries were the great nobles and the king's chief servants. Then came that class of country gentlemen and town burgesses who were so vital to the Tudor regime as JPs and commissioners. If we take the county of Lincolnshire as an example we find that no less than twenty-two grants of land were made to the Duke of Suffolk, who was already the leading landowner in the county. Next came Lord Clinton with nine parcels of property. Several county gentry also made successful application for territory. Notable among them were the Tyrrwhits, Henneages and Skipwiths, all of them prominent royal servants with court connections.

Another group of men who cashed in on the dissolution was the speculators. They were merchants and financiers who had made themselves useful to Cromwell and who now reaped their reward. In Lincolnshire the leading speculators were John Bellow and John Broxholme. Many were the estates and parcels of land which passed through their hands. But, in fact, everyone was speculating. Lands were bought, sold and resold. Estates were split up. Smaller units of land were joined together. For several years England was one vast land market as some fifteen per cent of landed wealth changed hands, much of it several times. Slowly things settled down. The new landlords established themselves, built their splendid country houses, set about exploiting their arable and pasture.

And what of the brave new world which the dissolution was supposed to usher in? Were funds made available for education and charity? Were the new landlords more aware of their social responsibilities than the idle monks and nuns? Alas, no.

As I walked alone
and mused on things,
That have in my time
been done by great kings,
I bethought me of abbeys
that sometime I saw,
Which are now suppressed
all by law.
O Lord, (thought I then)
what occasion was here
To provide for learning
and make poverty clear.
The lands and the jewels
that hereby were had
Would have found godly preachers
which might well have led
The people aright
that now go astray
And have fed the poor
that famish every day.[33]

6

'Wantonly and viciously brought up'

Crime and Punishment

A S A LAWYER – as, indeed, the first lawyer in the land – Chancellor More was concerned with the administration of what passed in the sixteenth century for justice. As a Christian humanist he believed passionately in the need for social reform, especially for softening the law against those forced by poverty into criminal acts or habits. In the Court of Chancery, over which he presided from 1529 to 1532, More had some opportunity to apply those principles and beliefs which, in his opinion, lay behind the written law and went to the heart of real justice. For Chancery was a court of equity. As More sat in his marble chair in Westminster Hall he had to give judgement not in accordance with statute or strict legal precedent but with regard only to natural justice, common sense and common fairness. The Court of Chancery existed to help those who, for whatever reason, could not obtain satisfaction through the common law courts. Tudor justice, save in a few cases where the king's interests were engaged, was impartial. If it was also harsh that was because society was harsh.

Vagrancy was the largest social problem throughout the sixteenth century. Beggars, thieves, unemployed labourers and craftsmen wandered the lanes and highways singly and in groups. Many of them were seeking work and a respected place within the order of society. Some had despaired of ever rediscovering security and self-respect. Some were second- or third-generation vagrants who had never known anything other than a shadow world on the despised fringe of the community. And some had discovered that they were not social animals at all and that they could make a good living by deliberately preying on a society that had rejected them.

Tudor commentators and legislators divided this army of the homeless, estimated (though the figure is necessarily only a guess) at about 10,000 strong, into categories – gypsies, sturdy beggars, the sick and infirm, out of work artisans, rogues (a term which included frauds, thieves and confidence tricksters) and whores. The truth, however, is not so tidy. In an age when violence was endemic and the insecurity deriving from social and economic change widespread, thousands of men and women were driven temporarily or permanently into a life of vagabondage. Their only immediate concerns were food and shelter. Sometimes they prevailed upon the charity of burgesses, priests and gentlemen. Sometimes they rifled fields and flocks to obtain their supper. Some interspersed periods of genuine job-seeking with robbery, violence or prostitution. Some linked up with bands of well-organised thieves, and either stuck to a life of crime or happened upon the lucky break which enabled them to earn an honest living once more.

Any society which could allow such an evil to become completely out of control was an unjust society. Medieval England had been no stranger to crime, poverty and vagrancy but these problems had grown much worse by 1495 and they were to increase steadily and alarmingly thereafter. The medieval solution to the problem had been threefold. The church taught people to be content with their earthly lot, assuring the poor that the record would be put straight in the next world. The church also enjoined the necessity of private charity upon all whom God had richly blessed. And for those who were 'wanton' enough to seek unlawful means of relieving their poverty there was the deterrent of harsh laws. The Tudors inherited this attitude but found it inadequate to the size of the problem. They had to find a fresh way of dealing with poverty and incipient crime. The ideas brought by the new learning and the Protestant ethic pointed towards this new way. Thomas More, Simon Fish, Robert Crowley, Thomas Starkey and a host of humanists and reformers, in sermons, books and pamphlets called for a reappraisal of the meaning of the 'commonwealth'. They demanded greater government intervention to secure social justice and, in the 1530s and 1540s, legislation did begin to reflect the new ideals.

But before we consider how the Tudors made the first, tentative steps towards a comprehensive national policy of poor relief let us examine some of the many sides of the problem. Because of the very nature of poverty, crime and civil disorder any attempt at neat analysis would be misleading. All we can do is look at some of the many cases that constables, magistrates, assize judges and the royal Council were having to deal with every day.

The worse kind of vagabonds were those trained in the martial arts, which theoretically meant every able-bodied man in the realm. All householders were compelled by law to provide 'harness' (i.e. armour and defensive accoutrements) and weapons for one or more fighting men, according to their social status and financial means. Magistrates were empowered to hold musters of military equipment and men fit for fighting. When the king would go a-warring the sheriffs called out the shire levies. Under their wapentake (an administrative unit found in many parts of eastern England similar to the hundred) and hundred leaders, they would turn out, a motley collection of unwilling soldiers culled from every walk of life, some able to draw a fair bow, others clumsy incompetents, strangers to the pikes they were now expected to wield. Such militia made up the bulk of the armies which Tudor generals took to France or Scotland in the sporadic campaigns of the era.

Most of them resented being called from their fields, shops and workbenches. Their resentment grew when, as frequently happened as a result of inadequate funds and poor commissariat, their wages fell into arrears, their beer and victuals went stale and they had to forage for their own food. In 1512, 10,000 disgruntled English soldiers, fed up with French wine, poor food, lack of tentage and an outbreak of dysentery, told their leaders bluntly that they would not stay at Bayonne beyond Michaelmas – and they suited their action to their words.

Having been paid off (if they were lucky), those fighting men were sent home to resume their disrupted lives. It was not always possible. More tells of those, 'that come home oute of the warres, maymed and lame . . . suche, I say, as put their lives in jeoperdye for the weale publiques or the kynges sake, and by reason of weakenesse and lamenesse be not hable to occupye their olde craftes, and be to aged to lerne new.'[1] Nor was it only the wounded who returned to a cold welcome. Employers were not averse to taking on replacements for men away at the wars. The absence of many able-bodied men from a village might provide a landlord with an excellent opportunity for enclosure and eviction. A farmer might discover that he could manage perfectly well with his depleted wartime workforce and see no need to take back the returning men.

What were they to do? The halt, the blind and the lame had every incentive and little alternative to capitalising on their injuries by a life of beggary. The able-bodied men who had been trained to violence, whose finer feelings had been blunted by the brutality of war, and who felt quite justifiably aggrieved, were a different matter. Comrades in

According to Sebastian Brant (1458?–1521), German humanist and author of *The Ship of Fools*, only simple and gullible people got into gambling schools at inns and beer-houses. There were plenty of professional card 'sharks' with marked packs and loaded dice ready to relieve them of their money. Such a 'vocation' was only one of many criminal pursuits into which men and women were forced by unemployment. For those caught punishment was public and severe

British Library Board

British Library Board

arms became comrades in crime. In large and small bands they wandered the shires visiting farms, manors, villages and even the smaller towns, demanding food and money 'with menaces'. They were so terrifying that the authorities were often too frightened to take any action. If a conscientious constable did raise the hue and cry he was likely to be told 'God restore your loss; I have other business at this time.'[2] If one of these ruffians was apprehended the wronged villagers were often content to regain their property and set him at liberty for fear of further vengeful visitations from the rogue's friends.

In October 1545 the citizens of Canterbury were pestered by a band of ruffians. These were not demobbed soldiers but men going *to* the wars. They were en route for Dover and France. Some of them were old campaigners who had for years been living as able-bodied vagrants. Now, as they swaggered through the streets they jostled people into puddles and helped themselves from the market stalls. They stopped aged Canterburians demanding change for a groat or a noble, and then running off with coin and change. The mayor was too frightened to take any action and it was left to Archbishop Cranmer to send men to arrest some of the malefactors. Even he was not prepared to be over-zealous. He put the men in the town goal for four hours to quieten them down, then released them and sent them on their way.[3]

The life of the professional mendicant, particularly if his whining occasionally took on an aggressive tone, could be very lucrative. At a time when a labourer was paid 6d a day it was not uncommon for beggars to receive several shillings and probably a free supper at a monastery into the bargain.

> This daye was brought into the Courte certeyne money of one Mother Arden who used daly to go a beggyng the strettys, viz., in olde grotes xxix^{li} xii^s iiii^d; too olde angelles; in slypper vi^{li} xiii^s vi ; more in slypper lxiii^s; and in new money lxxiii^s vii^d. And there was taken oute and delyvered to Mother Arden vi^s viii^d of the foresayde sume.[4]

Mother Arden's total horde (although we do not know how long it had taken to gather) was £44 3s 5d, more than a labouring man could earn in five years and much more than he could ever hope to save. This being so it is not surprising that many crafty idlers, especially old soldiers, feigned wounds, ailments and dire poverty to stir the generous sympathy of the populace. Thus, the well-organised bands of beggars travelled from town to town, 'some in rags and some in jags'. As the dogs barked and the children rushed out to look, the odd little procession came down the street, the 'upright man', their gang-leader, at the head perhaps even clad in an old velvet gown cast off by some wealthy benefactor. They presented a spectacle well worth the watching 'these ragged rabblement of rakehells, that under the pretence of misery do win great alms'.[5] Some limped along on crutches; others appeared blind or armless; the 'dommerers' or deaf mutes stumbled vacantly forward; some supposedly smitten with the falling sickness had to be supported by their colleagues; the show stealers were the Abraham men who had lost their wits and were suffered to march in chains, rolling their eyes, shrieking hideously, and darting in and out among the crowd until restrained. And always in the crowd were other members of the group, travelling incognito, cutting the purses of those who were slow with their voluntary almsgiving.

Peddling was frequently little more than a respectable cloak for robbery, trickery, fraud or prostitution. The itinerant tinker carried his worthless stock in trade of baubles and trinkets on his back but his most valuable asset was his tongue which he used to good effect on market and fair days persuading the gullible to pay good money for his tawdry merchandise. He probably found gambling a useful sideline and of an evening in the tavern would take on the locals at 'tables' (backgammon) or dice with loaded ivories, cards or shuffleboard, invariably leaving town with other people's hard-earned cash in his purse. Women had their own version of this kind of fraud:

These Bawdy Baskets be also wemen, and go with baskets and Capcases on their armes, wherein they haue laces, pynnes, nedles, white ynkell [linen tape], and round sylke gyrdles of al colours. These wyl bye conneyskins, and steale linen clothes of on hedges. And for their trifles they will procure of seruants, when their mystres or dame is oute of the waye, either some good peace of beefe, baken, or cheese, that shalbe worth xii pens, for ii pens of their toyes ... The vpright men [see above] haue good aquayntance with these, and will helpe and relieue them when they want. Thus they trade their lyues in lewed lothsome lechery.[6]

Not unrelated to the pedlars (as a social problem, at least) were 'the lords and earls of little Egypt', the gypsies, who first appeared in England in the early sixteenth century. These mysterious, dusky people of unknown origin were known as 'Bohemians', 'Tartars' and 'Heathen' in various part of the continent. Whatever they were called, they were everywhere hated and persecuted and England was no exception. In 1531 an Act was passed outlawing 'an outlandish people calling themselves Egyptians, using no crafte nor feate of merchandize, who have come into this realm and gone from shire to shire, and place to place, in great company, and used great, subtle, and crafty means to deceive people, bearing them in hand that they by palmestry could tell men and women's fortunes.'⁷ They were no worse in their behaviour and their means of obtaining a livelihood, than other vagrants, but they were foreign and this was enough to call down the full fury of the law upon them. Magistrates were empowered to hang all gypsies they could find without trial or the obtaining of any special commission. It was one thing to pass harsh laws; quite another to ensure that they were enforced. Thomas Cromwell complained to the Earl of Chester that although the king's 'poore subjectes be dayly spoyled, robbed, deceyved by them, yet his Highnes officers and Ministres lytle regarding their dieuties towards his Majestye, do permyt them to lynger and loyter in all partys, and to exercise all their falshods, felonyes, and treasons unpunished . . .'⁸

The number of felons, charlatans and rogues grew steadily. Justices reported hundreds of sturdy beggars wandering the country, putting fear into whole communities, rustling sheep, stealing whole cartloads of cheese, making away with draught animals and slaughtering them to furnish their own feasts. The increase in crime was due in part to the increase in population, in part to the increase of poverty and hardship, but there was another reason: the chances of a villain being caught and made to pay the awful price of his offences were minimal. The system of apprehension, detention and punishment was archaic and quite unable to cope with a crime wave of sixteenth-century proportions. It had been devised for a static community living in small, semi-isolated settlements. It could not work in the much more fluid society of Tudor England.

The men who bore the brunt of law enforcement at the parish level were the constables and their assistants. They had to keep the peace and confine those who broke it. They had to appoint watch-guards at night. They were responsible for suspected criminals detained in the town gaol or village cage. They inflicted minor punishments such as putting criminals in the stocks, flogging and branding. They had power to raise the hue and cry which, in theory, meant that anyone they called upon was obliged to help in tracking down wrongdoers. They could cope perfectly well with drunken peasants on holy days, with market stallholders accused of cheating and with common brawls. They were powerless against sharp-witted professional criminals and posses of armed louts who swaggered defiantly from parish to parish, shire to shire.

The constables' authority was openly flouted by criminals and poorly supported by the people. Men confined to the stocks were set free by their friends at dead of night. Villagers were loth to bring accusations because a full gaol meant several mouths to be fed at the expense of the parish. The constables did have the support of the justices of the peace. These were the leading local nobility and gentry,

> ... in whom at this time for the repressing of robbers, thieves, and vagabonds, of privy complots and conspiracies, of riots and violences, and all other misdemeanours in the common wealth the Prince putteth his special trust. Each of them hath authority upon complaint to him made of any theft, robbery, manslaughter, murder, violence, complots, riots, unlawful games, or any such disturbance of the peace and quiet of the realm, to commit the persons whom he supposeth offenders to the prison ... till he and his fellows do meet.[9]

The first two Tudors realised the importance of the ancient office of JP. The magistrates were the men who had both local power and local knowledge. These were the men the two Henrys relied on heavily to make the centralised state a reality throughout the realm. Because of the respect they commanded and the extra manpower they wielded they went a long way towards making up the deficiencies of the constables. But the magistrates were only human; they had their likes and dislikes, their prejudices and rivalries and these sometimes got in the way of justice. When, in 1538, James Clarke, constable of Barrow-on-Humber, presented one Laurence Bawmborough to Sir William Ayscough on a charge of seditious speech he found the magistrate quite unsympathetic. In fact Sir William accused Clarke of being a trouble-maker and sent him packing. Clarke left, but only to ride straight to the home of another justice, Sir Robert Tyrrwhit, who, as all the county knew, was Ayscough's sworn enemy. Tyrrwhit immediately clapped Bawmborough in Lincoln gaol. Clarke's problems were still not over; when he appeared before the bench to accuse Clarke, Sir William Ayscough claimed that Clarke had not submitted a formal, written charge. This the constable certainly had done but Sir William had thrust the paper into his purse. Trouble broke out between the magistrates in open court and it was only after a deal of wrangling that Clarke saw justice done to his satisfaction.[10]

Lacking the police force necessary to compel obedience to the law the Tudor monarchs first resorted to making the law so terrible that it would be a powerful deterrent.

> . . . if any person or persons being whole and mighty in body and able to labour . . . having no land, master, nor using any lawful merchandise, craft, or mystery, whereby he might get his living . . . be vagrant and can give no reckoning how he doth lawfully get his living . . . then it shall be lawful to the constables and all other the King's officers, ministers, and subjects of every town, parish, and hamlet to arrest the said vagabonds and idle persons and then to bring to any of the Justices of Peace of the same shire or liberty . . . and that every such Justice of Peace . . . shall cause every such idle person so to him brought to be had to the next market town or other place where the said Justices of Peace . . . shall think most convenient . . . and there to be tied to the end of a cart naked and be beaten with whips throughout the same market town or other place till his body be bloody by reason of such whipping. . .

> . . . if any impotent person . . . be vagrant and go a-begging . . . then the constables . . . shall cause every such beggar to be taken and brought to the next Justice of Peace . . . and thereupon the said Justice of Peace . . . shall command the said constables . . . that they shall strip him naked from the middle upward and cause him to be whipped within the town where he was taken. . . And if not, then to command such beggar to be set in the stocks in the same town or parish where he was taken by the space of 3 days and 3 nights, there to have only bread and water. . .[11]

So ran the Beggars Act of 1531. Sixteen years later the growing problem drove the government to pass one of the most savage and retrograde pieces of legislation of the whole Tudor era. On conviction as a beggar, a man or woman was to be branded with a 'V' and given over to the informant or to the parish as a slave who, for two years, had no rights and might be put to any kind of work, or sold. Fortunately, Tudor authorities found the Act both unduly harsh and impractical, and it was repealed after three years.

Punishment in Tudor times was public. It had been so from time immemorial and it would not have occurred to anyone that it should be otherwise. Justice must be seen to be done, especially by those who might be tempted to repeat the crimes of the convicted. Gallows were, therefore, erected in the most prominent places and felons hung there were not cut down for many days – usually until relatives begged the body or until the gallows were required again. The corpses of particularly heinous offenders were displayed in gibbets where they putrefied and disintegrated before the common gaze, much as farmers still display the broken bodies of foxes as a deterrent to others of their kind. We have already seen how the Duke of Norfolk was ordered to have the convicted rebels of 1536–7 hung, drawn and quartered, and their severed parts prominently displayed. Sixteenth-century men and women were quite used to the sight of blackened and rotting heads set up on poles and hacked limbs bleeding over the market cross.

They were also inured to the sight of barbaric executions. It was, admittedly, usually London and the major cities which were chosen as the sites for the garish execution of traitors and heretics but the crowds which these events always attracted suggest that a ghoulish fascination with hideously tortured flesh was not confined to urban man. Tudor man was close to death and suffering. Pain, whether toothache or dysentery, was something they had to bear; it could not be alleviated by a pill or an injection. They expected to lose children and loved ones in the prime of life. Because pain and death were not strangers in their homes they could more readily watch a man dragged through the streets on a hurdle, strung up on the gallows, cut down while still breathing, disembowelled, his entrails burned before his eyes, and his carcase cut in pieces. Yet of all the techniques of public execution practised in that barbaric age the worst was undoubtedly the burning of heretics and witches. When the church handed over a heretic to the secular arm it did so, 'requiring in the bowels of Christ that the execution of this worthy punishment to be done upon thee, may be so moderated that there be neither over much cruelty, nor too much favourable gentleness; but that it may be to the health and salvation of thy soul, and to the extirpation, fear, terror, and conversion of all other heretics unto the unity of the Catholic faith.' To burn someone alive and say that you hope it does not hurt too much sounds like the ultimate hypocrisy and, of course, in most cases the pain inflicted by this form of execution was quite appalling. There were too many variables involved. The faggots might be damp, in which case the victim would suffer the double anguish of inhaling smoke while his feet roasted. Strong winds might carry the flames to and fro, thereby prolonging suffering intolerably. The fire might be ill-laid causing the martyr's flesh to toast and smoulder long before the merciful fire reached his torso. No wonder that those who could afford to do so or had wealthy friends acquired bags of gunpowder which were dropped around them when they were tied to the stake.

There was a strong element of the theatrical about public punishment. Every recanted heretic had to carry a faggot around his home town or village, usually on three separate Sundays. The ducking of scolds was a cause of great amusement as was the pelting of offenders set in the stocks or pillory. Centuries of disuse have bereft the picturesque sight of age-worn stocks on the village green of all sinister overtones. The Tudor reality, whereby a malefactor, whatever the weather, was made to sit in a cramped position, in his own accumulating excrement, denied sleep, and subjected to every indignity heaped upon him by an audience keeping carefully upwind, came close to the techniques of mental and physical torture which we associate with Eastern Bloc countries. Many diverting kinds of public humiliation were invented. A market cheat might have his wares burned under his nose as he stood in the pillory. A perjurer might be made to ride backward on a donkey with a placard about his neck displaying his crime. One such was imprisoned in London for a year during which time he was brought out on four separate occasions,

> . . . without hood or girdle, barefoot and unshod, with a whetstone hung by a chain from his neck, and lying on his breast, it being marked with the words, 'a false liar'; and there shall be a pair of trumpets, trumpetting before him on his way to the pillory; and there the cause of his punishment shall be solemnly proclaimed. And the said John shall remain on the pillory for three hours of the day, and from thence shall be taken back to Newgate in the same manner.[12]

The great public executions had a ritual all their own. The specially erected stage ringed by soldiers, the procession of the condemned, the prayers, the declaration of the offender's crimes, the sermon (if the prisoner was a heretic), the last speech, the formal forgiveness of the kneeling headsman – these all served to hold large audiences spellbound. Even in the reign of Henry VIII such exhibitions were rare and most were confined to the capital but they excited widespread interest and for months afterwards details of the gruesome events went around, gossips relating in market and tavern how fine or abysmal an end the condemned had made. A burning or beheading always attracted a crowd and because crowds always attracted pedlars, minstrels, jugglers, ballad-mongers, strolling players and other street performers, there was a fair-like atmosphere at executions.

Nor should we too readily condemn the morbid curiosity of our forbears. Unlike us, they were not sated with entertainment in their own homes. Life was a drab monochrome and the colourful exceptions were the days when something different happened. Apart from the procession of saints' days, festivals and fairs, these exceptions included visits by friars and mummers, the guild plays, the passing of a great nobleman's or bishop's entourage and the public vengeance displayed against criminals.

Thomas More played the central role in what was to become the most celebrated public execution of the age. It took place, like so many others, on Tower Hill. The time was 9 am on Tuesday, 6 July 1535. For men and women accustomed to rising and retiring with the sun it was mid-morning, and a large crowd of Londoners had gathered to witness the end of such a public figure – the foremost opponent of the divorce and the supremacy. There was much jostling and good-natured banter. Happiest of all were the cutpurses who slipped profitably through the throng of close-pressed bodies. At last the little procession emerged from the gatehouse and made the short uphill journey. There was the armed escort, the lieutenant, the priest and the emaciated figure of the ex-Chancellor. Unkempt, his long beard straggling to his waist, More wore a simple gown of frieze (because, according to Stapleton, a wicked gaoler had stolen the more presentable garment More had decided to wear for the occasion) and carried a large, red cross before him. Noisily, the crowd displayed its emotions: some wept, some shouted encouragement but others jeered and gloated, like the woman who thrust through the line of pikemen to accost her old adversary, 'Do you remember, Master More, that when you were Chancellor you were my hard friend, and did me great injury in giving wrong judgement against me?'

Wearily, the condemned man put her aside. 'Woman, I am now going to my death. I remember well the whole matter; if now I were to give sentence again, I assure thee I would not alter it. Thou hast no injury, so content thee, and trouble me not.'[13]

Yet another bystander wanted to know what had happened to certain documents delivered into More's hands when he was in office. 'Have patience, I beseech you, for the space of one short hour. For then from the care of your documents, and from every other burden, the King's Majesty in his goodness will give me complete relief.'[14]

With taunts and interchange of this kind and with the press of people who wanted to shake More's hand or touch the martyr's robe, the three-hundred-yard journey was slowed down. Those closest the scaffold watched closely to see the demeanour of the prisoner; some of them regarded themselves as experts on how men faced death. They heard the last witticism of the man who was England's greatest wit – as More turned to the sheriff at the foot of the short ladder, 'I pray you see me safe up, and for my coming down let me shift for myself.'

But the watchers were to be disappointed over the matter of More's last speech. He had been expressly forbidden to make a long address and so, as one watcher was soon reporting to friends in Paris, 'He spoke little before his execution. Only he asked the bystanders to pray for him in this world, and he would pray for them elsewhere. He then begged them earnestly to pray for the King, that it might please God to give him good counsel, protesting that he died the King's good servant but God's first.'[15]

More knelt for his prayers and the crowd fell silent, ears straining to catch the words. They were recognised as lines from Psalm 51: 'Have mercy upon me, O God, after thy great goodness.' When his devotions were over it was the turn of the executioner to kneel and ask More's forgiveness. Even as a child Thomas had had a gift for acting. It had served him well throughout his public life and it did not desert him now. To say that he made the most of these last few moments is not to accuse him of shallowness or insincerity. The people expected him to make 'a good end'. It was important for himself and for the cause he believed in that he should not disappoint them. So now he embraced the headsman, gave him an angel-noble and said, loud enough for near spectators to hear, 'Thou wilt give me this day a greater benefit than ever any mortal man can be able to give me. Pluck up thy spirits, man, and be not afraid to do thine office. My neck is very short: take heed, therefore, thou strike not awry for saving of thine honesty.'[16]

He refused the executioner's offer to blindfold him, taking a piece of cloth he had brought with him and covering his own face. And so he knelt. And so the axe was raised. And so with one deft stroke his head was severed from his body to be held up, dripping, to the gaze of the onlookers with the traditional words, 'Behold the head of a traitor.' The body was packed into the waiting coffin, the officials returned to the Tower, the soldiers formed ranks and marched away, and men and women pressed forward to dip kerchiefs in the blood rapidly soaking into the sawdust.

Thomas More believed himself blameless according to the laws of God but he knew that he had been justly condemned according to the statute law of the land and it would not have occurred to him to challenge the king's right to extract the penalty prescribed by that law. But some laws More had certainly challenged as had other men who shared his humanist outlook. In *Utopia* he had protested against the very basis of the judicial attitude towards felons.

... this punyshment of theves passeth the limites of Justice, and is also very hurtefull to the weale publique. For it is to extreame and cruel a punishment for thefte, and yet not sufficient to refrayne and withhold men from thefte. For simple thefte is not so great an offense, that it owght to be punished with death. Neither ther is any punishment so horrible, that it can kepe them from stealynge, which have no other craft, wherby to get their living. Therfore in this poynte, not you onlye, but also the most part of the world, be like evyll scholemaisters, which be readyer to beate, then to teache, their scholers. For great and horrible punishmentes be appointed for theves, whereas much rather provision should have ben made, that there were some meanes, whereby they myght get their livyng, so that no man should be dryven to this extreme necessitie, firste to steale, and then to dye.[17]

More, and the inheritors of the humanist tradition who would, in the reign of Edward VI, be known as the 'Commonwealth Party', saw poverty as the root cause of crime and unbridled greed as the root cause of poverty. Everywhere, radical preachers were inveighing against the irresponsible accumulation of wealth. 'The rich man,' said one, 'so encroacheth, gathereth together and obtaineth so much into his own hands, that he alone possesseth the earth, liveth thereby and his poor neighbour ready to die for lack... These men, except they repent, cannot be saved.'[18] Protestantism was in the process of breaking down the barrier between priest and layman, and was propagating the notion of the priesthood of all believers. Charity was no longer predominantly the concern of the 'professional Christians' – the monks and clergy; everyman was responsible for his neighbour. If the rich, wrote Crowley, 'would consider themselves to be but stewards and not lords over their possessions, this oppression would soon be redressed. But so long as this persuasion sticketh in their minds: It is mine own, who should warn me to do with mine own as myself listeth? it shall not be possible to have any redress at all.'[19] More took this notion to its logical extreme when he posited 'Utopia', the land where all property is held in common. Like More, all the realistic reformers realised that the natural impetus to acquisitiveness, which, by the grasping and redistributing of monastic lands, Henry was encouraging, would not be stopped by sermons and pamphlets. Government action was necessary. 'Employ your study,' the anonymous *Supplication of the poore commons* urged the king, 'to leave [Prince Edward] a commonweal to govern and not an island of brute beasts, among whom the strongest devour the weaker.'

Not until the 1530s did the lawmakers of the realm make at least some response to the demands for social reform. The genius behind the sweeping attempts of this decade to deal with the problem was Thomas Cromwell, a man committed to Commonwealth principles. And, in this context at least, his record is more interesting for what he attempted than what he achieved. In this matter the most powerful man in England next to the king found himself up against vested interests capable of thwarting his designs.

First of all he tackled the enclosure problem. Earlier legislation had done no more than ineffectually forbid the pulling down of rural dwellings. Everyone knew that these statutes were universally ignored but they were ignored by the landed interest in the shires and it was that landed interest which was dominant in parliament. Private bills aimed at preventing enclosure were occasionally introduced but stood no chance against the closed ranks of abbots, nobles, gentlemen and burgesses who owned most of the enclosed land. Cromwell took an interest in the problem from the start and introduced a comprehensive bill in 1534 which dictated that no man was to own more than 2000 sheep, the amount of land a man might lease was controlled and he was obliged to keep at least one eighth of it as arable. Had this bill become law it would have reversed the trends towards larger holdings and increased pasture. It did not become law – at least not in its original form. In the Lords an organised opposition brought forward a host of objections and legal quibbles. The Act which finally emerged in 1536 was an emasculated piece of legislation but it did place restraints on leaseholding and provided a means of tackling the worse aspects of enclosure.

The fate of early Tudor vagrancy and poor laws was much the same. All legislation up to and including the Act of 1531 tried to prevent vagabondage by imposing 'deterrent' punishment. The operative Act for most of the period was the Beggars Act of 1495 which instructed local authorities diligently to seek out vagrants and punish them. It also enacted that, 'none apprentice nor servant of husbandry, labourer nor servant artificer, play at the tables . . . but only for meat and drink, nor at the tennis, closh [a game which involved driving a ball through a hoop with a spade-shaped implement], dice, cards, bowls, nor any other unlawful game in no wise out of Christmas, and in Christmas to play only in the dwelling-house of his master or where the master of any of the said servants is present. . .' This provision was an attempt to combat the activities of itinerant gamblers who deprived honest labourers of their wages. With the same evil in mind the statute empowered JPs to keep a close watch on ale-houses and, where necessary, close them down.[20] As we have seen, this approach was almost a total failure. By its failure to distinguish between the poor who were willing to work and those who had embraced a life of beggary and crime it drove many innocent people into a life of dishonesty. Once again, Cromwell's office completely re-examined the whole problem and came up with a revolutionary set of proposals. The relief of impotent poor was to remain the responsibility of the parish but the leaders of the community were to see to the efficient, regular collection and distribution of alms. The able-bodied poor were to be set to public works such as the repair of roads, bridges and ditches. There was to be a national 'council to avoid vagabonds' which was to be financed by a graduated income tax.

The last three words of that paragraph have always been among the most unpopular in the English language, and the whole package of proposals met with determined parliamentary opposition. Cromwell persuaded the king, in person, to present the bill in the Commons but the members refused to be overawed and once again the government had to be content with a very diluted piece of legislation. The Act of 1536 exhorted all men of substance to charity and directed authorities to compel 'sturdy vagabonds and valiant beggars to be set and kept to continual labour, in such wise as by their said labours they and every of them may get their own livings with the continual labour of their own hands.'[21] The collection of alms was to be on an organised basis but remained purely voluntary. Thus, even under the despotic Tudor regime, the upper classes of English society were able to defend their 'ancient liberties' through the institution of parliament.

Had he lived to see the fate of these reforming bills, Thomas More would have resented the power of ingrained conservatism and wealth to resist humanitarian progress. But other reactionary legislation would have won his wholehearted support. Such were the laws against heretics, sorcerers and traitors. In the official mind and in the minds of many Englishmen there was little or no distinction between those three categories. The heretic set himself against religious orthodoxy, the traitor against the political orthodoxy of the existing regime; both, like the sorcerer, were in league with the devil or, at the very least, were unwittingly doing the devil's work. About heresy we shall have more to say in a later chapter, so we now turn our attention to the other two members of this unholy triumvirate.

For Tudor men and women the unknown world, the world of spirits, angels, devils, fairies and elves, was always close at hand, overlapping with the known, influencing everyday life. The unknown

Superstition was a strong undercurrent in sixteenth-century life. Here, witches are conjuring up a hailstorm

always evokes both fear and curiosity and it was so in the sixteenth century.

Fear largely accounted for the prevalence of superstitious religion and the practice of magic arts in one form or another. The parish priest was just such a practitioner in the minds of most people. However nondescript or outrageous his personal life, however resented his behaviour, he was, nevertheless, a dangerous man to cross. He was the performer of strange rituals in a foreign, scholar's tongue. Sunday by Sunday, saint's day after saint's day, he made offerings and muttered incantations in the dim, religious atmosphere of the sanctuary. He had power over the eternal welfare of the dear departed. He had power to bless and power to curse the living. He had power to excommunicate those who were unfaithful over matters of tithes or irregular at confession and that meant consigning their souls to the fiery torments of hell so garishly displayed over the chancel arch. Above all, he had power to 'make God' in the mass, and there were many simple souls who regarded the consecrated wafer simply as a powerful charm to be carried away from church to afford protection at home just as cloves of garlic, sprigs of rue and lumps of coal were used to keep the evil one at bay (see below, pp. 205–206). Elements of ancient pagan religion survived side by side with the Catholic church. The maypole, midsummer ceremonies and other activities were indispensable elements of the annual cycle. Popular legendary heroes such as Robin Hood and Herne the Hunter started life as supernatural beings.

Fear and curiosity go a long way towards explaining the prevalence of witchcraft, astrology and occultism. Those who claimed or were generally believed to have access to the world beyond human knowledge exerted, sometimes unwillingly, great power over their neighbours. This is not to say that there was any similarity between the village crone and the academic star gazer. Their motives and beliefs were quite distinct: the witch probably had a basic knowledge of simples and a reputation for consorting with demons which she may or may not have believed in herself; the astrologer was a scientist in the strict sense of the word who probed the secrets of the physical universe and was convinced that the planets had an influence on human affairs. Between the two there was a wide gulf tenuously bridged by a host of more or less serious practitioners – alchemists, physicians, necromancers, magicians and charlatans. The only similarity between all these people was the similarity afforded them in the common mind. Most Tudor men and women found it difficult to distinguish between 'science' and 'superstition'. To the unlearned there is something almost miraculous about knowledge, and the assumption is easily made that that knowledge is supernaturally conferred.

But superstition was not the sole possession of the uneducated masses: kings and nobles had their horoscopes cast by court astrologers; university doctors and students dabbled in necromancy and sought the philosopher's stone; distracted yeomen and burgesses bought love potions from wizards and crones reputed to be wise in herb magic. Every level of society had its 'wise' men, some of them serious devotees, some of them self-deluded simpletons, some of them heartless charlatans.

At a time when the trained minds of Europe had shattered all the old barriers and were probing into new realms of knowledge it is not surprising that some bold spirits should venture beyond the 'natural'. In any case, where were the lines to be drawn between what a Christian scholar might and might not explore? The boundaries were as yet unfixed between alchemy and medicine, astronomy and astrology, philosophy and necromancy. The revival of classical studies reinforced the astrological world view, fully accepted in the ancient world. Physicians believed in the influence of heavenly bodies just as profoundly as did astrologers. Chemistry was beginning to emerge from its alchemical chrysalis but there was still general belief in transmutation. Scholars were still seriously trying to change base metals into gold and few of them lacked wealthy patrons who hoped to become wealthier.

The accomplishments of the celebrated magi of the age, though not Englishmen, illustrate the catholic nature of knowledge to which the more liberated members of the international intelligentsia subscribed. Paracelsus laid the foundations of medical chemistry but regarded astrology and theology as vital aids for the physician because the balance of forces in the body was controlled by astral spirits. Nostradamus practised medicine but was more famous for his astrological predictions. Agrippa von Nettesheim, sometime friend of John Colet, lectured in philosophy, practised as a physician and wrote treatises on magic which he regarded as the surest path to lead men to a knowledge of God. Meanwhile, in relative obscurity, a German philosopher was gaining a reputation as a necromancer, palmist, astrologer, soothsayer and sodomite. Within a few years the scandalous life and noteworthy death of Georg Faust would become a legend and a warning for all those who sought forbidden knowledge.

At the parish level sorcery was an accepted part of life. Whether it was the lonely and cantankerous old man or woman dubbed 'witch' by superstitious neighbours or the person who augmented his income by deliberately dabbling in necromancy and herb magic, every town and village boasted at least one specialist in the black arts. Health, sex and money were the motives which drove people to the expedient of seeking the aid of the wise man or woman. Simple people could not afford the ministrations of physicians or surgeons and had little alternative but to consult the local 'specialist'. This might be the parson, for many priests and monks are known to have dabbled in the forbidden arts. It might be the woman who doubled as village midwife and witch, for the attitude of people to these 'specialists' was ambivalent; they both feared them and needed them. Consulted about a pain or ailment the witch might prescribe an ointment or potion, the reciting of orthodox prayers or the performance of strange rites. A serious dabbler in the black arts might invoke the devil to transfer the affliction to someone else, like the woman who boiled up thirty herbs in a pot and then cast the concoction into the street to transfer her client's lameness to the first person who should walk on the potion-damped earth.

Tudor Englishmen had no doubt that witches were able to inflict disease as well as cure it. They believed that sorcerers could make themselves invisible and spirit themselves into people's homes or cattle sheds to work mischief. Such services were not infrequently commissioned by people who wished their neighbours harm. Conversely, misfortunes for which there was no other obvious explanation were often blamed on to those known to be witches. If a crop failed it was because an invisible sorceress[22] had flown behind the sower and removed the seed from the ground. Human or animal sickness was obviously the result of poison introduced to food or water by the unseen witch.

Love potions were probably the most commonly demanded and prescribed magical aids to living. Almost anything, it seems, could become an ingredient in a passion-inducing philtre; pulverised birds' bones, ashes from burned reeds, herbs, water in which feet had been washed, menstrual blood and human excrement are only some of the more easily acquired components known to have been obtained by the frustrated and the love-sick.[23]

In Suffolk a young swain was given this solemn advice on how to win the girl of his dreams:

Take new wax, and the powder of a dead man, make an image with the face downward and in the likeness of the person you wish to have; make it in the ouers of mars and in the new of the mone; under the left arm-poke place a Swaler's hart and a liver under the rite; you must have a new needal and a new thread; the Sprits name must be menchened, his Sign and his Character.

Once again, it was easy for a witch or sorcerer to become the scapegoat in affairs of passion. The adulterous wife or unfaithful husband, faced with an angry spouse, could affirm that his or her affections had been diverted by magical means, with some prospect of being believed.

Unlike the countries where the Inquisition held sway (in 1515 five hundred witches were executed in Geneva and four hundred in Toulouse), there were no vindictive witchhunts in England. Witchcraft and sorcery were matters for the ecclesiastical courts and, according to extant records, the few people convicted of such offences in the early sixteenth century were permitted to expiate their sins by means of penance. There were, apparently, no burnings, and no statute law against witchcraft existed until 1542. This is not to say that witches, sorcerers, necromancers and the like were not punished, far from it.

They were not, however, punished for being practitioners of black arts *per se*. They were punished for employing sorcery and invocation for purposes of murder, fraud or sexual depravity.

It was not difficult for the charlatan, the simpleton or even the serious student to fall foul of the law. Richard Jones of Oxford had a number of rich patrons who were impressed by the magical clutter of his dingy chamber – the stills, cauldrons, alembics, glass tubing and pestles, the carved sceptre used for conjuring 'the four kings', the box with a snake-skin inside and the shelves of magical and alchemical treatises. Here Jones laboured earnestly and long in his search for the philosopher's stone and paid for his researches by making astrological predictions and providing unguents and potions for the relief of various disorders. Some of his compounds may have worked but despite his confidence that within a year he could make the king all the silver and gold he could want, he never discovered the secret of turning base metals into bullion.

Whether Jones was always a charlatan or whether he was lured into crime by the gullibility and enthusiasm of his own clients we do not know. What we do know is that the scholarly magus soon got himself into serious trouble. It began when Jones became involved with William Neville, younger son of an ancient and noble Midlands family. Neville was the sort of client every spiritualist and medium prays for. He believed implicitly in magical powers and he was extremely ambitious. He had consorted with several wizards, sorcerers and necromancers before he was introduced to Jones. He came in quest of a magical ring 'that should bring a man in favour with his prince' fondly believing that other-worldly powers could make up the deficiencies of his own talents. Wolsey, he affirmed, had owed his advancement to such a ring and as for Cromwell, 'when he and I were servants in my lord cardinal's house,' he told Jones, 'Master Cromwell did haunt to the company of one that was seen in your faculty: and shortly after no man so great with my lord cardinal as Master Cromwell was.'

This was altogether too close to important people for comfort but Jones did play upon another of Neville's ambitions; he prophesied that Neville would inherit the earldom of Warwick. As the months went by sundry supernatural 'proofs' of this prophecy were manufactured and, carried away by his own inventive powers, Jones elaborated on just how, through battles and sudden death, the obstacles on the path to the earldom would be removed. Soon Jones found himself forecasting the imminent death of Henry VIII and his replacement by someone who would be well-disposed towards his client.

Unfortunately for Jones, he succeeded too well. Neville was so taken in that he began to tell everyone of his coming good fortune. After the king's death his successor, with the new Earl of Warwick at his right hand, would put all the realm's ills to rights and restore the ancient families to their proper place. Even to talk of the king's demise was treason for which others had already paid with their heads. Consorting with magicians to encompass the death of the sovereign was a certain passport to the scaffold. Jones was swimming in very murky waters and can scarcely have been surprised when a detachment of soldiers arrived to escort him from Oxford to London – and the Tower. For some six months he remained there while the Council considered the case very carefully. At his examinations he grovelled and claimed that the whole elaborate story had been invented in order to make fun of Neville. It is very unlikely that the king's ministers believed this excuse but they eventually decided that Jones was harmless and they let him go.[24]

The outcome of this case indicates the common-sense attitude normally taken by the government and the courts. However, it was a different matter when magicians deliberately involved themselves with politics. In 1537 Mabel Brigge, a thirty-two-year-old witch from Holderness, embarked on a three-day fast. This was a well tried technique for bringing harm upon other people. The theory was that before the fast was ended the person against whom it was directed would be dead or seriously injured. Witch Brigge had already had the gratification of breaking a man's neck by this means. This time, however, she was aiming higher; the intended victims of her magic were the king and the Duke of Norfolk. Information was laid before the Council in the North which wasted little time in condemning Mabel Brigge to death as a traitor.[25]

Between these two cases there lies an enormous variety of instances of magic directed against prominent figures. While most people employed witches and sorcerers for private matters there were those who felt so strongly about the activities of the government and the politically powerful that they resorted to supernatural means of combating them. Such consultations were the desperate acts of resentful individuals who lacked any political means of bringing pressure to bear on their rulers.

The last instance of this 'protest by magic' that we have space to consider is a case which created a considerable public stir in the early weeks of 1538. Seeing a crowd gathered in a London churchyard, one Fulk Vaughan went to discover what the attraction was. He found the parish priest gingerly scraping the earth away from what at first appeared to be a half-buried child. Closer examination showed it to be a large wax image wrapped around with 'a piece of cloth knit like a winding-sheet' and pierced by two pins. Everyone drew back in horror from this obvious piece of black magic but Vaughan said he knew someone who might be able to shed some light on the matter. He took the image to the shop of a scrivener named Pole in Crooked Lane. Pole was a well-known sorcerer who had previously tried to interest Vaughan in a search for buried treasure. Pole knew at a glance what the objective of the image-maker was and also that he was a bungling amateur. The model, he said, had been 'made to waste one, but . . . he that made it was not his craft's master, for he should have put it either in horse dung or in a dunghill'. Pole intimated that this piece of malevolent magic was aimed at Prince Edward, the heir to the throne. This was enough for the matter to come rapidly to Cromwell's attention and for him to send three of his closest colleagues to investigate. No culprit was ever detected but we may be sure that Vaughan, Pole and others underwent some very unpleasant grilling.

Gambling among the peasant and servant classes was proscribed by law but, of course, it continued. The only other means of getting rich quick was with the aid of magic. At least, that is what sufficient gullible people thought for frauds and cranks to make a living out of conducting searches for buried treasure and making charms guaranteed to bring the wearer wealth. Typical of this kind of roguery was the case of two men who told some Islington villagers that they could lead them to a cache of several hundred pounds worth of gold. By divination they knew that it was guarded by a demon until its original owner, now in purgatory, should be released by prayers, fasts and offerings to saints. If the good men of Islington would only provide the necessary funds they would be doing a charitable act for a poor, departed soul and would enrich themselves into the bargain. The tricksters obtained 40s in this way before royal justice caught up with them.

It was difficult for practising sorcerers not to contravene the laws. Their potions and unguents, composed of the most unsavoury ingredients, often made people ill and sometimes proved fatal. That was murder. They received money for useless incantations. That was fraud. Yet there were no witchhunts in England until well into the Puritan era and, by and large, necromancers had little to fear from royal justice. The same was not true of the rough justice of the parish. All too often foolish stories about cattle, crops or children being bewitched were eagerly believed. The impotent countryfolk in the grip of famine or murrain needed a scapegoat. By mutual encouragement the members of a community could overcome their fear of demonic reprisals. Then they might exact a fearful revenge involving torture by burning coals, branding or dowsing. Public lynchings were not unknown.

It was not, of course, only those inhabiting the no-man's-land between the terrestrial and spiritual worlds who manufactured potions, powders, purges and prophylactics. Every family, high and low, had its trusted remedies, which were administered when needed to members of the household and recommended to friends – not always with the best results:

> To-night, after midnight, I have taken your medicine, which has done me much good. It has caused the stone to break, and now I void much gravel. But for all that your said medicine has done me little honesty, for it made me piss my bed this night, for the which my wife hath sore beaten me, and saying it is children's parts to bepiss their bed. Ye have made me such a pisser that I dare not this day go abroad; wherefore I beseech you to make mine excuses to my lord and master Treasurer for that I shall not be with you this day at dinner. Madam, it is showed me that a wing or leg of a stork if I eat thereof will make me that I shall never piss more in bed, and though my body be simple, yet my tongue shall be ever good, and specially when it speaketh of women; and sithens such a medicine will do such a great cure, God send me a piece thereof.[26]

While life and death, pain and ease were at the mercy of such homely remedies and while the sciences of medicine and surgery were in their infancy there could be little real connection between treatment and health. Tudor man was a prey to so many ailments and diseases that we are not surprised to discover that the basic attitude to ill health, pain and lingering death was one of acceptance. A Venetian ambassador reported, 'they have some little plague in England well nigh every year, for which they are not accustomed to make sanitary provisions, as it does not usually make great progress. The cases for the most part occur amongst the lower classes, as if their dissolute mode of life impaired their constitutions.'[27] His observation is excellent but his diagnosis is at fault. The main reason why the poor were worse affected by epidemics was the dirty, rat-infested conditions under which they lived. As we have already seen the dwellings of ordinary people in both town and country were simple and evil-smelling in the extreme. They appalled and offended foreign visitors, like Erasmus. 'The floors are made of clay and are covered with layers of rushes, constantly replenished, so that the bottom layer remains for twenty years, harbouring spittle, vomit, the urine of dogs and men, the dregs of beer, the remains of fish, and other nameless filth.'[28] Moreover, the poor town-dweller could not take the only effective remedy against plague visitation – flight. Every summer the court left Westminster for the cleaner air of sundry royal manors in the home counties and the shutters were put up on all the town houses of the noblemen and leading gentry. It was an obvious precaution but it was not always enough, as Henry himself discovered in 1528. This was the worst year for epidemics in living memory. Both plague and sweating sickness were rife in London and other major population centres. July found the court at Tittenhanger from where Thomas Henneage, one of Wolsey's gentlemen, reported on the 5th to his master at Hampton Court,

> . . . the Kinges Highnes, this mornyng, being advertised Your Grace purposed to have com, and visited hym as tomorrow, commaunded me to write unto Your Grace . . . to desire Your Grace to differ your saide commyng, untill the tyme be more propiciouse; for as yet he feareth and thinketh not mete Your Graces company, and hys, shuld joyne in oon howse; and is mervelouse gladd that he is no nighe unto Your Grace, sayeng "I am right glad my Lordes Grace is so nere hand, for now, if any casualtie shuld happen, I may have redy and spedy word from hym;" assuring Your Grace, that His Highnes is so well contented, in all poyntes, with his lodginges, with the aire and site of this your place, as ever I sawe hym ells where to be. Further-more His Highnes willed me . . . to desire Your Grace to cawse generall processions to be made, unyversally thorough the realme, as well for the good wetheringes, to thencrese of corne and fruyte, as also for the plage that now reignethe.

Henry might have been 'well contented' with Tittenhanger on 5 July but events soon caused a change of heart. Four days later Henneage wrote again from an anxious (one might almost say panic-stricken) court and this time his talk was of wills and death:

> . . . this morneynge, [the King] hathe word, that my Lady Marques of Exeter ys syke of the comen sykenes, whiche causythe His Hynes to apoynt to remove, apon Seterday, frome hens to Amtyll [Ampthill], and hath comawyndyd that all suche, as where in my seyd Lord Marquys compeny, and my seyd Lady, to deporte in severall parcells, and so not contynue to gether; and so he desyreth Your Grace to do, yf any suche case shall fortune, as God forbede. And glad he ys to here, that Youre Grace hathe so good hart, and

that you have determyned, and made your wyll, and orderyd youre
selfe anenst God, as you have doyne, as His Highnes haythe semable
doyne. . . And also, this morneynge, Hys Hynes haythe knowledge of
the deythe of on of his chapell. . . And also he desyrythe Youre
Grace, that he may here every second day frome you, how you doo;
for I esewer you, every morneyng, assone as he comythe frome the
Quene, he haskythe, whether I here any thyng frome Youre
Grace. . .[29]

Though England was spared the devastating epidemics of the
fifteenth and seventeenth centuries, plague was seldom absent from the
land. The word 'plague' was used to cover a variety of diseases whose
effects were usually fatal. The most stubborn variety was still bubonic
plague which was carried by the fleas of the black rat and which
therefore flourished in insanitary, overcrowded towns. Equally deadly
was virus-borne pneumonia. However, it was generally realised that the
contagion was spread by the coughing of affected persons and that
isolation of victims was the only way to contain an outbreak.

Two new scourges entered England in the early Tudor period, small-
pox and the sweating sickness. The former arrived about 1514, though
it was another century before it was clearly distinguished from measles
and chicken pox. On the other hand the sweating sickness became the
first disease to be scientifically observed and described. The man
responsible for this pioneer work on diagnosis was Dr John Caius of
Cambridge who wrote *A Boke or Counseill against the Disease commonly
called the Sweate or Sweatyng Sicknesse* in 1552. (The particular
strength of this disease in England was acknowledged in Dr Caius's
later expansion of the book which was called *De Ephemera Britannica*.)
It seems very likely that the disease was introduced by Henry Tudor's
invading army in 1485, for the first reference to it occurs within days of
his landing at Milford Haven. Unlike other epidemics it struck in the
town and the country; it carried off high and low alike, which is how it
gained its common nickname, 'Stoop-knave-and-know-thy-master'.
The symptoms were high fever, headache, insatiable thirst, pains in the
joints and an overwhelming desire to sleep which, physicians soon
discovered, the patient had to resist at all costs. Its most appalling
characteristic, however, was the speed with which it took effect. It
could kill a man in two or three hours. No other disease struck such
terror into the hearts of Englishmen as the sweating sickness. We have
seen how Henry VIII and his court kept on the move to avoid it. In
1522 the muster commissioners in Lincolnshire had to report that they

In an age when plague was a frequent guest and the average life expectancy was about thirty-five years, death was a familiar figure. As Holbein pointed out in a series of woodcuts called 'The Dance of Death', the universal leveller was an impartial visitor

could not do their work because 'There is much harness in houses infected with the sickness, with which no one will meddle.'[30]

Diseases associated with infected food and water – typhus, cholera, dysentery – were very common, as was tuberculosis which claimed the lives of thousands, including Henry VII and Prince Arthur (and, later, Edward VI). Malaria and related fevers were rampant. Gaol fever was probably malaria. Mosquitoes flourished in damp, airless cells and dungeons where pools of stagnant water lay undisturbed for centuries. A long spell in such notorious prisons as Newgate and the Fleet was virtually a death sentence.

For none of these diseases did Tudor experts have any cure. If victims recovered it was in spite of, rather than because of, the ministrations of apothecaries, surgeons and physicians. The medical world was a bustling, backbiting concourse of more or less qualified astrologers, doctors, quacks and confessed amateurs. The man with a pain or a sick child could see little difference between all these practitioners with their latinised mumbo-jumbo and their talk of zodiacal signs. The university trained experts, however, were very jealous of their craft and the College of Physicians was founded in 1518 specifically to exclude 'common artificers, as smiths, weavers, and women who boldly and customarily take upon themselves great cures ... in which they use sorcery and apply medicines very noyous.'

The study of medicine was well established at Oxford and Cambridge but it could not be said to flourish. Often, there was only one resident teacher in the university to supervise those who, having proceeded BA, elected to go on to study medicine. Hippocrates and Galen still were the basic texts and astronomy was an important part of the course. Advances in anatomy and diagnosis which had been made by Islamic, Jewish and European pioneers were very slow in filtering through to England. Not until 1549 was it established that a student physician must perform two anatomies and effect three cures before being admitted to practice. Diagnosis was based upon the theory that the human body was composed of four 'humours' – hot, cold, moist and dry, corresponding to the four elements of earth, air, fire and water. Imbalance led to illness and to restore health it was necessary to restore the harmony of the humours, usually by blood-letting which could be achieved by opening a vein or applying leeches. But treatment could not be carried out at any time, not even if the patient was in great pain or in need of instant relief. The propitious moment could only be deduced by studying the motions of the heavenly bodies and by accurately casting horoscopes. In fact medicine had not progressed since the time of Chaucer who said of his 'doctour of physick'

> Well could he guess the ascending of the star
> Wherein his patient's fortunes settled were.
> He knew the course of every malady,
> Were it of cold or heat or moist or dry.

But slowly, very slowly, attitudes were changing. The new learning breathed its revivifying life into the comatose body of medical studies as into other disciplines. The great educational reformer, Juan Luis Vives, who was in England from 1522 to 1528, established the ground rules of empirical science: 'I call that knowledge which we receive when the senses are properly brought to observe things ... in a methodical way to which clear reason leads us on, reason so closely connected with the nature of our mind that there is no one who does not accept its lead. . . [This] knowledge . . . is called science, firm and indubitable. . .'[31] In 1540 the king personally endowed a professorship in medicine at Cambridge, which was rapidly becoming the more progressive of the two universities. Within a few years the celebrated Dr

Caius was lecturing on anatomy. Dr Caius had studied under some of the continental masters including the great Andreas Vesalius, who revolutionised the study of anatomy in 1543 with his *De humani corporis fabrica*. He may also have met Girolamo Fracastoro who was about to publish his *De Contagione*, suggesting that disease was carried in small particles transmitted from person to person by contact or through the air. It was a beginning.

A beginning was also made in the distinction between serious medical studies, astrology, magic and amateur doctoring. Just as the College of Physicians sought incorporation to distinguish itself from unqualified practitioners and 'mere surgeons', so too the surgeons sought to place their craft on a professional basis. The Company of Barber-Surgeons had been incorporated in 1461 but without disciplinary powers over its members. In 1540 the company was refounded and the court painter, Hans Holbein, was commissioned to produce a magnificent large picture to commemorate the important event. It was Holbein's last masterpiece; indeed, the finishing touches were added by another hand, for in the autumn of 1543 the great painter succumbed to the plague and was laid to rest in an unmarked London grave.

The surgeon's instruments were crude and he had, of course, no concept of clinical antisepsis. He operated on patients whose only means of escaping the pain inflicted by knife and saw was a liberal intake of alcohol – until, that is, they fainted in the chair or on the bench to which they were strapped. On the other hand the science of surgery was far freer from antique theories about the influences of heavenly bodies. The barber-surgeon learned by observation and experience. In fact, the master surgeon was capable of performing some remarkably complex operations (e.g. trepanning).

At the bottom of the professional ladder were the apothecaries. They, too, were concerned to be distinguished from the purveyors of useless or positively injurious concoctions. Most of their study was in the properties of herbs and plants. Slowly empirical methods transformed this branch of medicine. The medieval herbals with their attributions of fantastic properties to certain plants were replaced by works of genuine observation. Though, once again, it was continental scholars, such as Otto Brunfels, Pierandria Mattioli and Leonhard Fuchs, who led the way, English specialists were not slow to follow. William Turner, an active Reformation preacher, began the serious study of plant remedies while at Cambridge in the 1520s. He found little to help him in the existing literature: 'I could learne neuer one Greke nether Latin nor English name even amongst the Phisicions of

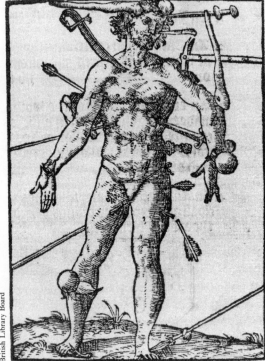

CERTAINE VVORKES
of Chirurgerie, nevvly compiled and
publiſhed by Thomas Gale, Maſ-
ſter in Chirurgerie.

British Library Board

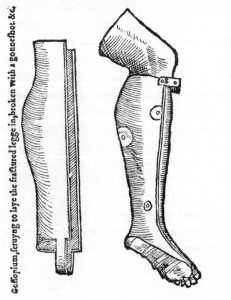

Goſſopium, ſeruyng to laye the fractured legge in, broken with a gonneſhot. &c.

Surgery or 'chirurgery'
was in its infancy when
Thomas Gale published
his treatise in 1563.
However, among the
many implements at the
surgeon's disposal was
the forerunner of the
plaster cast

any herb or tre, suche was the ignorance in simples [medicines composed of one substance] at that tyme.'[32] He became the first great English botanist and, although his contemporary reputation rested largely upon his scurrilous attacks on the church of Rome, generations of apothecaries were grateful to him for his catalogues of English plants and their properties.

Sixteenth-century doctors did not write up case histories, or, if they did, none have survived, so it is difficult for us to speculate on the treatment and care lavished by competent physicians in actual practice. Only one man's affliction is described in frequent letters of the period and that is the leg ulcers from which Henry VIII suffered. The first one appeared in 1528, the very summer when the thirty-seven-year-old king was hurrying from place to place to avoid a worse malady. It seems likely that the disease was osteomyelitis, a chronic bone infection, resulting possibly from an earlier wound sustained in the hunt or the tilt yard. (An alternative diagnosis canvassed by some historians is varicose ulcer. The scanty details of the symptoms will support either theory.) The thigh ulcers discharged pus and, later, pieces of necrosed bone. The royal physicians, prominent among whom were William Butts and Robert Huick (both able men of the new learning), applied the conventional leeches which, of course, did nothing. They then closed the wound with hot, evil-smelling poultices which can only have increased the pain. Henry insisted on riding everywhere, on hunting regularly and on over-indulging himself at table, all of which aggravated his condition. By 1537 both legs were affected and Henry had relief from appalling pain only after a discharge of matter lessened the tension within the wound.

For years the physicians had striven to close up the wounds, believing this would speed recovery. In the summer of 1537 they received a nasty shock; a blood clot detached itself and reached the area of the lungs where it caused a blockage. The king fell speechless and his face turned black. Possibly it was only his iron will and his incredible constitution that enabled him to survive until the obstruction cleared itself. Now all the doctors could do was keep the ulcers open to encourage discharge and apply soothing ointment, no easy task with such an ill-tempered patient. There were times when Henry could not bear anyone to touch his legs and, in the latter years, only Queen Catherine Parr was allowed to apply the bandages. Pain deprived the king of sleep and impaired his judgement but the physicians could do little for him. He had to be carried up and down stairs and he attended to his official duties leaning heavily on the shoulder of one or other of his attendants.

Sometimes the ulcers closed up and the poison in his system then brought on fevers, some of which were serious. But the king's subjects never saw Henry the patient, in shivering delirium, helpless with pain, his legs swathed in bandages. Always he appeared before them resplendent in heavily padded clothes which concealed the bulges under his hose, and seated on a massive charger. By the end of 1546 Henry could pretend no longer. Racked by ceaseless pain and recurrent fever, he locked himself up in Westminster Palace with only a handful of councillors and attendants and there he died in the small hours of 28 January 1547.

We have ventured some way from our discussion of crime and punishment yet the prevalence of disease and the inadequacy of treatment are far from irrelevant to these matters. Life was very uncertain and most people only had the present to live for. The chances of dying an unpleasant death before reaching middle age were high, certainly higher than the chances of being arrested and condemned for a felony. The potential criminal, therefore, had little to lose.

The worst crime on the Tudor statute book was treason and the law against it was severe. Few Englishmen, however, went in fear of this law. Only a handful of politically motivated magnates seriously considered compassing the king's death, levying war against the king or adhering to the king's enemies, and as we have seen, the first two Tudors effectively disposed of any threat to their crown arising in that quarter. Then, in the 1530s, the whole question of treason (like so much else) was radically altered. Between 1531 and 1543 no less than nine Acts passed through parliament which created new treasons and extended the power of the monarch over the deeds, words and even beliefs of the people. During that period many ordinary men and women who had never harboured a disloyal thought found themselves on trial for their lives.

The reason was, of course, the need to enforce the religious, political and social revolution that Henry VIII and Thomas Cromwell had set in hand. The new treason laws were the snarling watchdogs of the Reformation. The king and his minister were under no illusions about the enormity of the task they were undertaking; to confiscate ecclesiastical wealth and close the monasteries: to sever England's links with the church of Rome; to deprive the people of saints' days and religious images; to set the whole church and state administration on a more efficient footing; these were certain to arouse misunderstanding, resentment and opposition at all levels of society. The instigators of the new policies believed that 'them that be for us are more than them that be against us' but there were sufficient people in the latter category to render tightening of the treason laws desirable and justifiable.

The first problem to be dealt with was that of the vast number of people who sympathised with Catherine of Aragon and deplored Henry's marriage to Anne Boleyn. The First Act of Succession (1534) made it high treason 'by writing, print, deed or act' to 'procure or do or cause to be procured or done anything or things to the prejudice, slander, disturbance or derogation of the matrimony solemnised between Your Highness and the said Queen Anne'. The king's unfortunate and chequered matrimonial career made necessary further succession Acts as, one by one, royal wives were taken to bed and royal children bastardised (one result of the cancellation of Henry's first two marriages was the illegitimising of Mary and Elizabeth).

The royal supremacy over the church was safeguarded by four Acts which nominated as treason any attempt to refuse the king any of his titles, to refer any matter to papal jurisdiction, to attempt to escape the king's justice by fleeing abroad and 'slanderously or maliciously to publish and pronounce, by express writing or words, that the King our Sovereign Lord is an heretic, schismatic, tyrant, infidel or usurper'. Since the pope had employed spiritual sanctions against Henry and those who supported him, every Englishman was, by 1540, either an excommunicate or a traitor. Driven into such a corner there were few staunch Catholics who preferred martyrdom in this world to divine displeasure in the next. About forty-five Englishmen were executed under the treason laws for their adherence to the old church. One of them was Thomas More.

From his resignation of the Chancellorship in May 1532 until March 1534 More lived quietly at Chelsea trying to remain apart from politics, saying nothing in public about the divorce or the royal supremacy. But everyone knew what he was thinking. Other prominent men were also known to be silent sympathisers with Catherine and the old religion. Some were in correspondence with the Emperor Charles V, Catherine's nephew and the champion of papal Christendom. Henry bullied, threatened and browbeat. One by one the recalcitrant bishops, abbots and laymen came to heel. But there remained a hard core of mute resistance and around it a grumbling and discontented populace. Henry demanded a more positive measure and in March 1534 parliament passed an Act requiring all adult males to swear an oath recognising the succession to the throne of the lawful issue of Henry and Anne. For More this was the sticking point. Implicit in the swearing of the oath was recognition of the legitimacy of the royal marriage and

Catherine of Aragon, by Michael Sittow

the divorce of Catherine and that meant agreeing that the king had been right in setting aside the authority of the pope. More would not take the oath and he was sent straight to the Tower. Later that year the Treason Act embraced all those who refused the oath and Thomas More's fate was sealed.

But we should not, perhaps, focus our attention on the well-known story of Thomas More. We can obtain a yet more vivid impression of the impact of the treason laws if we consider the cases of ordinary people all over the country who were informed against, examined, imprisoned, put on trial and frightened out of their wits as the royal agents sought to impress upon the populace the authority and power of the king.

Nicholas Heath, Prior of Lenton, was executed for saying, 'I hear say the King is now married and to one of the same generation as evil as the other Queen was before. The devil is in him, for he is past grace; he will never amend in this world. I warrant him [to] have as shameful a death as ever king had in England. A vengeance on him!'[33]

John Henmarshe, priest of Postington, Bedfordshire, was tried and condemned as a traitor for telling his congregation in 1536, 'Take ye heed what ye do, for the Lincolnshire men are up, and they come for a common wealth and a good intent, and their opinion is good and yours is nought.'[34]

Dr Robert Holdsworth, vicar of Halifax, was reported to Cromwell for uttering treasonable words: 'If the King reign any space he will take all from us of the Church that ever we have, and therefore I pray God send him a short reign; . . . upon Harry all England may weary.'[35] Cromwell apparently regarded the matter more lightly than the people of Halifax, for Holdsworth was dismissed with a caution.

The second half of Henry VIII's reign was, then, a time when people had to watch carefully lest their tongues should run away with them. They had to be careful, too, what enemies they made, for accusations could easily be aired and magistrates and royal agents were only too willing to show their zeal by sending up to London men and women of a 'proud stomach'.

7

'Which church is the very church?'

I. The Old Religion

As to the statement in my Epitaph that I was a source of trouble for heretics – I wrote that just to be smart. I find that breed of men absolutely loathsome, so much so that, unless they regain their senses, I want to be as hateful to them as anyone can possibly be; for my increasing experience with those men frightens me with the thought of what the world will suffer at their hands.[1]

So wrote More to his 'darling' Erasmus in the summer of 1533 and the character revealed by these words contrasts strongly with the urbane, devout, good-humoured Christian champion portrayed by Catholic hagiographers and modern playwrights. In fact, they point to the issue which increasingly dominated More's life, the issue which is central to any realistic description of sixteenth-century England: the conflict between the old religion and the new religion, in a word, the Reformation. An age like ours, which sets great store by tolerance (the eldest child of indifference), finds it hard to understand the passionate hatred More felt for heretics, a hatred based on contempt for their beliefs and fear of their growing influence.

It was the 1520s which witnessed what was for More and all Catholic leaders an alarming resurgence of heresy. In the universities and inns of court, excited students were already reading Erasmus's *Novum Instrumentum* with its implied questioning of traditional doctrines. Now they began to study inflammatory pamphlets and treatises by the German monk, Martin Luther, who did not hesitate to call the pope 'antichrist'. As if that were not bad enough, in 1526 the first edition of William Tyndale's English *New Testament* appeared and, despite fervent efforts at suppression, copies were smuggled all over the country by a secret and efficient colportage system. No other single book has made more impact on the course of English history. It made Holy Scripture for the first time available to all men and women who could read or who could gather in secret at the feet of one of the 'gospellers' who gave instruction from the new book. Tyndale's *Testament* contained glosses pointing out the errors into which the historic church had fallen. But for More and the Catholic world he represented it was the reformers who had fallen into catastrophic and heinous error: they had substituted the authority of the Bible for the authority of the church (by which was meant the papacy and the priesthood). More had always been dubious about the wisdom of making the Word of God available to the unlearned. In an early poem he had warned that only disaster could follow

> When an hatter will go smatter
> In philosophy,
> Or a pedlar wax a meddler
> In theology.[2]

He had even parted company with Erasmus over this issue. In the preface to his *Novum Instrumentum*, the Dutch scholar had affirmed: 'I should wish that all good wives read the Gospel and Paul's Epistles; that they were translated into all languages; that out of these the husbandman sang while ploughing, the weaver at his loom; that with such stories the traveller should beguile his wayfaring.' Erasmus, the pure scholar, believed that the transformation peacefully overtaking the academic world would overtake the whole of Christendom as men read and began to live by the Gospel. More was too much of a realist and too much of a conservative to follow his friend down this path.

More, as we have seen, was highly critical of ecclesiastical abuses but this was because he was passionately devoted to the concept of a united Christendom under papal leadership acting as a civilising, redemptive force in the world and, therefore, distressed by anything which marred it. Because the growing waves of heresy threatened to engulf the whole edifice of the medieval church More realised that he had to employ all his talents and influence in opposing it. He turned his back on the technique of dignified, scholarly debate as he explained to Erasmus:

> I am keenly aware of the risk involved in an open-door policy towards these newfangled, erroneous sects . . . some people like to give an approving eye to novel ideas, out of superficial curiosity, and to

dangerous ideas, out of devilry; and in so doing they assent to what
they read, not because they believe it is true, but because they want
it to be true . . . All my efforts are directed toward the protection of
those men who do not deliberately desert the truth, but are seduced
by the enticements of clever fellows.[3]

Thus, More the elegant man of letters, the radical humanist, became in
his forties More the reactionary, the hammer of the heretics.

His appointment as Chancellor provided him with a unique opportunity to bring the weight of the law to bear upon suspect men and
books, as he was very quick to see: 'The more I realise that this post
involves the interests of Christendom, my dearest Erasmus, the more I
hope it all turns out successfully.'[4] It did not. More found himself
hampered first of all by an anti-clerical House of Commons and then
by a king, whose conflict with the pope over the divorce obliged him to
seek the support of radical elements. Lacking parliamentary backing,
the Chancellor issued two proclamations which listed banned books
and obliged law officers and all others 'having governance of the
people' to take an oath before entering office to extirpate heresy and give
all assistance to the bishops in bringing suspected offenders to trial. If
this policy had been fully implemented England would have had her
own version of the Inquisition. As it was, for two years anti-heretical
activity reached a peak and rumours of persecution and torture (how
well founded it is difficult to know) abounded. One government agent
complained to Cromwell:

Would God the King would look to these punishments, which
threaten more hurt to the realm than the ministers who execute
them conjecture; for his subjects will be forced to leave the realm in
great numbers, and live in strange countries, where they will practise
not a little hurt to England. Instead of punishments, tortures and
death ridding the realm of erroneous opinions, and bringing men
into such fear that they will not be so hardy as to speak or look . . . it
will cause the sect in the end to wax greater. . . By driving men
away, they will make the company in strange countries greater, and
four will write where one wrote before.[5]

More found himself in increasing difficulty over his inability to give
the royal divorce proceedings his active support in Council and parliament, but it was the government's growing attack on the English
church which eventually rendered his position intolerable. In the
spring of 1532 Henry, with strong parliamentary backing, launched an
attack on the legislative powers of Convocation and the church courts.

The king thundered in the Commons against the clergy whom 'we thought ... had been our subjects wholly, but now we have well perceived that they be but half our subjects, yea, and scarce our subjects'. These were worrying days for More, as his friend Chapuys, the imperial ambassador, reported:

> Parliament is discussing the revocation of all synodal and other constitutions made by the English clergy, and the prohibition of holding synods without express licence from the King. This is a strange thing. Churchmen will be of less account than shoemakers, who have the power of assembling and making their own statutes. The King also wishes bishops not to have the power to lay hands on persons accused of heresy, saying that it is not their duty to meddle with bodies, and they are only doctors of the soul. The Chancellor and the bishops oppose him. He is very angry especially with the Chancellor and the Bishop of Winchester, and is determined to carry the matter.[6]

On 15 May the southern Convocation was bullied into resigning its legislative independence. Two days later Thomas More resigned the Great Seal.

This did not signal the end of the battle. More had been forced to lay down some of his weapons but he now wielded with all his might the one he had left. It was in 1528 that he had yielded to the persuasion of his friend Cuthbert Tunstall, Bishop of London:

> Because you, dearest brother, can rival Demosthenes in our vernacular as well as in Latin, and are a frequent and brilliant advocate of the Catholic position whenever it is publicly challenged, you will never find a better way of spending any leisure hours you can snatch away from your official duties than in publishing in English for the common man some books that would help him see through the cunning malice of heretics and so keep him alerted and better fortified against these traiterous subverters of the church.[7]

More set to work immediately and for the remainder of his life he spared neither time nor effort in waging literary warfare on the heretics. Between 1528 and 1534 he produced seven major works of Catholic polemic; some of it couched in the polished, urbane prose of which he was a master; some of it expressed in the gutter language of unrestrained controversy; all of it burning with zeal for the cause More had found so late in life. And that cause was the preservation of the traditional church with all its teachings, institutions and customs.

All the whole churche from the beginning this XV C yere hath belieued that good workes wrought in faith, hope and charity, shall be rewarded in heauen, and that it is well done to go in pilgrimages, and to pray to saintes, and to pray for all christen soules, and that the prayour and [charitable] deedes of good christen folke here, doth helpe to relieue the soules in the paynes of purgetory, that the very blessed body and blood of Christ is in the sacrament of the aulter, and that therfore it is ther to be honoured, and that no person professing and vowing chastitie, may for hys pleasure lawefully breake his vow and wedde.[8]

The greater part of More's contribution to the literary war was made after May 1532 and he expressed himself most fully in his exchanges with Tyndale.[9] There was no common ground between the protagonists. Tyndale argued for an invisible church of individuals saved by their faith in Christ as revealed in Scripture. More believed that salvation was only possible in and through membership of the historic church and obedience to its leaders. From these platforms More and Tyndale pelted each other with proof texts from the Bible and the Fathers, with subtle argument and unsubtle abuse. It was a dialogue of the deaf and Tyndale's complaint about his adversary could just as well have been turned against himself: 'I have answered you unto that and many things more . . . against which ye reply not, but keep your tune, and unto all things sing cuckoo, cuckoo, "We are the Church and cannot err".'[10]

This is not the place to analyse the arguments on both sides nor to outline the major events of the English Reformation. What we must try to do is to see the two churches, the two communities, the two ideologies which confronted each other. We start with the old, traditional church. To obtain a vivid picture of just what it meant to be a good sixteenth-century Catholic let us go in imagination into a large bedchamber in a substantial house on the edge of London. In that room Sir John Skevington, a wealthy merchant, lies dying. He has been told the end is near. He has composed his mind and is ready to face the unknown. All his affairs are in order but Sir John, being a careful, methodical person, wishes to make sure that every provision has been made for his soul's repose and for his family. So the priests and kinsmen are asked to withdraw and the old knight listens attentively while his lawyer itemises the contents of his long will.

To the Crossed Friars for the new building of their conventual church, £50; for a marble tomb, with my image and that of my wife, if she chooses to be buried there, with our children at the feet, £40; to the high altar of St Michael's, Cornhill, for tithes forgotten while I lived in the parish, 20s; to the high altar of St Mary Wolnoth, Lombard Street, where I am now a parishioner, 20s ... for new casting the roof in the middle aisle of St Mary Wolnoth, £10 ... to Christopher Stevynson, parish priest of St Mary Wolnoth, to pray for my soul, 20s; to old Agnes Dycar, to pray for my soul, 6s 8d ... to the parish church of Skevington [Leics] where I was born, a vestment, etc, with my arms or the cross, worth £6 13s 4d; to our Lady of Bradley in Leicestershire, a white damask vestment, with like arms, worth 53s 4d ... to the Grey, Black, Augustin and White Friars of London, to pray for my soul, and bring my body to burial, £8 ... To the houses of the Friars Observant at Greenwich and Richmond, 40s ...[11]

Then there were the heavy expenses of a lavish funeral to be provided for – black gowns for relatives, friends and neighbours, poor people to follow the coffin and pray for the deceased, mortuary dues, sombre coverings for the bier, candles (which were to be distributed to various churches after the funeral). Only when he was sure he had discharged all his religious obligations could Sir John turn with an easy mind to the business of making provision for his wife and children.

The church was a monumental institution far more real to English men and women than the machinery of royal government. It was absolute in time and space for it extended as far as they knew over all this world and, through the communion of saints, it was co-extensive with the world to come. In England it owned between a third and a fifth of all the landed wealth. Its cathedrals, episcopal palaces and abbeys were the finest buildings in the land, easily dwarfing the residences of kings, dukes and earls. In jewels and plate, bedecked shrines and ornate reliquaries it surpassed the combined riches of all the monarchs of Europe. Its personnel were ubiquitous and its organisation touched the life of the realm at every level. The Archbishop of Canterbury and several other higher clergy were as much officers of state as leaders of the church.

The rulers of the great religious houses and the bishops' officers were among the leaders of county society, regularly hunting and exchanging hospitality with the nobles and gentlemen. Ecclesiastical courts, touching, as they did, matters of matrimony, probate of wills and disputes involving clergy, were closer to most Englishmen than royal courts. Itinerant friars and pardoners were as familiar on the roads as pedlars and highwaymen. And, of course, every town and village was dominated by the regular pattern of Sunday and saint's day worship centred on its parish church. Even if the priest was an unlettered, rural clod or an indigent curate put in by an absentee incumbent he nevertheless possessed the grace of orders, could make God in the mass and pray for souls in purgatory. From him ran a direct chain of command which ended in Rome with the one who held the keys of heaven and hell.

The devotion of some Englishmen to this church was total. They believed in the priestly miracle, the efficacy of masses and of prayers to the saints as implicitly as they believed in Black Shuck, Robin Goodfellow and witchcraft. Those who wished to ensure their soul's salvation took the only certain road to heaven which began at the main gate of a monastery or nunnery. The majority of the devout contented themselves with faithful attendance at mass, liberal contributions to the upkeep and rebuilding of their parish churches, and charity towards friars and other mendicants.

But there was a growing number of critics who found intolerable the obvious gap between what the church preached and what it practised. Avarice, sexual licence, ignorance, tactlessness and inefficiency were not confined to ecclesiastical representatives but when those representatives exhorted others to holy living, heard confessions and threatened to withhold divine grace, this was more than some Englishmen could bear. They complained, they grumbled, sometimes they became violent. A few, a very few, gave their allegiance to the 'other church', that underground society of Lollards, Lutherans and miscellaneous heretics which had thrown off once and for all the old authority of the pope and his minions and replaced it with an allegiance to the written word of God. Heretical groups were growing in size and number but they would remain a small minority until the 1530s, when the king himself joined the ranks of those who challenged the authority of the pope. And the reason why even the most disgruntled anti-clerical did not join the heretics was fear of the spiritual power of the priesthood.

The church's most important role in Tudor society was that of gatekeeper at the portal of death. The average parishioner had little interest in the niceties of religion. He attended mass on Sundays and saints' days. He received communion once or twice a year. He went to confession with greater or lesser regularity. He fasted in Lent and attended the major festivals and processions. He put the occasional coin in the friars' alms-dish. Perhaps once or twice in his life he would make a journey to gaze on the celebrated relics or shrines of the saints, although a new scepticism had done much to undermine the devotion which had once impelled men to 'goon on pilgrimages'. For the rest, he was content to leave religion to the professionals – the rector, the chantry priest and the monk.

But death, either his own or that of his loved ones, was another matter. Death and its aftermath were ever-present realities and familiarity in this instance certainly did not breed contempt. Only a minority died of old age. Every family had buried new-born children. Every parish church had on its walls the sad, fading circlets of flowers that betokened the death of virgins. Funerals were the most frequent of all the occasional services. Should any man ever forget the need to pray for the departed or to make provision for his own demise the church was ever zealous to remind him. Lurid 'dooms' were depicted on most chancel arches which showed Christ the Judge calling forth men from their graves at the general resurrection. Some were carried by white-robed angels into eternal bliss, but others were handed over to hideous demons to be cast into the everlasting flames of hell. The books of sermons used by parish clergy were stuffed with anecdotes designed to recall trembling parishioners to a consideration of their eternal well-being.

It happened also beside the abbey of Lilleshall that four men stale an ox of the abbot's of the same place to their larder. And the abbot did a sentence cursed therefore, with the abbey; so three of them were shriven and asked mercy and were assoiled, but the fourth died and was not assoiled and had not forgiveness. So, when he was dead, the spirit went by night and feared all the people about, that after sun going down durst no man walk. Then, as the parish priest went on a night with God's body to housel a sick man, this spirit went with him, and told him what he was and why he went, and prayed the priest to go to his wife, and they should go both to the abbot and make him amends for his trespass, and pray him for the love of God of forgiveness, and so to assoil him; for he might have no rest. Anon the abbot assoiled him, and he went to rest and joy for evermore.[12]

There were many ways a man might ensure his eternal salvation and minimise the duration of his stay in purgatory. A good and charitable life was valuable but far more important was his devotion to the church which, for all practical purposes, meant the religious establishment. He must pay his tithes and other dues faithfully, he must receive communion regularly, not doubting but that after the miracle of the mass the bread and wine were really changed into the body and blood of Christ.

He must pay priests and monks to pray for his soul, for great was the effectiveness of the petitions of men who were holy, not by the piety of their lives but by virtue of the grace of orders. He must make offerings to the shrines of saints and contribute to the work of the church.

Therefore, the people of England bought masses for the dead and installed chantry priests to pray perpetually for themselves and their families. Therefore Sir John Skevington left a considerable sum of money to various churches and religious houses. Therefore, John Roger of Otford bequeathed money to the parish church for the maintenance of 'sevyn pounde tapers five of them before our Ladye and one before the ymage of Saynte Thomas'.[13] And, therefore, parishioners grudgingly paid their ecclesiastical dues and made provision in their wills for 'tithes and oblations forgotten'.

Tithes and payments for specific services were the principal sources of clerical income and they were widely resented. The tithe was a tax of ten per cent on a man's annual profit from his labours. It might be collected in cash or kind and was payable direct to the incumbent. Where a benefice was held by a religious house the crops and offerings had to be brought to the great tithe barn where they were meticulously checked off in the steward's register. No man, be he householder, tenant or servant, rich or poor, rejoicing in a good harvest or acutely suffering the effects of a bad one, was exempt from tithing. The tax was established by canon law and scrupulously exacted by the clergy (who often relied on it for their sustenance). The parish priest of St Peter's, Nottingham, was hauled before the constables by his angry flock 'for ower sessyng of poor foulkes and menes servantes at Estur for theyr tyes and other duttes' and the parson of Swainsthorpe, Norfolk, rode round the parish to collect tithes with his reputed mistress riding pillion behind him.[14] Nothing caused more anger in rural and urban society than punctilious and tactless collection of tithes. Clergy whose own glebe land was farmed in a lackadaisical manner were not well regarded when they claimed their share of the crops of more diligent neighbours. Frequently clergy and monastic agents were mishandled. But protest was always useless, for the church had the whip hand. Behind the parish priest was the ecclesiastical court and always there was the ultimate sanction of the curse, solemnly pronounced with cross, burning taper and tolling bell before the whole congregation.

By the authority of the Father and of the Son and of the Holy Ghost and of our Lady St Mary God's Mother of heaven, and all other Virgins, and St Michael and all other Angels, and St Peter and all other Apostles, and St Stephen and all other Martyrs, and St Nicholas and all other Confessors, and of all the holy Saints of heaven; we accursen and bannen and departen from all good deeds and prayers of Holy Church, and of all these Saints, and damn into the pain of hell, all those that have done these articles that we have said before, till they come to amendment: we accursen them by the authority of the court of Rome, within and without, sleeping or walking, going and sitting, standing and riding, lying above earth and under earth, speaking and crying and drinking; in wood, in water, in field, in town; accursen them Father and Son and Holy Ghost! accursen them Angels and Archangels and all the nine Orders of Heaven! accursen them Patriarchs, Prophets and Apostles and all God's Disciples and all holy Innocents, Martyrs, Confessors, Virgins, Monks, Canons, Hermits, Priests and Clerks! that they have no part of mass nor matins nor of none other good prayers that be done in holy church nor in none other places, but that the pains of hell be their meed with Judas that betrayed our Lord Jesus Christ! and the life of them be put out of the book of life till they come to amendment and satisfaction made! *Fiat, fiat. Amen.*'[15]

The spirit world touched Tudor England at many points, peopling it with hobgoblins, ghosts, familiars and demons who were as instantly recognisable to the parishioner as the man standing next to him in church. Such a curse was real and terrible to him indeed and vested the priest, whatever might be his shortcomings, with awful power. The urbane Erasmus might complain of those who preyed on the gullibility of the superstitious masses but hardly a one dared to stand up to pedlars of extravagant curses and spurious miracles:

The next to be placed among the regiment of fools are such as made a trade of telling or inquiring after incredible stories of miracles and prodigies: never doubting that a lie will choke them, they will muster up a thousand strange relations of spirits, ghosts, apparitions, raising of the devil, and such like bugbears of superstition, which the farther they are from being probably true, the more greedily they are swallowed, and the more devoutly believed. And these absurdities do not only bring an empty pleasure, and cheap divertisement, but they are a good trade, and procure a comfortable income to such priests and friars as by this craft get their gain.[16]

Scarcely less burdensome – and certainly more distressing – than tithes were mortuary dues. When a parishioner died the priest had a claim to a not inconsiderable fee. It usually took the form of the best animal or the best gown. When, as sometimes happened, the parson called for payment upon a family in bitter mourning, ill-feeling ran high. The taking of the best animal often caused real hardship. Sometimes the best animal was the only animal.

These were the main charges made by the church on the Tudor purse. But there were others. Four times a year the priest received an 'oblation' or free-will offering. He could charge for weddings, churchings and funerals and even for confessions and taking communion to the sick. There were other circumstances which an enterprising priest could turn to good account. The desire of a wealthy parishioner to be buried in the chancel might be granted for a consideration. Dispensations for infringements of canon law might similarly be obtained for a fee: 'for a licence to remain in marriage contracted in ignorance within the third and fourth degree of affinity, 23s 4d'; 'To contract matrimony in the fourth degree of consanguinity, 23s 4d'; 'for marriage without bans, 20s'.[17]

That Englishman was fortunate indeed who did not at some stage of his life encounter the exactions and delays of the church courts. The inefficiency and partiality of ecclesiastical justice aroused enormous bitterness. One writer colourfully described the archbishop's court as 'the filthy quake-mire and poisoned plash of all the abominations that do infect the whole realm' and the commissaries' court as 'a petty little stinking ditch that floweth out of that former great puddle, robbing Christ's Church of lawful pastors, of watchful seniors and elders, and careful deacons'.[18]

In 1521 a marriage contract was drawn up between Henry Byrd of Coventry and Marjery Pysford, who was at that time under age. It was a marriage of convenience, concerned more with lands than affections. But Marjery was a strong-willed girl. When, later, she fell in love with William Norton she gave herself to him (or as the official documents put it she 'unlawful contracted marriage *de facto*' with him). The angry Byrd went to the Archbishop of Canterbury's court and obtained letters inhibitorial to prevent the solemnisation of the liaison. William and Marjery counteracted by eloping. At the chapel of Temple Grafton they bribed or conned a lax priest into marrying them without calling banns or obtaining a licence from their own rector.

But Byrd had not given up; he cited the couple before John Cocks, a canon lawyer, in the bishop's court. With the aid of witnesses he proved his case to Cocks's satisfaction – a task made easier by the non-appearance of the runaways. The bishop's officers apprehended

William and Marjery and the girl was placed in the custody of Julian Nethermyll, Mayor of Coventry. She ran away to Leicester, was caught again and entrusted to the keeping of William Wygeston, worthy of that town. He proved as unable as Nethermyll to hold the spirited girl and we next find the star-crossed lovers in London.

Byrd was relentless. He tracked them down and obtained a third sequestration order. This time Marjery was held on pain of excommunication at John Heryng's house in Paternoster Row. Cocks now determined the case 'finally' (he had already taken a couple of years to give judgement). The relationship between William and Marjery was pronounced adulterous and Marjery's contract to Henry legally valid.

All was not lost. There existed a cumbersome system of appeal which William and Marjery now set in motion. They persuaded Miles Spencer, Canon of York, to obtain from Rome a commission empowering Geoffrey Wharton, Canon of St Paul's, to re-examine the case. Several anxious months later, Wharton had all the contestants and their witnesses before him and reconsidered the affair. Alas for William and Marjery, Wharton only confirmed Cocks's judgement.

The young couple had now lived together as husband and wife (though in something rather less than settled domesticity) for four years. They were happy together. They hated the belligerent Byrd and his clerical friends and they simply refused to accept an ecclesiastical law which would separate them because of a piece of paper written when Marjery was no more than a child. They now appealed to the Rota, the supreme court. Pending the consideration of their case by the holy doctors in Rome, they obtained letters of inhibition preventing Cocks and Byrd from proceeding further.

And that is virtually the last we hear of the case. Four years later all parties were still awaiting a decision from the ponderous and overworked Roman court. William and Marjery continued to live together, though as far as their neighbours and their priest were concerned their relationship was adulterous. They were denied the comforts of holy church. Their children (and by this time there presumably were children) could not be baptised. They had spent a great deal of money in legal fees and probably more in greasing the palms of officials who promised to expedite their business. And all for nothing. Henry VIII was not the only one whose matrimonial problems were intolerably exaggerated by the Roman church.

The canon law provided that crack in the church's shell into which the Reformation wedge was hammered. The operation of the ecclesiastical courts was so blatantly cumbersome and corrupt that even dedicated churchmen called for reform. By 1530 most of the bishops were scholars who had qualified at the inns of court where the civil lawyers were jealous of their own traditions and resentful of a rival code which exempted clergy from prosecution in the royal courts and which controlled large areas of jurisprudence. When the crisis came, there was little opposition from the bench to the breach with Rome. It was only giving concrete form to the absolute supremacy of royal power which all the bishops acknowledged.

And what of the religious life proper? Monks and nuns had always been admired by one section of the community and hated by another. There was nothing very remarkable about Simon Fish's scurrilous broadsheet, *The Supplication of Beggars*, which advised the king,

> Set these sturdy loobies abroad in the world, to get them wives of their own, to get their living with their labour in the sweat of their faces, according to the commandment of God . . .
>
> Tie these holy, idle thieves to the carts, to be whipped naked about every market town, till they fall to labour, that they by their importunate begging, take not away the alms that the good Christian people would give unto us, sore, impotent, miserable people, your beadmen.[19]

The same opinions would have been expressed two centuries earlier by the people of Bury St Edmunds who, at the culmination of a summer of fearful violence, virtually razed the abbey to the ground, murdered many of the monks and rampaged through twenty-two abbatial manors. Stories of monastic immorality, debauchery and perversion were always swapped in alehouses and there was persistent resentment at those whose stout walls and grasping bailiffs protected them from harsh economic reality.

In fact, there was some justification for the complaint that the religious had fallen away from the stringent observance of their founders' rules. In 1524 Wolsey called the rulers of all the Benedictine houses to a conference in London and intimated that certain reforms in their pattern of life and worship were long overdue. In their cautious reply they agreed that some of the Cardinal's suggestions should be followed up. Others, however, were 'too austere for these times'. Any attempt to carry through all the measures Wolsey demanded might drive the weaker brethren into flight, apostasy or rebellion and would certainly deter others from entering the order. It was, they said, diffi-cult to keep their houses filled without fresh difficulties being put in the way of recruits – 'now the world is drawing to its end, very few desire to live an austere life'.[20]

It is easy to point to flagrant instances of corruption, laziness or over-indulgence, and just as easy to quote examples of holy, disciplined living. What is important is that the spirit had gone out of monasticism. Most of the vast, cavernous abbey churches echoed to the chanting of dwindling choirs. Between 1500 and 1534 the approximate number of religious in England and Wales fell from 12,000 to 11,000. By the time of the dissolution many houses had less than five inmates. In some establishments inefficient accounting had wasted the endowments so that the communities could no longer feed and clothe themselves. A number of small foundations were closed during Henry VII's reign and Wolsey dissolved twenty-nine houses in order to endow his new colleges at Oxford and Ipswich.

Dwindling monastic numbers made the disproportionate distribution of wealth even more noticeable. Vast abbeys were maintained by considerable staffs for the benefit of a handful of monks. At Butley Priory there lived 12 canons. They were served by 2 chaplains, 11 domestic servants, a master of the children (to look after a small school for 7 children), 3 cooks, one slaughterman, one sacristan, one cooper, 3 bakers, 3 brewers, 2 horse-keepers, 2 maltsters, one porter, 6 laundresses, 2 bedemen and 34 estate workers. The monasteries certainly laid out some of their income in alms, hospitality, education and care of the sick but such disbursements bore no relation to the sums expended on maintaining their state.

The secular clergy also used the church's money in ways which showed a disregard of public opinion. Plurality and absenteeism were the rule rather than the exception. Well-endowed benefices were given by religious and secular patrons as rewards or payments for faithful service. Their recipients were not expected actually to reside in their cures and tend the souls committed to their charge. They would be teaching at the universities or serving as chaplains, tutors or clerical staff in great households. The parish work was left to curates who were poor, ill-qualified and only too happy to accept a pittance for their inadequate talents. Not all benefices, however, were sufficiently well-endowed to make attractive gifts for ambitious place-seekers. The majority would support only a humble, poorly educated class of peasant-priests. As Archbishop Lee of York complained to Cromwell,

Many benefices be so poor, £4, £5, £6, that no learned man will take them, and therefore we be forced to take such as be presented, as long as they be honest of conversation and can competently understand what they read and minister sacraments and sacramentals, observing the due form and right. . . And in all my diocese I do not know secular priests that can preach, any number necessary for such a diocese, truly not twelve, and they that have the best benefices be not here resident.[21]

The reason for the poverty of most livings was the dwindling value of ancient endowments, exacerbated by the early Tudor price rise. Nothing illustrates this more clearly than the many reports of dilapidated chancels. This part of the parish church was the financial responsibility of the incumbent, who in most cases simply could not afford to meet his commitments. In every locality there were churches whose chancels had broken windows, gaping roofs or even more serious structural defects. The problem was even more pointed by the spate of church rebuilding which went on in the fourteenth and fifteenth centuries (see below, pp. 208–9). Wealthy congregations, especially those of wool-rich East Anglia and the West Country, spent thousands of pounds enlarging, embellishing and furnishing their parish churches as never before. New naves, towers, porches, side aisles, chapels and chantries were raised by the wealth and piety of the laity but the splendid buildings thus created were often attached to chancels which were crumbling and weather-beaten eyesores.

At the other end of the ecclesiastical scale were the bishops who lived in a style many people considered excessive. True, they were leaders of society, expected to offer hospitality to ambassadors, nobles and princes. True, they needed several residences if they were to travel round their dioceses effectively. But the extravagance of their building programmes and their retinues could not fail to excite comment.

Archbishop Warham was certainly not another Wolsey. On the contrary, he was a man of holy and simple life, an ascetic, a scholar and a close personal friend of Erasmus and More. Yet Warham did not think it at all incongruous that he should embark, in 1514, on the building of a spacious new palace. The moated edifice which grew rapidly under an army of masons, carpenters and glaziers eventually sprawled over four and a half Kentish acres. An impressive though irregular conglomerate of towers, courtyards, imposing gateways, great hall, soaring chapel, state rooms, domestic offices, stables, privy garden, galleries, walks and arbours, it cost Warham about £30,000 and was sufficiently grand to arouse the envy of the king, who confiscated it in 1537. What must have piqued the local people was the fact that this splendid new archiepiscopal palace of Otford was only three miles away from Warham's equally magnificent establishment at Knole.[22]

None of these abuses was new. They were of the kind endemic to all religious establishments which can rely on the loving respect – or, failing that, the fear – of the masses. But the spirit of the times was changing. There was a new independence of thought abroad. The church could no longer assume that the people would tolerate in blind faith what common sense told them to be wrong.

Few Englishmen had any clear idea of what they believed. Christianity was, for them, a rag-bag of doctrines and stories culled from scripture, the lives of the saints, popular legends and spurious miracles. And the miraculous was of first importance; it validated the whole sacramental system of the church.

It was alarming to Colet and his men of the 'new learning' that the doctrine of transubstantiation should be open to grossly materialistic interpretations which, once shown up for empty superstition, might destroy the credibility of the church in the popular imagination. No less worrying was the common devotion to 'miracle-working' images, shrines and altars. Every church was stuffed with statues of the Virgin and other saints before which burned eternally a multitude of votive candles. The walls were daubed with pictures of St Nicholas, St George, St Catherine and allegorical scenes, vying in colourful profusion with the riot of stained glass. These were supposedly the 'books of the unlearned' which, in default of systematic teaching from the clergy, were to impart to them the fundamentals of the faith. In fact, they had become objects of devotion in themselves. Peasants made their prayers to these representations of the Virgin and the saints and looked to them for signs of favour.

Many shrines and tombs were revered for their miraculous properties. In an age when medicine was rudimentary and there was no relief from pain whatsoever it is not surprising that Somerset toothache sufferers should resort to the tomb of the thirteenth-century Bishop Bytton in Wells Cathedral for a cure. There was, perhaps, less excuse for the London ladies who offered oats to the statue of St Uncumber in St Paul's: this spurious saint reputedly had the power to remove unwanted husbands. The shrines and altars were kept in good repair by collections, donations and bequests. At Prescot, Lancs, there were eight collections a year for lights before the images of SS. Katherine, Stephen and Anthony.[23] In larger parishes church workers were grouped into guilds (not to be confused with urban and trade guilds): friendly societies which, as well as organising poor relief, kept up the fabric of the church and, particularly, cared for the shrines to which they were dedicated. Many churches, as well as abbeys, possessed relics which were still greatly treasured. They varied from the famous precious blood of Hailes (a phial of the Saviour's blood which, miraculously, never dried out) and Reading Abbey's armoury of 242 relics, to the head of St Lawrence owned by Croston parish church (Lancs) of which the beneficent owners had presented a fragment to Chorley chapel.[24]

The Tudor parishioner lived in the world of tangible things; he was less comfortable, less secure in the world of ideas. Until the Reformation the grace of God was mediated to him through material objects – consecrated bread, holy relics, images and altars. Things were the vehicles of his devotion – candles, rosaries and offerings in money or kind. When those things were removed by zealous reformers crusading against 'superstition', he was confused. The familiar externals of religion were more important to him than the doctrines which were the underlying cause of that religion.

The dominating external was the parish church. It soared above the village, as permanent as the peasants' lath and plaster hovels were impermanent, as painstakingly and lovingly built as their dwellings were hastily thrown up, as beautified and adorned as the parishioners' houses were starkly functional. The contrast was so complete that it was natural for the villager to believe that the smoky, incense-pervaded interior, where the freshly-painted blue and gold of the madonna's robe glowed mysteriously in dim light filtered through stained glass, was the very threshold of heaven. The people were proud of their churches. These sacred edifices had been built and added to by their fathers and fathers' fathers over countless generations. They were permanent memorials to devotion and sacrifice.

On St Matthew's Day (21 September) 1536 royal subsidy commissioners visited St James's church, Louth. A servant of one of the king's men tactlessly remarked that the fine silver alms-dish would make a suitable present for their liege lord. Within the hour the news was all round the town that the king intended to despoil the parish churches of all their treasures. Angry, anxious crowds appeared in the streets, for the men of Louth were very sensitive about St James's. Well within the memory of most of them was that summer's day of feasting and thanksgiving when 'William Ayleby, parish priest, with many of his brethren priests, hallowed the ... weathercock and the stone that it stands upon ... and then the priests sang *Te Deum Laudamus*, with organs and the churchwardens rang all the bells, and caused all the

The Old Religion: many aspects of traditional devotion were stoutly maintained throughout most of the period. Monasteries continued to produce beautiful illuminated service books. Most parish churches had a 'doom' painted over the chancel arch warning worshippers of the day of judgement. The state could sometimes be relied upon to dispose of troublesome heretics

people there present to have bread and ale.'[25] That day in 1515 had seen the culmination of fourteen years of work, prayer and sacrifice. At a cost of £305 8s 5d the soaring 295-foot spire had been built and that was only the crowning achievement of decades of repairing, rebuilding and redecorating which had made St James's, Louth, one of the most beautiful churches in Lincolnshire. Despite the assurances of the commissioners, the conviction persisted that King Henry was bent on spoliation. At the Michaelmas procession one of the singing men urged his neighbours, 'Go ye and follow the crosses, for if they be taken from us, we are like to follow them no more.'[26] Four days later Louth rose in revolt. It was the beginning of the Pilgrimage of Grace.

The reigns of the first two Tudors saw the accomplishment of some magnificent churches. Indeed, no other period in our history has seen such a spate of church building. In the Perpendicular Gothic style masons and carpenters seem almost to have combined air with stone and wood, to have carved light and engraved space. Slender columns of Purbeck marble foliated into exuberant fan tracery. Wide clerestory windows trapped sunlight in their panes.

Some of the parish churches enlarged or rebuilt at this time were grandiose. In 1485 the lord of the manor of Lavenham, in wool-wealthy Suffolk, was John de Vere, Earl of Oxford who, as Captain-General, had just won the battle of Bosworth for Henry of Richmond. Visiting the parish soon afterwards he suggested to the burgesses that, as a thank offering to Almighty God for the great victory, they might like to rebuild their church. Enthusiastically the merchants, under the leadership of rich clothier Thomas Spryng, took up the idea. Work began almost immediately. Down came the fourteenth-century nave and the people of Lavenham worshipped in the chancel for many years while the building work went ahead. A new, massive tower began to grow on the ancient site above the village and only when it had settled could the new nave be keyed into it. It took forty years to build SS. Peter and Paul, Lavenham, the finest Perpendicular parish church in England. Before it was completed, de Vere and Spryng, both of whom had contributed handsomely towards it, were dead. Even Spryng's son, another Thomas, did not live to see the accomplishment of a work in which he had been closely involved. He and the men of his generation built slowly and surely and they built for the future. Theirs was the dedication of those who work for a far higher aim than their own satisfaction. When Thomas Spryng came to make his will in 1523 he instructed that he was to be buried 'in the Church of Lavenh'm before the Awter of St Kateryn where I will be made a Tombe with a Parclose

thereabout at the discretion of myn executors.' The parclose is there to
this day with its carved emblems – Catherine's wheel and Spryng's
wool mark. Also there is the beautiful lady chapel for which the clothier left a large sum of money, and round the parapet the inscription
'Pray for the souls of Thomas Spryng Esq., and of Alice his wife, who
caused this chapel to be built in the year of our Lord, 1525.'

While local pride reared fine new churches and ensured a following
for local saints, the great days of national pilgrimage were over. The
changing attitude which the Christian humanists both exemplified and
feared was already displaying itself in a growing scepticism. In the first
year of its existence (1220) £1142 had been offered at the shrine of St
Thomas in Canterbury. In 1535 the income was £36. This pattern was
repeated at all other ancient centres of pilgrimage except Walsingham.

The new scepticism was a characteristic of a new breed of
Englishman – the literate layman. Before Caxton established his press
in London books were handwritten, they were expensive and they were
in Latin. Even the scholar's horizon was limited by problems of the
cost and availability of his raw material. By the early years of the
sixteenth century vernacular books were pouring forth in a flood (fifty-
four new titles in 1500; 700 published between 1492 and 1535 by
Wynkyn de Worde alone). Every man prepared to con his letters might
now set forth on a seemingly limitless voyage of discovery. The excitement and zest this brought into life can scarcely be imagined.

> Bliss was it in that dawn to be alive
> But to be young was very heaven.

So wrote Wordsworth about the exhilarating effect of political freedom
in the early days of the French Revolution. The impact of novel,
liberating ideas on More's generation was just as thrilling.

New knowledge, new learning was available. Old knowledge could
be, must be, questioned. Colet and his friends were aware of this
movement. They welcomed it, for they believed the church had nothing to fear from the truth. What was essential, in their view, was that
the church should keep up with the new movement. That meant that
the clergy must be better educated. William Melton, a close friend and
confidant of Colet's, put the issue clearly to ordinands in 1509.

> . . . the chief remedy against idle sloth is the constant reading and
> conning of the books of the laws of God and of the Scriptures, which
> holy fathers and teachers before us have published. In their works,
> which are now plentiful in print, even the moderately learned can

gain a pleasant solace of various kinds. Such study belongs to the true priestly art. Every craftsman who uses his hands has, besides the stall for his wares outside, a workshop for his craft within, and if he does not work diligently in it for many days, he will not easily earn for himself through his craft the necessities of life; similarly, besides the temples and the shrines of God, in which by daily prayer and psalms we, as it were, display our wares to passers by, we must make useof our inner workshop or study with sacred reading and teaching, that we may become rich in learning and have no lack of the necessities of life eternal. . . Nor may we have any other source to expound to the people the holy consolation of God's Word.[27]

Alas for pious hopes. Forty years later Bishop Hooper examined the 311 clergy of his Gloucester diocese: 168 could not recite the Ten Commandments and thirty-three could not locate them in the Bible. Ten could not recite the Lord's Prayer, thirty-nine did not know where to find it in the Bible and thirty-four did not know who its author was. Between 1500 and 1550, 869 East Anglian clergy died leaving wills to be proved in the consistory court at Norwich. A study of these wills yields the following statistics relating to the education of the clergy: only 158 possessed any books at all, fifty-eight owned only service books, seventy-nine had collections of sermons and anthologies of sermon illustrations (of the 'miraculous' type). Only seventeen clergy had Bibles to bequeath.

Of course, there were always glowing exceptions to the rule, saints and mystics whose lives of meditation and service were an inspiration to thousands. The fifteenth century witnessed the spread of an influential spiritual movement, the *Devotio Moderna*, throughout much of northern Europe. Contemporary and earlier works of devotion were now available in print for the first time. (Thomas à Kempis's *Imitation of Christ*, for example, was among the first books to be printed. It appeared at Augsburg, *c.* 1471–2.) For him who had ears to hear, prophetic voices were not infrequently raised proclaiming the necessity of personal devotion and warning against reliance on ritual. There was, therefore, nothing 'new' about the spiritual content of the reformers' message. Nor were the theological issues raised by the Reformation novel. Such problems as the authority of Scripture and tradition had been debated by orthodox Catholic academics for centuries.

But never before had mystical, hortatory and academic elements coalesced into a movement. The Christian humanists, for all their devotion to the new learning, believed themselves to be standing in a perfectly respectable tradition of Catholic protest. Erasmus had no conception that he was setting his shoulder to the wheel of revolution when he published his *Novum Instrumentum* or advocated in his *Enchiridion Militi Christi*: 'Perhaps you sacrifice every day and yet you live to yourself. You worship the saints, you like to touch their relics; do you want to earn Peter and Paul? Then copy the faith of the one and the charity of the other and you will have done more than if you had walked to Rome ten times.'[28] Most of Erasmus's writings were intended for the international community of scholars who, by reason and reflection on scripture, should lead the church into a golden age of enlightenment. Yet it was the *Novum Instrumentum* which set Thomas Bilney, Cambridge's first Protestant martyr, on the road to the stake, and the scholar who translated the *Enchiridion* into English was William Tyndale.

When did Thomas More first begin to be fearful of the direction in which the humanist impulse was pushing Christendom? Was it when he saw known Lollards flocking to Colet's sermons and agreeing enthusiastically with the preacher? Was it when he read in the preface to the *Novum Instrumentum* Erasmus's ambition that the words of scripture should be available

> ... for the ploughboy to sing them to himself as he follows the plough, the weaver to hum them to the tune of his shuttle, the traveller to beguile with them the dullness of his journey. . . . Other studies we may regret having undertaken, but happy is the man upon whom death comes when he is engaged in these. The sacred words give you the very image of Christ speaking, healing, dying, rising again, and make him so present, that were he before your very eyes you would not more truly see him.

These were the marks of that other church, that persecuted – and, in More's view, rightly persecuted – congregation of heretics which was growing alarmingly. There was never any question in More's mind that heretics might be tolerated. No more than any other man in Tudor England did Thomas More believe in complete freedom of the individual conscience. 'I pray God that some of us, as high as we seem to sit upon mountains, treading heretics under our feet like ants, live not the day that we gladly would wish to be at league and composition with them, to let them have their churches quietly to themselves so that they would be content to let us have ours quietly to ourselves.'[29]

It is to those other 'churches' that we must now turn our attention.

8

'Which church is the very church?'

II. Lollards and Protestants

ANY STREAMS poured into the river of the English
Reformation. Traditional devotion, anti-clericalism, humanism and the political issues attending Henry VIII's divorce,
all added to the flow of revolutionary ideas and events. But the main
tributaries were Lollardy and continental Protestantism.

The Lollard 'church', the secret church which based its beliefs on
the English Bible and the teachings of Wycliffe, had been in existence
for over a hundred years and had successfully resisted many sporadic
outbreaks of persecution. Its members were to be found in most parts
of the country – numerous enough in some places, such as Kent, Essex
and the Chilterns, to dominate whole communities; appearing in others
only as isolated, inward-looking cliques.

Who were these men and women, these strange, earnest folk dismissed by their neighbours as Lollards, those who 'lolled' or muttered
their beliefs to each other? There was Henry Tuck, a Bristol wine-
drawer who had learned the book of Revelation off by heart. There was
wealthy Richard Sanders of Amersham and his wife Alice. Woe betide
any who crossed them in religion: for informing on suspected Lollards
to the bishop several men of the town lost the Sanders's favour – and
lost their livelihood too. There was William Sweeting, a servant at St
Osyth's Abbey in Essex, whose proselytising was so successful that he
converted the prior. There was Thomas Man who peddled his religion
through Newbury, Henley-on-Thames, Uxbridge, Billericay,
Chelmsford and throughout Suffolk and Norfolk, claiming to have
made six or seven hundred converts, before being captured and burned
at Smithfield. There was Edward Walker of Maidstone who held
regular Bible studies in his home and Richard Gavell of Westerham

who went ostentatiously to the inn at sermon time and declared over his flagon, 'Now the prest standeth in the pulpet and he doth no thyng but chide and brawell ffor I loke more one his dedes thane of his wordes whate so ever he saith thair.'[1]

Most Lollards came from the growing class of literate artisans and small-town traders, men whose work trained them to think for themselves and who had widespread contacts. Some had given themselves up to a life of evangelism and wandered the shires, their scrips stuffed with handwritten tracts and fragments of scripture. The guile of the Lollard missionary was, in More's opinion, boundless. He lived 'everywhere and nowhere . . . for he walked about as an apostle of the devil from shire to shire and town to town, through the realm, and had in every diocese a diverse name. By reason whereof he did many years much harm before he could be found out.'[2] The preachers linked the isolated conventicles and spread news of the new spirit stirring in the land. As the faithful gathered in barns and upper rooms of merchants' houses or sat around the textile worker's silent loom, the itinerant preacher told of the Dean of St Paul's who preached what the Lollards had believed for years. He told of Oxford students buying English Bibles and Wycliffite tracts which they had once dismissed as fit only for ignorant peasants. He showed copies of Lollard pamphlets in *print*, pressed on foreign machines and smuggled into England. They were thrilling signs for the members of the 'other church' – signs that God was answering their prayers to bring England to the truth. Few of them could have guessed how much violence, bitterness and bloodshed lay ahead.

They were not violent people. For the most part they were openly conformist and were regarded by their neighbours as harmless. There was even considerable sympathy for Lollards particularly during outbreaks of persecution. In 1532 parliament complained about bishops who were over-zealous in the seeking out of heretics. Once, the populace would have supported any purge against unorthodox beliefs. Now there was alarm when harmless neighbours were interrogated under torture and forced to go about with an embroidered faggot displayed on their clothes – the sign of a recanted heretic.

'Lollardy' covered a wide spectrum of beliefs. Some heretics held extreme opinions that could scarcely be called Christian. At the other end of the scale were ill-equipped armchair theologians whose 'heresy' ran to little more than a rejection of pilgrimage and veneration of images. But there was a common corpus of doctrine to which most Lollards subscribed. They rejected the power of the priesthood and the

miracle of the mass. They rejected prayers for the dead and the invocation of saints. These were the religious shackles that thousands of
Englishmen longed to throw off but dared not. What gave the Lollards
greater boldness was that they had found a new authority. For them
the Bible had replaced the church, and the Bible told them that every
individual was free to make his peace with God without the need for a
mediating priesthood. Thus fortified with the certainty of eternal life,
Lollards were able to bear the searing, lurid flames of death. John
Browne was burned at Ashford in 1513. In an attempt to frighten him
into submission the archbishop's officers had forced Browne to walk on
hot coals. The prisoner reported this to his wife when she came to visit
him. His mentors thought, he said, 'to make me to deny my Lord,
which I will never do; for if I should deny my Lord in this world, he
would hereafter deny me. I pray thee, therefore, good Elizabeth, continue as thou hast begun, and bring up thy children virtuously, and in
the fear of God.'[3]

But it was not the martyrdom of John Browne which brought the
conflict between the two churches into the open. The *cause célèbre*
which set London and England buzzing with indignation and hate was
the case of Richard Hunne. Hunne was a respected and reputable
London merchant of considerable substance. In 1511 he and his wife
rejoiced in the birth of a son. Their jubilation was short-lived: five
weeks later the child died. He was duly buried and, as was the odious
custom, the parish priest, Thomas Dryffeld, demanded the dead
child's winding sheet as a mortuary fee. Angry at the rector's insen-
sitiveness and at the power of the church which entitled the clergy to
press their petty demands even at a time of family grief, Hunne refused
to pay. Feelings on both sides must have run very high; threats, insults
and recriminations flew back and forth for months and what should
have been a storm in a teacup escalated into a tragic trial of strength.
Each contestant saw the other as representative of a detestable community: Dryffeld stood for the corrupt, grasping, unspiritual clergy;
Hunne, for dangerous, anarchistic heretics. (Hunne was posthumously
condemned as a heretic but there is good ground for believing he was
no more than an angry anti-clerical.)

In 1512 Dryffeld brought a suit against Hunne in the archbishop's
court. To counter, Hunne filed a writ of praemunire against the clergy
involved in the case. In doing so he created a test case which concentrated the long-running conflict between canon law and common law.
The praemunire statutes dated back to the time of Edward III and
were designed to inhibit those who sought, by appeal to ecclesiastical

(and therefore to papal or 'foreign') courts, to evade the king's justice.[4]

The case now became the focus of widespread attention. The city lawyers, fascinated, followed its slow course. Students at the inns of court debated it hotly. Time and again, the case was adjourned on one technicality after another but an ultimate conclusion was inevitable and, at length, Bishop Fitzjames of London took a hand. He was alarmed at the spread of heresy in his diocese and angered at the failure of an attempt he had recently made to silence Colet. He knew what encouragement the enemies of the church would derive if Hunne was able to secure a favourable verdict. Somehow the case must be stopped and the troublesome merchant silenced.

It was not easy to move against a respected freeman of the city and a prominent member of the merchant community, especially when that man, to all outward appearances was a devout Christian, scrupulous in attendance at mass. The bishop's only lever against the man was the faint suspicion of Lollardy attaching to him. In October 1514 Fitzjames sent men to arrest Hunne and search his house. Hunne was lodged in the Lollard's Tower, a prison which was part of the St Paul's complex. His gaoler was Charles Joseph, one of the men named in Hunne's praemunire suit. The search of the Whitechapel house brought forth some Lollard writings and a Wycliffite Bible, possession of which was technically sufficient to sustain a charge of heresy in the church courts. Hunne's preliminary examination by the bishop took place on 2 December and that night he was returned to his cell.

The following morning – a Sunday – the shocking news flashed round the city 'Hunne is dead!' The merchant's body was hanging by the neck from a beam in his prison. London was in an uproar. No one accepted the suicide theory and everyone clamoured for justice against the murderous agents of a tyrannical and reactionary bishop. Incredibly inept and unmoved, Fitzjames took heed neither of public opinion nor of strict legality. He continued the case against Hunne, pronounced him guilty of heresy and handed his dead body over to the secular arm for burning. This involved the confiscation by the crown of all the condemned man's possessions. The church had thus destroyed its enemy and ruined his family. Vengeance was complete.

It was a hollow victory. The coroner's jury brought in a verdict of murder against Charles Joseph, Fitzjames's chancellor and one other. The bishop complained that the verdict was untrue and appealed to Wolsey on behalf of his servants. He admitted that feeling in the city was such that, 'if my Chaunceler be tryed by any xij men in London, they be so maliciouslie set, *in favorem hereticae pravitatis* (that is are so set apon the favoure of heresie) that they will cast and condemn my clarcke thowght he was as innocent as Abel.'[5] Thanks to the Cardinal's intervention the accused were never brought to trial which inevitably aroused a fresh furore of resentment.

The 'heretical' merchant was dead but his spirit effectively haunted the church for many years. When the next parliament assembled in 1515 the Commons immediately demanded full restitution for Hunne's family, as well as launching fresh attacks on mortuary fees and clerical privileges. By the time More wrote his *Dialogue Concerning Heresies* in 1529 the ghost had still not been laid. More devoted a large section of his book to justifying Hunne's condemnation and the dismissal of the murder charge. It was a piece of specious writing unworthy of a great and independent mind. In More's scarcely concealed opinion Hunne was a heretic and his death, however encompassed, was justifiable. He asserted his belief in the suicide story and attempted to dismiss the murder charge by ridiculing some of the evidence brought against the accused. It was witty but it was neither dignified nor honest. Another parliament met in that same year, a parliament bent upon destroying the power of the church hierarchy. In the person of Thomas Wolsey the anti-clericals had a perfect target. The Cardinal seemed to embody all that was bad in the church – arrogance, love of luxury, misuse of wealth and power.

There was a limit to the amount of flagrant injustice that even Tudor men and women could stomach. The battle between the church and its critics escalated steadily during the 1520s and 1530s. Scurrilous pamphlets and ballads flooded the streets. Action against suspected heretics grew more intense. Tavern arguments led to brawls and minor acts of desecration were perpetrated. And some not so minor:

In the same year of our Lord 1532, there was an idol named the Rood of Dovercourt, whereunto was much and great resort of people: for at that time there was great rumour blown abroad amongst the ignorant sort, that the power of the idol of Dovercourt was so great that no man had power to shut the church door where he stood; and therefore they let the church door, both night and day, continually stand open, for the more credit unto their blind rumour. This once being conceived in the heads of the vulgar sort, seemed a great marvel unto many men; but to many again . . . it was greatly suspected, especially unto . . . Robert King of Dedham, Robert Debnam of East Bergholt, Nicholas Marsh of Dedham and Robert Gardner of Dedham. . . Wherefore they were moved by the Spirit of God to travel out of Dedham in a wondrous goodly night, both hard frost and fair moonshine . . . from the town of Dedham to the place where the filthy Rood stood . . . and found the church door open . . . for there durst no unfaithful body shut it. This happened well for their purpose, for they found the idol, which had as much power to keep the door shut, as to keep it open; and for proof thereof, they took the idol from his shrine, and carried him a quarter of a mile from the place where he stood, without any resistance of the said idol. Whereupon they struck fire with a flint-stone, and suddenly set him on fire, who burned out so brim, that he lighted them homeward one good mile of the ten.[6]

Anti-clericalism alone would never have sparked off the Reformation. Indeed, there was a sense in which, paradoxically, attacks on the ecclesiastical establishment helped to preserve the fundamental beliefs on which that establishment was based. For complaints about the misused power of the clergy sprang largely from a frustration felt by a laity which realised that the clergy did have a real, spiritual power. It was only when that belief was challenged, when men came to reject the priestly miracle, the necessity for confession, the efficacy of masses for the dead, that they could break with the old religion. The Lollards had made this break but they were only, to most people, a minority of simple cranks. It was the influence of the continental Protestants which was decisive.

The speed with which the influence of Martin Luther reached England and spread here is little short of breathtaking. By about 1517 Dr Luther had established a new kind of theology at Wittenberg University and in October of that year he challenged the doctrine of indulgences (remission of eternal punishment granted by the pope or his agents in return for acts of penance – usually involving financial payment) in the Ninety-five Theses which he nailed to the door of the castle church. This aroused not only opposition but stirrings of sympathetic action in some of the academic centres of Europe. During the next couple of years Luther printed an explanation of his theses and a handful of sermons but it was not until 1520 that he thought through the implications of his doctrines and published his first major pamphlets challenging the establishment. Yet it was at the end of that same year or early in 1521 that there was a public burning of Lutheran books in Cambridge. Since 1519 members of the White Horse group had been eagerly laying hold on the works of the Wittenberg reformer and discussing them at their meetings. Nor was interest in Luther confined to a group of radical students at Cambridge. In May 1521 Wolsey himself presided over an elaborately staged bonfire of Luther's works at St Paul's. Clearly the works of the reformer were circulating in England in their thousands.

Nothing demonstrates more clearly the nation's readiness for a religious revival, a cultural revolution, than the eagerness with which the increasing output of the heretical presses was snapped up despite desperate efforts by the bishops to inhibit imports and to track down Lutheran cells. Hundreds of people who had business abroad – merchants, scholars, government agents and others – brought back the forbidden books with them. So great was the demand that captains, merchants and colporteurs found it profitable to take considerable risks to smuggle the banned works in vats and bales and distribute them around the shires. The secret network of Lollard contacts and conventicles was revitalised and expanded to cope with the new trade. The new heresy had a different clientele to the old. Its devotees were to be found among scholars, monks, clergy, country gentlemen and members of the court.

This strange phenomenon of heresy stepping out of the gutter and transcending social barriers took the authorities by surprise. Persecution was sporadic and, in some cases, half-hearted. Bishops were reluctant to proceed against gentlemen and tended to be tolerant of what they chose to regard as academic peccadilloes. But the movement soon had its first martyr, the small, earnest, gentle Thomas Bilney, fellow of Trinity Hall, Cambridge.

Bilney's life was turned upside down not by Luther's *Babylonian Captivity* but by the *Novum Instrumentum*. Bilney bought the new translation for the sake of the Latin but the message of the New Testament and particularly of one verse in the First Epistle to Timothy,

did so exhilarate my heart, being before wounded with the guilt of my sins, and being almost in despair, that immediately I felt a marvellous comfort and quietness, insomuch that my bruised bones leaped for joy.

After this the Scripture began to be more pleasant unto me than the honey or the honey-comb; wherein I learned that all my travails, all my fasting and watching, all the redemption of masses and pardons, being done without trust in Christ, who only saveth his people from their sins; these, I say, I learned to be nothing else but even . . . a hasty and swift running out of the right way.[7]

The convert gave himself up to rigorous personal devotion, works of charity among prisoners and the local poor, and preaching. Throughout East Anglia he travelled to bring to others the joy he had found. Inevitably this aroused opposition. He was arrested, accused of spreading Lutheran heresies and forced to abjure. His recantation broke him. He was cast into bitter depression by the conviction that he had betrayed his Lord. At length, despite the entreaties of his friends, 'St Bilney' left Cambridge setting his face, he said, towards Jerusalem. Bilney's 'Jerusalem' was Norwich where Bishop Nix was a sworn enemy of the reformers. On a summer's day in 1531 Thomas Bilney was burned to death in the Lollards' Pit.

Persecution, or the threat of it, drove some Protestants abroad and in so doing gave the new movement enormous impetus. Although their enemies branded all heretics as 'Lutherans', most English religious radicals certainly did not go all the way with the Wittenberg monk. But when John Frith, George Joye, William Tyndale and others went to the Low Countries and Germany they came into much closer contact with more virulent forms of heresy. Not only were they themselves won over, they wrote books and pamphlets for the benefit of their countrymen.

By far the most important of the exiles was William Tyndale. This student of both universities imbibed the atmosphere of Erasmian and early Lutheran Cambridge. About 1522 he decided to take upon himself the burden of producing an English Bible. It did not seem to him a wildly revolutionary idea. Many reformers, including Colet and Erasmus, had advocated it. Tyndale went first to London hoping that the humanist Bishop Tunstall would be his patron in the task. He was soon disillusioned. The year 1524 saw him setting sail for Antwerp, never to return. In 1526 the first edition of Tyndale's New Testament was published at Worms and smuggled into England. No other book has ever had such an impact on English society. The production and distribution of the New Testament was controlled by the Christian Brethren, a secret organisation headed by wealthy London merchants such as Tyndale's patron, Humphrey Monmouth. Concealed in boxes and bales of cloth the forbidden merchandise came ashore at the city wharves and at the east coast ports. From there an underground network of colporteurs carried them throughout the country to be bought by Lollard groups, university students, gentlemen, merchants and priests. Some were even distributed free, as More discovered: 'I was by good honest men informed that in Bristol ... there were of these pestilent books some thrown in the streets and left at men's doors by night that where they durst not offer their poison to sell, they would of their charity poison men for naught.'[8] The trade was brisk as the books were bought, sold and bartered throughout the country. We can only catch glimpses of this clandestine commerce – a London friar selling a New Testament for 3s 2d to some Lollards from Steeple Bumpstead; a law student's rooms in Gray's Inn serving as a distribution centre; a Gloucestershire priest accepting a load of hay for a New Testament; an Oxford distributor winning the confidence of students with harmless Greek and Latin books before offering more dangerous fare.

It would be impossible to overestimate the impact of this book, the fervour with which it was sought, the diligence with which it was read and committed to memory, the rapidity with which it spread at all levels of society (Anne Boleyn had her own copy and Tyndale's book was certainly read by the king). At least one man looked back nostalgically on the 1520s: 'The fervent zeal of those Christian days seemed much superior to these our days and times, as manifestly may appear by their sitting up all night in reading and hearing: also by their expenses and charges in buying of books in English, of whom some gave five marks, some more, some less, for a book; some gave a load of hay for a few chapters of St James or of St Paul in English.'[9] For the first time many English men and women could read the word of God for themselves and find their own way to salvation without having to rely on priests. It was an intoxicating experience and, though the 1526 edition and subsequent editions were banned, a vital point had been made, as a contemporary pamphleteer stated: '. . . it is proved lawful, that both men and women lawfully may read and write God's law in their mother tongue, and they that [forbid] this, they show themselves heirs and sons of the first tormentors, and worse; for they show themselves the very disciples of Antichrist . . . in stopping and perverting of God's law.'[10] It was an opinion shared by some who were certainly not Protestants, for there was something incongruous about bishops and priests burning the Holy Bible. For over a decade scholars and politicians contended for an official English Bible. They achieved their goal in 1539 with the production of the Great Bible, a copy of which was, by royal injunction, ordered to be set up in every parish church.[11]

Protestants might consider the 1520s to be 'Christian days': Thomas More could not. As he approached his fiftieth year he looked out on a world hideously distorted by evil – heresy rampant, the church and its clergy openly despised, ancient truths rejected, old customs overthrown, the seamless garment of Christendom being torn in shreds by

Lollards and sceptics had long ridiculed such practices as pilgrimage and veneration of images. In this tract a carpenter is observed worshipping an image he has just made. When the new ideas really took hold they completely swept away monasticism. Much Wenlock priory, Shropshire, was typical of many monasteries which were partly turned into secular dwellings and partly left to decay

British Library Board;

Christina Gascoigne

Lutherans, Zwinglians, Lollards and Anabaptists. Pandora's box had been opened and the suspicion must have lurked in his mind that he and his humanist friends had, perhaps, turned the key.

> ... wisdom were it for us to perceive, that like as folk begin now to delight in feeding their souls on the venomous carrion of those poisoned heresies of which may well be verified the words of holy writ 'death is in the pot' our Lord ... to revenge it beginneth to withdraw his gracious hand from the fruits of the earth, diminishing the fertility both in corn and cattle and bringing all to death much more than men can remedy or fully find out the cause. And yet besides this ... he sendeth war, sickness and death to punish in the flesh that odious and hateful sin of the soul, that spoileth the fruit from all manner of virtues, I mean unbelief, false faith and infidelity, and to tell you all at once in plain English – heresy.[12]

More had personal reasons for feeling so strongly about heresy; it had intruded into his own home. In 1525 his eldest and favourite daughter Margaret married a young lawyer called William Roper and the young couple lived in More's household. The two men were close friends but Roper was by degrees drawn into the Lutheran fold. When the family went to mass on holy days Roper sat at home with his Bible. He bought banned books on the underground market. He challenged More's Catholic friends at More's own table. He was indiscreet about the public proclamation of his new faith. Eventually he found himself before Wolsey on a charge of heresy and More had to use his influence to gain his son-in-law's release.

Those were difficult years in the Chelsea household. 'Megge,' More told his daughter, 'I have borne a longe time with thy husbande; I haue reasoned and argued with him in those pointes of religion, and still geuen to him my poore fatherly counsaile; but I perceaue none of all this able to call him home.'[13] It was a problem increasingly common to thousands of households, high and low, throughout the land.

Unfortunately for More and those other churchmen who were prepared to pin their reputations and their lives to the old religion, they were now facing not only heretics but the government. The king's 'great matter' first came to the fore in 1527. Henry justified from the Bible his intention to rid himself of Catherine of Aragon. When Rome would not or could not grant the nullification he required, the whole issue of royal justice versus 'foreign', papal allegiance was raised again. An absolute monarch discovered that he was not absolute after all. The pope's courts held sway alongside his own and 'all the prelates whom he had looked on as wholly his subjects were but half his subjects, for at their consecration they swore an oath contrary to that which they swore to the Crown, so that it seemed that they were the pope's subjects rather than his.'[14]

One by one Henry severed the juridical and economic ties between England and Rome. He removed from office Cardinal Wolsey, the symbol of ecclesiastical power and wealth. He stopped appeals to Rome. He diverted the flow of papal taxation into the royal coffers. He established himself as supreme head of the church in England. Long before this ultimate position was reached More realised he had gone as far as he could along the path this king had chosen. He had spoken unequivocally in the Council against the anti-papal legislation that Henry and his new agent Thomas Cromwell were intent on forcing through. In May 1532, after only two and a half years in office, Thomas More resigned the chancellorship.

Flatterers, heretics and reformers about the king had encouraged him in his divorce proceedings but More had the majority of English men and women behind him when he opposed the increasingly frenzied royal attempts to be rid of Catherine. (Most reformers saw the divorce as a means to a highly desirable end – the severing of links with Rome. It is interesting that William Tyndale, another hero of the early Tudor age who was, like More, scrupulously honest but who was More's theological enemy, also opposed the king in his 'great matter'.) The queen was popular; Anne Boleyn was not. It was an irrational gut reaction. The people knew that Catherine had passed child-bearing age and that there was no male heir to the throne. Fear of anarchy, weak rule and insecure succession went deep but the English sense of fair play went deeper. There was widespread outrage that the king proposed to set aside a virtuous wife in favour of a chit of a girl who was nothing better than a Frenchified whore. Hugh Lathbury, a hermit, took it upon himself to leave his cell and tour the Midlands drumming up support for 'Catherine Queen of Fortune'. He achieved considerable support and claimed that Catherine 'would make ten men against the king's one' and that before long she would be restored to her crown.[15] At Barrow-upon-Humber a stallholder at the Easter fair set up a picture of the king and 'pinned upon the body of the said picture a wench made in cloth, holding a pair of balances in her hands. In the one balance was two hands together and in the other balance a feather, with a writing over her head saying that love was lighter than a feather.'[16] The justices in Nottinghamshire sent up to London a sixty-nine-year-old veteran soldier ('sore bruised in the king's wars') because he had complained about Henry's forsaking 'so noble a lady, so high-born and so gracious'.[17]

But it was to Aldington, in Kent, that the more determined opponents of the divorce flocked in excited droves to see and be blessed by Elizabeth Barton, the Holy Maid. This wonder of the hour, who convinced even bishops with her sanctity and divine powers, was an emotionally disturbed servant girl whose affliction showed itself in trances, and hysterical outbursts of religious fervour. Her master and her parish priest convinced themselves that Elizabeth's ravings were divinely inspired and the poor girl believed that they must be right. In 1526 Edward Bocking, a monk of Christ Church, Canterbury, was sent to examine her. Bocking was to become the Maid's Svengali. Realising that a live prophetess was more valuable than a churchful of dead relics, Bocking saw Elizabeth's potential as a restorer of faith in traditional religion. He taught her the legends of the saints and tutored her in simple Catholic dialectic. Then he put her on show.

From far and wide they came in their thousands. They crammed into the chapel of Our Lady in Court-at-Street and gazed open-mouthed at the prostrate figure shrouded in white before the altar. The hairs of their heads rose as the Maid spoke out of deep trance in sepulchral tones not her own. The voice – was it the Virgin herself? – told of the joys of heaven, the pain of hell and urged the congregation to venerate images and holy days, masses and pilgrimages. With lightened hearts and tears of joy the hearers went back to their towns and villages to tell their neighbours of the Holy Maid's miracles and prophesies.

As soon as Elizabeth was installed at a nunnery in Canterbury her religious experience (or, perhaps, her imagination) was intensified. She was taken up to heaven by the Virgin who also revealed to her the secrets of the future – both as regards the nation and individuals. Unfortunately, among the individuals who were the subjects of her vision was numbered Henry VIII. She plainly avowed in the name of God that if Henry put away his lawful wife, within a month 'he should no longer be king of this realm' and that he should 'die a villain's death'. It was an age of divine miracles and demon possession, of black magic and of the direct intervention of the spirit world into our own. Charlatans and fakes abounded and made a good living by battening on the gullible until they were exposed. Church leaders were experienced in distinguishing between the genuine mystic and the mountebank, but they failed to detect Elizabeth Barton. Her accomplishment or her self-deception were of a rare order. Among her disciples she could number

Archbishop Warham, Bishop Fisher of Rochester – and Thomas More. Perhaps their critical faculties were numbed because the Maid said what they wanted to hear. At a time when the church was under great pressure it seemed that God had sent a messenger to put heart into the faithful. More was very circumspect in his dealings with Elizabeth, warning her to keep off political matters, but he certainly treated her with reverence – until September 1533. Then Thomas Cranmer, the new Archbishop of Canterbury, extracted a full confession from the Maid and her accomplices, that 'she never had visions in all her life, but all that she ever said was feined of her own imagination, only to satisfy the minds of those which resorted to her and to obtain worldly praise.'[18]

When Henry put an end to papal jurisdiction he certainly did not regard himself as a heretic. He was a Catholic king; had he not personally written a book refuting the errors of Luther? He would simply set in hand a reform of those abuses in the external life of the church which everyone agreed needed reform. Thomas More knew better; you cannot divorce faith from practice. The implications of royal supremacy were most clearly seen by Christopher St Germain, perhaps the greatest civil lawyer of his day. He drew logical conclusions from the king's new position which were to lie at the root of England's constitutional problems for a century or more. Ultimate authority in spiritual matters lay only in the Bible. Who, then, had the right to expound the Bible? St Germain's answer is 'the king and people', which for all practical purposes means 'the king in parliament'. There was another man who also knew better; the man behind the growing volume of statutes and royal injunctions which revolutionised the religious life of the nation; the man who dominated English life for a decade and achieved more in such a brief time than any British statesman before or since.

Thomas Cromwell was a political realist unhampered by any sentimental attachment to ancient forms. Where More saw a pope with 1500 years of authority behind him, Cromwell saw a foreign prince controlled by the imperial house of Habsburg who wielded a totally unjustified power in the free nation state of England. While More longed for the religious life and venerated those who had immured themselves within an atmosphere of prayer and contemplation, Cromwell resented the idle communities of monks and nuns who kept a vast, stagnant treasure while the government was in danger of failing for lack of funds. More cautiously accepted the need for reform of educational standards among the clergy. Cromwell knew that nothing would suffice but the sweeping away of all the paraphernalia of images, shrines, holy days, doctrines of purgatory and penance by which an unworthy priesthood had dominated the life of the people, and the setting forth of an English Bible which would be a light of learning and true doctrine for clergy and laity alike. Thomas More was content with a modest pruning of the ecclesiastical tree; Thomas Cromwell was intent on cutting back to the old wood and grafting on a new and more vigorous stock.

By 1534 the severance of the English church from the church of Rome was complete. In 1535 the executions of More, Fisher and the Carthusian leaders served as a warning that Henry was determined to enforce universal acceptance of the new national church. In 1536 the attack on the monasteries began and the new Vicar-General, Thomas Cromwell, issued injunctions to the clergy which showed the theological direction in which he was moving. In these and subsequent injunctions the calendar of holy days was drastically trimmed, offerings to images were forbidden, preaching against idolatry and superstition was enjoined, parents were admonished to teach children the Paternoster and the Ten Commandments in English. In 1538 the clergy were ordered to set up prominently in their churches 'one book of the whole Bible of the largest volume in English'. In 1539 the Great Bible (of which the New Testament was largely the work of the condemned and executed heretic William Tyndale) was published.

Cromwell was not naïve enough to suppose that the beliefs and practices of the nation would be radically altered by royal edict. He set in motion a vast propaganda machine the like of which England had never seen. Books, pamphlets and tracts, authorised by the Vicar-General, poured from the presses. Preachers were licensed to tour the dioceses and set forth the royal supremacy. However, it was one thing to put a man in a pulpit but quite another to control what he said once he was up there. Where was Cromwell to find his preachers – men with the training and the zeal to persuade the people to accept the new regime? The only substantial pool of such men was the propagandists of heresy who had for years been secretly proselytising and spreading Lutheran literature. It is, therefore, not surprising that complaints were soon littering the tables of Cromwell and other ministers. The Bishop of Lincoln complained about Thomas Garrett, a man 'of little learning and less discretion' who was preaching 'novelties', and distributing Lutheran books. The Archbishop of York had taken upon himself to dismiss a friar for teaching 'new things and that very slanderously to the offence of the people'. A Sussex parson had one of

Cromwell's preachers put in the stocks for two days.[19] Over and over again the champions of orthodoxy affirmed that the people 'much grudged' against the new preachers. Certainly William Glaskeryon of Bristol was an embittered man: 'a vengeance upon the Bishop of Worcester,' he cried out during a sermon he did not like, 'I wish he had never been born; I trust before I die to see him burned.'[20]

The object of Glaskeryon's wrath was the greatest (or, in the opinion of many) the most notorious preacher of the age, Hugh Latimer. He had already stirred up controversy many times and in many places by his forthright denunciations of the old order and his advocacy of reformed doctrines before August 1535 when Cromwell, by a deliberate act of policy, installed him as Bishop of Worcester. Now, the West Country heard his fiery oratory from hundreds of its pulpits:

> we have to do with strong, mighty princes and potentates; that mighty prince, that great conqueror of this world, the devil. . .
>
> Think you not that this our enemy, this prince with all his potentates, hath great and sore assaults to lay against our armour? Yea, he is a crafty warrior, and also of great power in this world; he hath great ordnance and artillery; he hath great pieces of ordnance, as mighty kings and emperors, to shoot against God's people, to persecute or kill them. . . Yea, what great pieces hath he had of bishops of Rome, which have destroyed whole cities and countries, and have slain and burnt many! What great guns were those!
>
> Yes, he hath also less ordnance evil enough . . . some bishops in divers countries, and here in England, which he hath shot at some good Christian men, that they have been blown to ashes. So can this great captain, the devil, shoot his ordnance. He hath yet less ordnance . . . he hath hand-guns and bows, which do much hurt, but not so much as the great ordnance. These be accusers, promoters and slanderers; they be evil ordnance, shrewd hand-guns and bows; they put a man to great displeasure; oftentimes death cometh upon that shot. For these things, saith the text, 'take the armour of God'.[21]

Not only did Latimer preach extensively himself; he also filled the pulpits of his diocese with reforming orators who, secure in the knowledge that they had a powerful protector, exercised no self-restraint. Some congregations were stirred to white-hot fervour so that they tore down their statues and broke up their altars. Others complained loudly: Thomas Bell, sheriff of Gloucestershire, tried to enlist the Duke of Norfolk's support against this 'whoreson heretic' Latimer and his chaplains. Richard Cornewell, a foul-mouthed and immoral priest, voiced the resentment many of the clergy felt when their secure power and position were threatened. Having been disciplined by Latimer for wenching, Cornewell went around telling anyone who would listen that the bishop would be burned. This heretical prelate would be perfectly happy for priests to marry; if I wedded my mistress Latimer 'would be contented that I tilted up her tail in every bush'.[22]

The conservative clergy did not take the challenge lying down. Soon town congregations had a new entertainment to fill their Sundays: rival priests, thundering at each other from their pulpits in neighbouring parishes. In 1533 the people of Bristol went back and forth between two churches where Latimer and William Hubberdyne regularly slanged each other. Alas for Hubberdyne's fervour; on one occasion his enthusiasm carried him to such excesses of gesticulation that the pulpit gave way beneath him with fatal results. But then, as the churchwardens sanguinely remarked 'we made our pulpit for preaching, not dancing'.[23] In 1540 Londoners were divided between the followers of Edward Crome and Nicholas Wilson. Entertainment of another kind was offered by John Divale, priest of Wincanton, who threatened to punch any parishioner he caught reading the Bible and to thrash any 'new-fangled' preacher he came across. Clearly, with all this activity and counter-activity going on, the complaint of Thomas Corthop of Harwich was no exaggeration. He inveighed against sermonisers who preached three times in a day creating 'such divisions and seditions among us as never were seen in this realm'.[24]

There was scarcely a community in the country untouched by religious controversy. Men fell to arguing about the new ideas over their ale. William Senes, a choirmaster at Jesus College, Rotherham, got into a slanging match with the clergy of the college when he ridiculed masses for the dead. 'Thy father was a liar and is in hell,' he confidently told one opponent, 'and so is my father in hell also; my father never knew Scripture and now it is come forth.' So embittered was the argument that the staff of the college could scarcely speak civilly to each other and, at length, they all had to be marched off to the local magistrate. William Hunte, a minstrel, of Finchingfield provoked William Smyth of Shalford by urging him to read the New Testament and by singing at a wedding a song railing against saints and images. Smyth was eventually goaded into criticising the king for usurping the power of the pope. He, too, found himself trying to explain his outburst to the local magistrate.

The activities of the gospellers provided another cause of friction.

These were men and women who took it upon themselves to read and expound the scriptures to their illiterate neighbours. The people were curious to know about the large book which was chained to its new desk in the nave and wanted to know what it contained but when they asked the priest about it he shrugged his shoulders or warned them, with oaths, not to go near it. When, however, they came to mass they found a knot of parishioners gathered around while a local merchant or, perhaps, the steward from the manor read to them. The priest, murmuring away in the dimly-lit chancel, was completely ignored, for here was something new and exciting, and if it had been set forth by the king was it not their duty to hear it? Bishop Bonner had to put up a notice over the Bible in St Paul's Cathedral urging people to read quietly to themselves and not to attempt unlicensed exposition.

Preachers were not the only government agents, for royal policy had to be enforced as well as proclaimed. Cromwell had at his disposal an army of gentlemen, lawyers and court hangers-on only too willing to travel through the shires collecting news of clergy who would not preach the supremacy, encouraging informers to reveal latent opposition to the religious changes, seeking out objects of superstition which had not been removed. From these agents, as well as from sheriffs, constables, church officials and private persons, reports poured in to Cromwell's office.

In Nottinghamshire, to consider just one county, the Vicar-General's men were led by Sir John Markham, a substantial local landlord. In the spring of 1534 he reported the prior of the Observant Friars in Newark for preaching a 'seditious' sermon. A few months later it was the wife of a certain Allan Hey who attracted attention with uncomplimentary words about Anne Boleyn. The following April Markham and his colleagues were examining the proctor of Beauvale Priory, whom they found to be a stubborn papist. When William Senes of Rotherham found himself in trouble it was to another of Cromwell's agents, John Babington, that he appealed, with the immediate result that Senes's case was removed from archiepiscopal to royal jurisdiction – and dismissed. The year 1538 was a busy one for the agents of reform in Nottinghamshire. They sent the vicar of Newark to London for persistently urging his flock to follow the old devotional ways and to shun all English books. Their next assignment was the examination of a pair of very contumacious papists. Prior Heath of Lenton and Ralph Swenson, one of his monks, had clearly spoken treasonable words and proved quite unrepentant. Markham reported his findings to Cromwell and back came the order. Heath and Swenson were hung, drawn and quartered. Soon afterwards John Hercy, another of Markham's colleagues, had fresh news to report back to Cromwell.

> I have been informed that Sir Edward Eland, Chaplain to Dr Knolys, Vicar of Wakefield, has been teaching young folks seditious songs against your Lordship and others... Have pity for the poor men of Cottam, sure vexed by Anthony Neville, who ... threatens them with a lunatic priest put to them by the Archbishop of York's officers... I wish you would be pleased to take the [statue of the] Lady at Doncaster away, and send some good preachers into the country.[25]

So it went on – keeping their ears to the ground anxious to detect every sign of disaffection; hearing informers who came under cover of darkness; sifting true evidence from malicious gossip; examining, persuading, cajoling, bullying; supporting government preachers; writing reports; confining men in gaol and under house arrest; standing up to irate bishops and powerful magnates, like the Earl of Shrewsbury; above all, trying to impress upon everyone, high and low, that the new order had come to stay.

And the common people? What did they make of it? Here the historian is up against a real problem – how to define the state of mind of a populace living in the midst of a cultural revolution. All the evidence is conflicting. There were those who welcomed the Reformation. There were those who rejected it. There were those – probably the vast majority – who were completely bewildered by it. There were some who seem to have been unaffected by the changes taking place around them.

When Henry VIII died in January 1547 the Reformation had by no means run its course. There would be more changes – services in English, the disappearance of chantries, the stripping of more images and pictures from the churches. There would be attempts to put the clock back and there would be greater polarisation of theological viewpoints before the establishment of the Elizabethan *media via*. Thus, at the end of our period the religious life of England was still in a state of flux and the Reformation had made a greater impact in some parts of the realm than others.

If we take as an example a 1547 visitation of the diocese of Bath and Wells we find that twelve parishes had no Bible, while at Freshford and Queen Camel the parsons had Bibles but would not allow the laity access to them. The people of Stringston had not heard a sermon in three years and in at least a dozen other parishes there was no effort at regular preaching. Littleton still had no pulpit. Most of the rich livings had no resident rectors and there was a scarcity of churches without curates.[26] If many priests were dilatory in carrying out government orders it was because the bishop's officers were far from zealous in enforcing change and also because government policy veered wildly back and forth. After Cromwell's fall and death in 1540 conservative and radical factions on the Council fought for control. Official doctrine was defined and re-defined. The Act of Six Articles (1539) established transubstantiation, penance and other Catholic beliefs and led to a bout of heresy-hunting. It was reinforced by the *King's Book* and the Act for Advancement of True Religion (both 1543), which Act forbade anyone under the rank of yeoman to read the Bible. But soon after, the leaders of the conservative faction, Bishop Gardiner of Winchester and the Duke of Norfolk, were in disgrace, Protestant preachers were again encouraged and heresy proceedings were suspended. The court see-saw continued to rise and fall until, literally, the last hours of Henry's life.

With such confusion and conflict at the centre there could scarce be anything other than confusion and conflict throughout the country. A Yorkshire priest is reported for marrying his mistress and claims that he thought the king had given permission for celibate vows to be broken. A Cambridge rector is in trouble for giving communion to his people in both kinds. All over the country men responsible for the payment of obits (annual masses for the soul of the departed) failed to render account. A good, but bewildered and embarrassed West Country gentleman wrote to Hugh Latimer on the subject of the preachers in the diocese

> Only God knoweth the certain truth, which is committed to us, as our capacity may comprehend it, by faith . . . there have been those who have the zeal of God but not according to knowledge. Among which I repute not you, but to this purpose I write it, that to call this or that truth, it requireth a deep and profound knowledge, considering that to me, unlearned, that I take for truth may be otherwise, not having a wise spirit, as St Paul saith, to discern between good and bad: and it is showed me, that an opinion or manner of teaching which causeth dissension in a Christian congregation, is not of God . . . And like as the word of God hath always caused dissension among men unchristened, wherupon hath ensued and followed martyrdom to the preacher, so in Christ's congregation, among them that profess Christ's name, and one Lord, one baptism, one faith, they that preach and stir rather contention than charity, though they

can defend their saying, yet their teaching is not to be taken as of God, in that it breaketh the chain of Christian charity, and maketh division in the people, congregate and called by God into a unity. . .[27]

By 1545 religious life in England was in a state of turmoil. The new teaching created dissension and, so far from eradicating old abuses, had only made them worse. Given time, the medicine would work its healing magic but before it did so it produced alarming and distressing symptoms. Some extracts from the 1545 visitation of Colchester arch-deaconry amply illustrate the point. Henry Bankes of Great Totham no longer kept a light burning in the church as a rental for a piece of land. Robert Dawe of Great Tey removed a sanctuary carpet donated by his father. William Lynne, constable of Wormingford, ordered ale houses to provide meat and drink for sale during divine service. John Case of St Peter's, Colchester, would not attend church and openly kept a mistress. The priest of Walden was too drunk to attend to his duties. At Tolleshunt Major the church windows were broken, the chancel unpaved and the vicar kept a woman. At Little Tey wind and rain blew through the unglazed chancel but it mattered little, for the parson hardly ever said mass there. The rector of Bergholt had preached two sermons in two years and was more familiar with the tavern than the church. John Ellys of White Notley when he received bread at com-munion gave it to his dog.[28]

The truth about the state of the church was so appalling that it penetrated even King Henry's thick hide. On Christmas Eve 1545 he came down to parliament to address the Lords and Commons for what would be the last time.

My loving subjects, study and take pains to amend one thing which surely is amiss and far out of order, to the which I most heartily require you, which is that charity and concord is not amongst you, but discord and dissension beareth rule in every place . . . what love and charity is amongst you when the one calleth the other heretic and anabaptist, and he calleth him again papist, hypocrite and phar-isee? Be these tokens of charity amongst you? No, no. . . I must needs judge the fault and occasion of this discord to be partly by you the fathers and preachers of the spirituality. . . I see and hear daily of you of the clergy who preach one against another, teach one contrary to another, inveigh one against another without charity . . . and few or more preach truly and sincerely the word of God, accord-ing as they ought to do. How can poor souls live in concord when you preachers sow amongst them in your sermons debate and discord. To you they look for light, and you bring them darkness. Amend these crimes I exhort you and set forth God's word both by true preaching and good example-giving, or else I, whom God hath appointed his Vicar and high minister here, will see those divisions removed and those enormities corrected, according to my very duty, or else I shall be accounted an unprofitable servant and untrue officer ... you of the temporality be not clean and unspotted of malice and envy, for you rail on bishops, speak slanderously of priests, and rebuke and taunt preachers, both contrary to good order and Christian fraternity. If you know surely that a bishop or preacher careth or teacheth perverse doctrine, come and declare it to some of our Council, or to us, to whom is committed by God the high authority to reform and order such causes and behaviour, and be not judges of your own fantastical opinions and vain expositions, for in such high cases you may lightly err. And although you be permitted to read Holy Scripture, and to have the word of God in your mother tongue, you must understand that you have this licence only to inform your own conscience, and to instruct your children and family, and not to dispute and make Scripture a railing and a taunting stock against priests and preachers as many light persons do. I am very sorry to know and hear how unreverently that most precious jewel, the word of God, is disputed, rhymed, sung and jangled in every alehouse and tavern, contrary to the true meaning and doctrine of the same. And yet I am ever as much sorry that the readers of the same follow it doing so faintly and coldly. For of this I am sure: that charity was never so faint amongst you and virtuous and godly living was never less used, nor God himself amongst Christians never less reverenced, honoured or served. Therefore, as I said before, be in charity one with another, like brother and brother. Love, dread and serve God (to which I, as your Supreme Head and sovereign lord, exhort and require you) and then I doubt not the love and league ... shall never be dissolved or broken between us.[29]

We are told the king's words brought tears to the eyes of all who heard them. We may well believe it.

The Man Against the Age

... in my daydreams I have been marked out by my Utopians to be their king forever; I can see myself now marching along, crowned with a diadem of wheat, very striking in my Franciscan frock, carrying a handful of wheat as my sacred scepter, thronged by a distinguished retinue of Amaurotians, and, with this huge entourage, giving audience to foreign ambassadors and sovereigns; wretched creatures they are, in comparison with us, as they stupidly pride themselves on appearing in childish garb and feminine finery, laced with that despicable gold, and ludicrous in their purple and jewels and other baubles. Yet, I would not want either you or our friend, Tunstal, to judge me by other men, whose character shifts with fortune. Even if heaven has decreed to waft me from my lowly estate to this soaring pinnacle which, I think, defies comparison with that of kings, still you will never find me forgetful of that old friendship I had with you when I was but a private citizen. And if you do not mind making the short trip to visit me in Utopia, I shall definitely see to it that all mortals governed by my kindly rule will show you the honor due to those who, they know, are very dear to the heart of their king.

I was going to continue with this fascinating vision, but the rising Dawn has shattered my dream – poor me! – and shaken me off my throne and summons me back to the drudgery of the courts. But at least this thought gives me consolation: real kingdoms do not last much longer.[1]

Few passages of self-revelation go deeper than this extract from one of More's letters to Erasmus. Throughout this book we have used

Thomas More as a convention, as a representative man of the early Tudor period. The extract just quoted underlines the truth that has forced its way through our narrative at several points: Thomas More was fundamentally a man at odds with his age. He was a family man who hankered for the ascetic life; a scholar trapped by ambition and obligations into earning a living in the law and the royal service; a humanist ultimately unable to travel the same road as most of his friends and colleagues; a loyal subject who resisted his king and paid the inevitable penalty. When More died, he died alone. Old friends like Tunstall and Gardiner reasoned with him and were puzzled by his stubborn refusal to follow them in taking the oath. Even his beloved Meg failed to understand why her father had to take the stand he did take.

This is not a biography and so we can only ponder superficially on the central secrets of More's character, and make merely a few, inadequately supported, assertions about this lovable, complex man. In a sense the fact that he was so lovable, so admirable, has served to obscure the truth about him. He has been claimed as a champion by apologists of Erasmian, Catholic and even Marxist persuasion. In fact, he was a man apart, representative of no cause except his own convictions.

More's individuality is seen most clearly in his *Utopia*, the only work of the early Tudor age to be widely read and argued about throughout the succeeding centuries down to our own day. The book presents a vision of a holy commonwealth. It is the product of an imagination which soared above that of all his contemporaries and revealed the highest aspirations of Renaissance humanism. Utopia is a land where all men are equal, where all resources, including human resources, are directed to the benefit of the whole community. It is an austere society where no citizen is permitted to transgress the laws of equality, love and righteousness.

Utopia was not a programme for reform; its concluding words make that quite clear: '. . . so must I nedes confesse and graunt that many thinges be in the Utopian weale publique, whiche in our cities I maye rather wishe for, then hope after.'[2] The book is almost a council of despair. What More is really saying is that the Utopians, without any Christian revelation, lead a life which is virtuous and so ordered as to encourage virtue, whereas the nominally Christian Europeans are manifestly evil and even their religion is little more than superstition and empty ceremonial. More criticises and ridicules most aspects of contemporary society – the pursuit of private wealth and the greed of the upper classes; legal chicanery (significantly, there are no lawyers in Utopia); punishment of criminals; the military power élite of medieval society and the frequent wars to which its existence led; oppressive taxation; the luxury and pomp which civil and ecclesiastical leaders were expected to display.

Other humanist visionaries of the age laboured for the realisation of their dreams. They wrote books and pamphlets. They sought influential positions at the courts of kings. More was not such a man of action. He was a rare compound of dreamer and realist. He knew his ideals could not and would not be put into practice by Henry VIII and he did little or nothing to influence the king in matters of policy. To be sure, he gave his advice when called upon to do so and in his performance of his own duties he applied as far as possible those high principles for which he was well known. But it was left to Thomas Cromwell and his colleagues to try to realise, at least in part, the vision of the Christian commonwealth.

And More did not support them. He withdrew from the political arena before the bulk of the Reformation parliament's social legislation was introduced and he opposed Cromwell on one of the fundamental aspects of his policy. Henry VIII and his Secretary had decided that 'this realm of England is an empire' in which the king in parliament had total omnicompetence. Upon that rock the Henrician Reformation was built. More's opinion was radically different. For years he refrained from voicing that opinion. He used every legal trick to avoid making what he knew was, by current law, a treasonable statement. Only after his condemnation did he make his position clear.

> This realm, being but one member and small part of the Church, might not make a particular law dischargable with the general law of Christ's holy Catholic Church, no more than the City of London, being but one poor member in respect of the whole realm, might make a law against an act of Parliament.

More believed in the indivisibility of Christendom under the leadership of the pope, who retained the primacy in all spiritual matters. Having forsaken that principle, the Reformation, whatever admirable changes it might seek to effect, could not fail to lead men astray. Indeed, More was convinced that the programme put forward by the reformers was based on lust, greed and avarice. England was not witnessing, as many of More's friends believed, a transformation under an enlightened king to a new and better order. She was being dragged on a downhill course which could have only one destination. '. . . my dear

Cochlaeus, when I view the present situation with its rapid deterioration, from day to day, I imagine that, in the near future, someone will rear his head and preach the utter rejection of Christ. And if some senseless clown does rear his head, with the present frenzied state of the masses, there will be no lack of supporters.'[3]

More's execution evoked enormous resentment at home and abroad. This has led to the erroneous view that he represented a considerable Catholic reaction against the English Reformation. The truth is not so simple. Thomas More was a well known and popular figure. His opposition to Henry's divorce from Queen Catherine was common currency. (The Spanish ambassador, Chapuys, reported to his master on More's acceptance of the Chancellorship: 'Everyone is delighted at his promotion, because he is an upright and learned man, and a good servant of the Queen.')[4] Now, Catherine was extremely popular throughout the country; it would probably be true to say that most English men and women sympathised with her. It was therefore very easy for the people to believe that the ex-Chancellor was persecuted because of his support for Catherine and his opposition to the Boleyn marriage. They were quite wrong. In March 1534 More wrote to Cromwell avowing

... so am I he that among other his Gracis faithfull subgiettis, his Highnes being in possession of his marriage and this noble woman really anoynted Quene, neither murmure at it, nor dispute uppon it, nor neuer did nor will, but with owt eny other maner medlyng of the matter among his other faithfull subgiettis faithfully pray to God for his Grace and hers both, long to lyve and well and theyr noble issue. . .[5]

It was not the king's marital arrangements which troubled More's conscience but the authority which lay behind those arrangements. More knew this and Henry knew it and Henry was determined that More, like everyone else of consequence, should publicly support the new powers he had assumed. In 1533 he married Anne Boleyn. In the following year parliament passed the Act of Succession which adjudged the former marriage to Catherine of Aragon 'to be against the laws of Almighty God and . . . of no value or effect'. This was because the pope had no authority to grant a dispensation for Henry to marry his deceased brother's widow: 'No man of what estate, degree or condition soever he be, hath power to dispense with God's laws.' The king's subjects were required to swear an oath 'abjuring any foreign potentate' and declaring that they would 'truly, firmly and constantly, without fraud or guile, observe, fulfill, maintain, defend and keep, to their cunning, wit and uttermost of their powers, the whole effects and contents of this present act'. Many good Catholics cheerfully took the oath, believing that it merely confirmed the king's authority to decide such important matters of state as his marriage and the succession to the throne. More understood clearly that there were theological issues at stake. He refused the oath not because he believed the divorce to be against the laws of God, but because the pope said it was against the laws of God and in such matters the pope's decision was final.

Henry was reluctant to bring his old friend to the block. More remained in the Tower for over fourteen months before he was placed on trial. He might have stayed there and died years later, old and forgotten. But other factors intervened, Henry's patience snapped, he was determined to have More's obedience or his head.

So Thomas More died. The Reformation went on. England did not descend into atheism and anarchy. But had More lived he would have found little to please him. The downfall of the monasteries would have distressed him. The authorisation of the vernacular Bible would have filled him with alarm. Even the Counter Reformation when it came would have aroused mixed feelings. Among the actions the pope took to stem the tide of heresy was the banning of all Erasmus's books. There would have been no place for Thomas More in such a world.

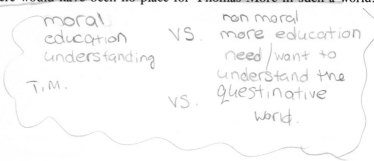

moral education understanding

T.M.

VS. non moral more education need/want to understand the

VS. questinative world.

REFERENCE NOTES

Prologue
The Man and the Age

1 *In Praise of Folly* (Sesame Library Edition, 1915), p. 46
2 I have argued this case more fully in *The People and the Book: The Revolutionary Impact of the English Bible 1380–1611*, pp. 34–91
3 cf. R. B. OUTHWAITE, *Inflation in Tudor and Early Stuart England*
4 THOMAS BECON, *The Jewel of Joy* in *Works* (Parker Society), ed. J. Ayre, p. 435
5 E. F. ROGERS, *St Thomas More: Selected Letters*, p. 170
6 MORE, *Works*, VIII, i, p. 12
7 P. S. and H. M. ALLEN (eds.), *Opus Epistolarum Desiderii Erasmi Roterodami*, VIII, 2228
8 ERASMUS, *Novum Instrumentum*, Introduction
9 *Confutation of Tyndale's Answer* (1532–3) in *Works*, VIII, i, pp. 178–9
10 *Letters and Papers of the Reign of Henry VIII*, IV, iii, 6179. (Hereinafter referred to as *L and P*)
11 RICHARD WHITFORD in P. S. and H. M. ALLEN (eds.), op. cit., I, 423
12 P. S. and H. M. ALLEN (eds.), op. cit., I, 118
13 R. WHITTINGTON, *Vulgaria*, ed. White, p. 64
14 *Utopia*, p. 40; *Works*, IV, p. 101. (All quotations from More's writings are taken from the Yale University Press edition of *The Complete Works* (1963–   ) unless otherwise stated)

Chapter 1
'Your world and impery of England' I

1 MORE, *Works*, II, p. 9
2 J. STOW, *A Survey of London*, ed. C. L. Kingsford, p. 139
3 *Utopia*, pp. 63–5; *Works*, IV, pp. 121–3
4 A letter of Andreas Franciscus, cf. C. H. WILLIAMS (ed.), *English Historical Documents 1485–1558*, p. 189

5 One landowner who fell victim to Cromwell's building plans was the father of John Stow, the chronicler, who 'had a garden there and a house standing close to the south pale [fence]; this house they loosed from the ground, and bare upon rollers into my father's garden twenty-two feet, ere my father heard thereof'. J. STOW, *Survey of London*, p. 142. After Cromwell's fall the house became the hall of the Drapers' Company

6 SIR THOMAS WYATT, *Collected Poems* (ed. J. Daalder), pp. 103–4

7 C. A. SNEYD (ed.), *A Relation, or rather a True Account, of the island of England . . . about the year 1500*, Camden Society, XXXVII, pp. 42–3

8 *Greyfriars' Chronicle*, p. 50

9 E. HALL, *The Union of the two noble and illustre Famelies of Lancastre and Yorke* (ed. H. Ellis), p. 799

10 CHARLES WRIOTHESLEY, *A Chronicle of England* (ed. W. D. Hamilton), Camden Society, I, pp. 99–100

11 John Leland was the father of English topography. He was a scholar priest with an unquenchable curiosity and an eye for detail. When the king wanted a survey of the realm in 1530 it was Leland he commissioned. The little parson took an extended sabbatical from his clerical duties and spent several years touring England from Berwick to the Lizard. Everywhere he went he made notes on the use of the land, the customs of the people and the men who ruled the shires. He interviewed burgesses and ferreted about in monastic libraries. Sadly 'he fell beside his wits' before he was able to write up his findings, but the detailed notes survived – a portfolio of close studies by a fascinated observer.

12 JOHN LELAND, *The Itinerary* (ed. L. Toulmin Smith, 1906–10) IV, p. 114. (Hereinafter referred to as *Itinerary*)

13 A. R. BRIDBURY, *Economic Growth: England in the Later Middle Ages*, pp. 112–13

14 *L and P*, XIII, 749

15 G. R. ELTON, *Reform and Renewal*, pp. 107–9

16 J. STOW, *Chronicle*, p. 192

17 C. PLATT, *The English Medieval Town*, pp. 49–50

18 *Statutes of the Realm*, 14–15 Henry VIII, c, vi

19 *Itinerary*, V, pp. 78, 102, 72, I, p. 68

20 SNEYD (ed.), op. cit., p. 34

21 J. FORTESCUE, *Works*, I, p. 466

22 H. S. BENNETT, *The Pastons and Their England*, pp. 136–7

23 *L and P*, XV, i, 295

24 *Itinerary*, I, p. 278
25 *Itinerary*, I, p. 145
26 *Itinerary*, II, p. 98
27 *Itinerary*, II, p. 21
28 *Itinerary*, V, p. 47
29 *Itinerary*, V, p. 53

Chapter 2
'Your world and impery of England' II
1 W. CAXTON, *Encydos* (Early English Text Society), p. 3
2 *L and P*, XI, 888
3 W. G. HOSKINS, *The Age of Plunder: The England of Henry VIII, 1500–1547*, p. 81
4 JOHN SPEED, *Theatre of the Empire of Great Britain*, Bk. I, Fol. 63–4, p. 2
5 T. ELYOT, *The Book Named the Governor*, I, xxvii
6 D. LYSONS, *The Environs of London*, I, *The County of Surrey*, pp. 226–9
7 *Robin Hood and the Potter* in R. B. DOBSON and J. TAYLOR *Rymes of Robyn Hood: An Introduction to the English Outlaw*, p. 125. The authors of this excellent book have an interesting section on the social significance of Robin Hood's popularity in the early Tudor period
8 Quoted by M. CAMPBELL, *The English Yeoman*, p. 228
9 *Itinerary*, I, p. 208
10 *Itinerary*, I, p. 34
11 *Itinerary*, V, p. 13
12 26. Henry VIII, c. vi, cf. G. R. ELTON, *The Tudor Constitution*, p. 211
13 *Itinerary*, I, p. 98
14 *Itinerary*, I, pp. 18–19
15 *Itinerary*, I, p. 21
16 *L and P*, XIII, i, 973
17 This treatise was pirated by Andrew Boorde in 1542 when he amalgamated it with some writings of his own under the title *A Compendyous Regyment or Dyetary of Helthe*
18 F. G. EMMISON, *Tudor Secretary, Sir William Petre at Court and Home*, p. 32. Chapter 3 of this classic study contains a long description of Ingatestone Hall and its buildings
19 ROBERT WYER in A. Boorde, op. cit.
20 *Itinerary*, V, p. 60
21 W. CAMDEN, *Chorographia*, quoted in G. M. FRASER, *The Steel*

Bonnets, p. 44. This is a useful study of the border families but, infuriatingly, the author does not give detailed references
22 Ibid.
23 *Itinerary*, V, p. 63
24 *State Papers*, IV, p. 2
25 G. M. FRASER, op. cit., p. 218
26 Ibid., p. 221
27 G. R. ELTON, *The Tudor Constitution*, p. 344
28 Letter of Lorenzeo Pascuaglio quoted in P. J. HELM, *England under the Yorkists and Tudors, 1471–1603*, p. 42
29 Ibid.
30 H. ELLIS, *Original Letters Illustrative of English History*, 1st ser., II, p. 126
31 *Utopia*, pp. 4–5; *Works*, IV, pp. 49–51

Chapter 3
'Them that sue for great men's friendship'
1 *Works*, II, *Richard III*, ed. R. S. SYLVESTER, p. 90
2 EDMUND DUDLEY, *The Tree of Commonwealth* (ed. D. M. Brodie), p. 44
3 DUDLEY, op. cit., p. 45
4 A state paper attributed to Lord Burghley, cf. R. FIDDES, *Life of Cardinal Wolsey*, p. 531
5 *L and P*, IV, 5967
6 K. B. MCFARLANE, *The Nobility of Later Medieval England*, p. 110
7 *Utopia*, p. 16; *Works*, IV, p. 66
8 *Joyfull* v. *Warcoppe* in Star Chamber, 1500. G. R. ELTON, *The Tudor Constitution*, pp. 176–7
9 J. R. TANNER, *Tudor Constitutional Documents*, p. 9
10 *L and P*, IV, i, 25
11 A. R. MADDISON, 'Lincolnshire Gentry during the Sixteenth Century', *Lincs A.A.S.R.*, XXII (1893), p. 209
12 PRO E 36/226, pp. 149, 151, 203
13 G. E. COKAYNE, *The Complete Peerage* (ed. V. Gibbs and others), IX, 719
14 *L and P*, IV, iii, 6117
15 *L and P*, III, ii, 3227
16 *L and P*, XIII, ii, 1184, iii
17 *Utopia*, p. 15; *Works*, IV, p. 63
18 *L and P*, XI, 534
19 *L and P*, XV, 229

20 W. H. WOODWARD, *Desiderius Erasmus Concerning the Aim and Method of Education*, pp. 166–7

21 *A Relation of the Island of England*, ed. C. A. Sneyd (Camden Society, 1847) p. 24

22 WILLIAM ROPER, *The Life of Sir Thomas More* (ed. E. V. Hitchcock, 1935), p. 5

23 T. STAPLETON, *The Life and Illustrious Martyrdom of Sir Thomas More* (ed. P. Hallett), I, p. 156

24 From the *Glossa Ordinaria*, cf. R. L. P. MILBURN in *The Cambridge History of the Bible*, II, p. 295

25 A. A. MUMFORD, *Hugh Oldham*, pp. 107–8

26 SIR JOHN FORTESCUE, *De Laudibus Legum Angliae* (ed. J. Selden, 1616), pp. 112–13. Fortescue's account was written about 1468, though not printed until 1537

27 P. S. and H. M. ALLEN (eds.), *Opus Epistolarum Desiderii Erasmi Roterodami* IV, 999, p. 17

Chapter 4
'The King is in the room of God'

1 WILLIAM TYNDALE, *The Obedience of a Christian Man* (1528)

2 *Rotuli Parliamentorum*, VI, p. 8

3 EDMUND DUDLEY, op. cit., pp. 103–4

4 T. CRANMER, *Works* (ed. J. E. Cox), Parker Society, 1844–6, II, pp. 188–9

5 THOMAS STARKEY, *Dialogue between Cardinal Pole and Thomas Lupset* (ed. S. J. Herrtage), Early English Text Society

6 *Utopia*, p. 44; *Works*, IV, p. 110

7 CRANMER, *Works*, II, pp. 185, 196

8 S. GARDINER, *Answer to Bucer*, quoted by P. JANELLE in *Obedience in Church and State – Three Political Tracts by Stephen Gardiner* (1930), p. 205

9 *Utopia*, p. 158; *Works*, IV, p. 241

10 *Utopia*, p. 47; *Works*, IV, p. 116

11 *L and P*, XI, 622

12 *State Papers of Henry VIII*, i, 538–9

13 ROPER, op. cit., pp. 100–101

14 *Greyfriars' Chronicle*, p. 27

15 *L and P*, III, i, 706

16 S. ANGLO, *Spectacle Pageantry and Early Tudor Policy*, pp. 212–14

17 JOHN SKELTON, *Poetical Works: with some account of the author and his writings*, ed. A. Dyce (1843), p. 39

18 ERASMUS, *In Praise of Folly* (Sesame Library edition), pp. 160–161

19 *Utopia*, pp. 43–4; *Works*, IV, p. 95

20 A parish register of 1563 gives the population of South Kelsey as 'Kelsey St Mary's. Rectory. 57 families. 1 Hamlet – Winghale with 1 family. Kelsey St Nicholas. Rectory. 31 families. cf. H. C. BREW-STER, *South Kelsey Notes* (1898), pp. 50–51. (This is a manuscript book in Lincoln Cathedral Library)

21 cf. D. WILSON, *A Tudor Tapestry: Men, Women and Society in Reformation England*, pp. 21ff.

22 *L and P*, XIII, ii, 307

23 J. R. LANDER, 'Bonds, coercion, and fear; Henry VII and the peer-age', in *Florelegium historiale: essays presented to Wallace K. Ferguson*, p. 339

24 ROPER, op. cit., pp. 7–8

25 T. CRANMER, *Works*, II, p. 168

26 The figures used are those which applied to the parliament summoned in 1529, cf. S. E. LEHMBERG, *The Reformation Parliament, 1529–1536*, pp. 9ff

27 SIR FRANCIS BACON, *History of the Reign of Henry VIII* (ed. Lockyer), pp. 148–9

28 *L and P*, III, ii, 3082

29 The commissioners for Kent to the king, 3 May 1525. *L and P*, IV, i, 1305

30 A. FLETCHER, *Tudor Rebellions*, p. 19

31 *State Papers of Henry VIII*, I, ii, p. 840

32 EDWARD HALL, *The Union of the two noble and illustre Famelies of Lancastre and Yorke* (ed. H. Ellis, 1809), pp. 424–5

33 SIR THOMAS WYATT, *Collected Poems* (ed. J. Daalder), p. 185

34 *Utopia*, pp. 40–41; *Works*, IV, pp. 91–3

35 P. S. and H. M. ALLEN (eds.), *Opus Epistolarum Desiderii Erasmi Roterodami*, III, 688

36 *Utopia*, pp. 46–7; *Works*, IV, p. 87

37 Orders for the Council, *c.* 1516. G. R. ELTON, *The Tudor Constitution*, p. 190

38 cf. I. S. LEADAM, *Select Cases in the Court of Requests, 1497–1596*

39 T. STAPLETON, *The Life of Sir Thomas More* (ed. P. Hallett), VII, p. 230

40 SIR THOMAS WYATT, *Collected Poems* (ed. J. Daalder), p. 103

41 J. FOXE, *Actes and Monuments of the Christian Religion*, VIII, pp. 24–6. Hereinafter referred to as Foxe

42 P. S. and H. M. ALLEN (eds.), op. cit., VI, 1770

43 Cal. S. P. Ven., IV, 824
44 Ibid., p. 130
45 *L and P*, IV, iii, 5860
46 E. HALL, *Chronicle*, p. 132
47 A. TREVISANI, *Relation of the Island of England*, p. 12
48 cf. S. B. CHRIMES, *Henry VII*, p. 306n.
49 E. HALL, *Chronicle*, pp. 517–19
50 CRESACRE MORE (ed. J. Hunter), *Life of Sir Thomas More*, p. 263

Chapter 5
'Unsatiable Cormorant'
1 *Utopia*, pp. 18–19; *Works*, IV, pp. 65–7
2 Quoted by P. RAMSEY, *Tudor Economic Problems*, p. 24
3 E. H. PHELPS BROWN and S. V. HOPKINS, 'Wage Rates and Prices: Evidence for Population Pressure in the Sixteenth Century', *Economica*, XXIV, p. 306
4 A. G. DICKENS, 'Estate and Household Management in Bedfordshire *c.* 1540', in *Bedfordshire Hist. Rec. Soc.*, XXXVI, 1956
5 E. LAMOND (ed.), *A Discourse of the Common Weal of this Realm of England*, pp. 19–20
6 Ibid., pp. 56–7
7 *L and P*, VI, 1526
8 cf. W. K. JORDAN, *Philanthropy in England*, p. 62
9 M. BERESFORD, *The Lost Villages of England*, p. 143
10 THOMAS WILSON, *The State of England Anno Dom. 1600* (ed. F. J. Fisher), Camden Society, LII, p. 18
11 Quoted by F. J. FISHER, 'Commercial trends and policy in sixteenth-century England', *Essays in Economic History* (ed. E. Carus-Wilson), I, p. 157
12 RICHARD CAREW, *Survey of Cornwall*, p. 78
13 *The Diary and Family Book of Robert Furst* (ed. H. Carpenter), *Devonshire Transactions*, XXVI, p. 170
14 R. THOROTON, *Antiquities of Nottinghamshire*, p. 460
15 *L and P*, IX, ii, 47, 74
16 *L and P*, IX, 632
17 *L and P*, XIII, i, 1085
18 *L and P*, IX, 231
19 *L and P*, IX, 708
20 *L and P*, IX, 42
21 *L and P*, IX, 722. For the best account of the 1535–6 visitation see D. KNOWLES, *The Religious Orders in England*, III, ch. 22

22 R. CROWLEY, *A Supplication of the Poore Commons*, Early English Text Society, p. 79

23 J. M. CLAY (ed.), *Yorkshire Monasteries: Suppression Papers*, Yorks Archaeological Society Records Series, xlviii, p. 48

24 J. R. TANNER, *Tudor Constitutional Documents*, p. 68

25 *L and P*, XIII, i, 192

26 R. B. WALKER, 'A History of the Reformation in the Archdeaconries of Lincoln and Stow, 1534–94' (Liverpool Ph.D. thesis, 1959), pp. 90–92

27 *L and P*, XIII, ii, 303

28 J. J. SCARISBRICK, *Henry VIII*, p. 341

29 *State Papers*, I, pp. 463–70

30 *State Papers*, I, pp. 538–9

31 Exact tallies of the executions carried out by Henry's agents 1586–7 are difficult to arrive at; cf. M. H. and J. R. DODDS, *The Pilgrimage of Grace*, II, pp. 226f and G. R. ELTON, *Policy and Police*, pp. 389f

32 *L and P*, XIII, i, 24

33 R. CROWLEY, *Select Works*, p. 7

Chapter 6
'Wantonly and viciously brought up'

1 *Utopia*, p. 15; *Works*, IV, pp. 61–3

2 R. H. TAWNEY and E. POWER (eds.), *Tudor Economic Documents*, II, pp. 339–46

3 J. RIDLEY, *Thomas Cranmer*, p. 250

4 *Norwich Corporation Court Books*, fol. 29

5 TAWNEY and POWER, op. cit., II, p. 305

6 TAWNEY and POWER, op. cit., III, pp. 414–15

7 H. ELLIS, *Original Letters Illustrative of English History*, 1st series, II, pp. 100–101

8 Ibid., p. 102

9 SIR THOMAS SMITH, *De Republica Anglorum* (ed. L. Alston), II, ch. 19

10 D. WILSON, *A Tudor Tapestry*, pp. 156–8

11 J. R. TANNER, *Tudor Constitutional Documents*, pp. 476–7

12 H. T. RILEY (ed.), *Memorials of London and London Life*, p. 316

13 R. W. CHAMBERS, *Thomas More*, p. 348

14 T. STAPLETON, *The Life of Sir Thomas More* (ed. F. E. Reynolds), p. 188

15 R. W. CHAMBERS, op. cit., p. 349

16 T. STAPLETON, op. cit., p. 189

17 *Utopia*, p. 14; *Works*, IV, p. 61

18 JOHN HOOPER, *Later Writings* (Parker Society), p. 97

19 R. CROWLEY, *The Way To Wealth* (Early English Text Society), p. 157

20 J. R. TANNER, *Tudor Constitutional Documents*, p. 474

21 Ibid., pp. 479–80

22 Invisibility was almost as much a fixation in Tudor times as the philosopher's stone. For example, William Neville paid to have a cloak of invisibility made for him. It was created from layers of linen and buckskin which had been treated with a compound of powdered horse bones, chalk, glass, skin and rosin, cf. G. R. ELTON, *Policy and Police*, p. 50

23 R. KIECKHEFER, *European Witch Trials, Their Foundation in Popular and Learned Culture, 1300–1500*, p. 57

24 G. R. ELTON, *Policy and Police*, pp. 50ff

25 Ibid., pp. 57–8

26 Lord Edmund Howard to Lady Lisle; *L and P*, VIII, 797

27 Quoted by P. J. HELM, *England under the Yorkists and Tudors, 1471–1603*, p. 347

28 P. S. and H. M. ALLEN (eds.), *Opus Epistolarum Desiderii Erasmi Roterodami*, I, p. 217

29 *State Papers*, I, pp. 308, 312–13

30 *L and P*, III, ii, 2531

31 J. L. VIVES, *On Education* (translated and edited by Foster Watson), pp. 170–171

32 W. TURNER, *A New Herball wherein are conteyned the names of Herbes*, preface

33 G. R. ELTON, *Policy and Police*, p. 359n

34 Ibid., p. 350

35 Ibid., pp. 348–9

Chapter 7
'Which Church is the very church?' I

1 Letter of More to Erasmus June (?) 1533. P. S. and H. M. ALLEN (eds.), *Opus Epistolarum Desiderii Erasmi Roterodami*, X, 2831; E. F. ROGERS, *St Thomas More: Selected Letters*, p. 178

2 From an early poem by More, *A merry jest how a Sergeant would learn to play the Friar*, cf. R. W. CHAMBERS, *Thomas More*, p. 90

3 More to Erasmus, 14 June 1532. ALLEN, op. cit., X, 2659

4 More to Erasmus, 28 October 1529. ALLEN, op. cit., VIII, 2228

5 Stephen Vaughan to Cromwell, 9 December 1531. *L and P*, V, 574

6 Chapuys to Charles V, 13 May 1532. *L and P*, V, 1013

7 E. F. ROGERS, *St Thomas More: Selected Letters*, p. 387

8 *Works*, VIII, pp. 1033–4

9 The course of the debate was as follows: In 1528 More challenged most of the reformers' main points in *A Dialogue Concerning Heresies*. Tyndale covered some of More's objections in *The Practice of Prelates* (1530) but the more deliberate *Answer Unto Sir Thomas More's Dialogue* was published the following year. More now set about a ponderous, line by line rebuttal. *The Confutation of Tyndale's Answer* appeared in two parts (1532, 1533). The crossfire between the two major protagonists ended there but More aimed other literary missiles at individual Protestants and at the massed ranks of the heretics.

10 W. TYNDALE, *Works* (ed. J. Walter), Parker Society, III, p. 119

11 *L and P*, IV, i, 952

12 JOHN MYRC, *Liber Festivalis* (1502), this quotation from the Early English Text Society edition, 1905, p. 104

13 D. CLARKE and A. STOYEL, *Otford in Kent, A History*, p. 107

14 PRO E 101/519/31, fos. 34, 7ᵛ

15 JOHN MYRC, *Instructions for Parish Priests*, Early English Text Society (1868), pp. 21–3

16 *In Praise of Folly*, pp. 85–6

17 *L and P*, IV, i, 2359

18 G. W. PROTHERO, *Select Statutes and Other Constitutional Documents*, p. 199

19 FOXE, IV, p. 664

20 *L and P*, IV, i, 953

21 *L and P*, VIII, i, 963

22 D. CLARKE and A. STOYEL, *Otford in Kent, A History*, pp. 100–106

23 C. HAIGH, *Reformation and Resistance in Tudor Lancashire*, p. 67

24 C. HAIGH, op. cit., p. 67

25 R. C. DUDDING (ed.), *The First Churchwarden's Book of Louth*

26 cf. H. MAYNARD SMITH, *Henry VIII and the Reformation*, p. 38

27 WILLIAM MELTON, *Sermo Exhortatorius cancellarii Eboracensis hiis qui ad sacros ordines petunt promoveri*

28 J. HUIZINGA, *Erasmus of Rotterdam*, p. 52

29 ROPER, op. cit., p. 22

Chapter 8
'Which church is the very church?' II

1 J. A. F. THOMSON, *The Later Lollards, 1414–1520*, p. 186

2 T. MORE, *A Dialogue Concerning Heresy, English Works*, p. 213

3 FOXE, IV, p. 28

4 By 27 Edward III, l.c.l, 1353, any subject who 'shall draw any out of the realm in plea whereof the cognizance pertaineth to the king's court, or of things whereof judgements be given in the kings court' was to be punished by outlawry, forfeiture of lands and goods and imprisonment at the king's pleasure. Later statutes had given further definition to this law and, by 1496, it had become established that the trial in an ecclesiastical court of any 'temporal cause' was a case of praemunire. Hunne had, after taking advice, found a legal technicality which appeared to bring his case within the scope of praemunire action. The law concerning mortuary dues permitted the priest to take a fee from the deceased person's goods. Since infants do not possess goods, Hunne claimed that an unlawful claim was being made upon him and that this was a temporal cause within the meaning of the act. For a full treatment of the entire Hunne case see A. OGLE, *The Tragedy of the Lollard's Tower*.

5 Quoted by Jeffries Davis in *EHR* XXX, p. 477, cf. also FOXE, IV, p. 196

6 FOXE, IV, pp. 706–7

7 FOXE, IV, pp. 635–6

8 *Works* (ed. Rastell), p. 344

9 FOXE, IV, p. 217

10 FOXE, IV, p. 676

11 cf. D. WILSON, *The People and the Book*, pp. 58–71

12 MORE, *Works*, VIII, i, p. 3

13 NICHOLAS HARPSFIELD, *The Life and Death of Sir Thomas More* (ed. E. V. Hitchcock), p. 87

14 E. HALL, *Chronicle*, p. 788

15 *L and P*, VIII, 809

16 H. ELLIS, *Original Letters*, Second Series, V, cviii

17 *L and P*, V, 628

18 J. STRYPE, *Memorials of Archbishop Cranmer*, II, p. 272

19 *L and P*, X, 891, 172; IX, 1130

20 cf. G. R. ELTON, *Policy and Police*, p. 119

21 *Sermons by Hugh Latimer* (ed. G. E. Corrie), Parker Society, pp. 27–8

22 cf. G. R. ELTON, *Policy and Police*, pp. 30–31

23 FOXE, VII, p. 478

24 ELTON, *Policy and Police*, pp. 33–4

25 *L and P*, XIII, i, pp. 387–8

26 R. DUNNING (ed.), *Christianity in Somerset*, pp. 30–31
27 FOXE, VII, pp. 490–491
28 cf. J. E. OXLEY, *The Reformation in Essex to the Death of Mary*, pp. 146–7
29 E. HALL, *Chronicle*, p. 865; J. STOW, *Annals*, p. 590

Epilogue
The Man Against the Age
1 P. S. and H. M. ALLEN (eds.), *Opus Epistolarum Desiderii Erasmi Roterodami*, II, 414. *Selected Letters*, p. 85
2 *Utopia*, p. 93; *Works*, IV, p. 281
3 E. F. ROGERS, *St Thomas More: Selected Letters*, p. 168
4 *L and P*, IV, iii, 6026
5 E. F. ROGERS, *St Thomas More: Selected Letters*, p. 199

SELECT BIBLIOGRAPHY

This list is, of necessity, very brief. It consists, first, of the major contemporary records which are in print and can be obtained through many libraries. Then follow some of the more recent books on specific issues. Many of the latter carry excellent bibliographies. In addition, the Notes in the present book will be found to contain references to a larger number of primary and secondary sources.

PRIMARY WORKS

The Complete Works of St Thomas More, Yale (1963–)

FOXE, J., *Actes and Monuments*, ed. J. Pratt (1877)

LELAND, JOHN, *The Itinerary*, ed. L. Toulmin Smith (1906–10)

Letters and Papers Foreign and Domestic of the Reign of Henry VIII preserved in the Public Record Office, the British Museum and elsewhere, ed. J. S. BREWER, J. GAIRDNER and R. H. BRODIE (1862–1910)

VERGIL, POLYDORE, *The Anglica History*, ed. Hay, Camden Society lxxiv (1950)

SECONDARY WORKS

(*a*) Political and Constitutional History

CHRIMES, S. B., *Henry VII* (1972)

DODDS, M. H. and R., *The Pilgrimage of Grace 1536–1537 and the Exeter Conspiracy* (reprinted 1971)

ELTON, G. R., *The Tudor Constitution* (1960)

—— *The Tudor Revolution in Government* (1953)

LEHMBERG, S. E., *The Reformation Parliament, 1529–1536* (1970)

MCCONICA, J. K., *English Humanists and Reformation Politics under Henry VIII and Edward VI* (1965)

SCARISBRICK, J. J., *Henry VIII* (1968)

WERNHAM, R. B., *Before the Armada: The Growth of English Foreign Policy 1485–1588* (1966) (*b*) Social and Economic History

The Agrarian History of England and Wales, IV, *1500–1640*, ed. J. Thirsk (1967)

CONNELL-SMITH, G., *Forerunners of Drake* (1954)

HOSKINS, W. G., *The Age of Plunder* (1976)

OUTHWAITE, R. B., *Inflation in Tudor and Early Stuart England* (1969)

RAMSEY, P. H., *Tudor Economic Problems* (1963)

SIMON, J., *Education and Society in Tudor England* (1966)

THOMAS, K., *Religion and the Decline of Magic – studies in popular belief in sixteenth and seventeenth century England* (1971)

(*c*) The Reformation

Church and Society in England Henry VIII to James I, ed. F. Heal and R. O'Day (1977)

CLEBSCH, W. A., *England's Earliest Protestants, 1520–1535* (1964)

CROSS, C., *Church and People 1450–1660: The Triumph of the Laity in the English Church* (1976)

DICKENS, A. G., *The English Reformation* (1964)

DICKENS, A. G., *Lollards and Protestants in the Diocese of York* (1959)

ELTON, G. R., *Policy and Police: The Enforcement of the Reformation in the Age of Thomas Cromwell* (1972)

HAIGH, C., *Reformation and Resistance in Tudor Lancashire* (1975)

KNOWLES, D., *The Religious Orders in England*, III (1959)

THOMSON, J, A. F., *The Later Lollards, 1414–1520* (1965)

WILSON, D. A., *A Tudor Tapestry: Men, Women and Society in Reformation England* (1972)

—— *The People and the Book: The Revolutionary Impact of the English Bible 1380–1611* (1976)

(*d*) General

BURTON, E., *The Early Tudors at Home* (1976)

ELTON, G. R., *England Under the Tudors* (2nd edition 1974)

HELM, P. J., *England Under the Yorkists and Tudors 1471–1603* (1972)

INDEX